South Africa's options

F VAN ZYL SLABBERT
AND DAVID WELSH

South Africa's options
Strategies for sharing power

ST MARTIN'S PRESS : NEW YORK

Printed in South Africa

First published in the United States in 1979

ISBN 0-312-74696-2

Library of Congress Cataloging in Publication Data

Van Zyl Slabbert, Frederik.
South Africa's options.

Bibliography: p. 184.
Includes index.
1. South Africa—Politics and government—1961–. 2. South Africa—I
relations. 3. Blacks—South Africa—Politics and government. I. Welsh, Da
John, joint author. II. Title.
DT779.9.V36 1979 320.9'68'06 78-23291
ISBN 0-312-74696-2

Contents

Preface

This book is the fruit of long friendship and common involvement in academic and political life. Both of us are academics by profession, but in 1974, unbeknown to each other, we decided that it was time to climb out of our ivory towers and enter the political arena. As Progressive Party candidates we contested the adjoining Cape Town constituencies of Groote Schuur and Rondebosch. Slabbert won his seat and still represents Rondebosch for the Progressive Federal Party; Welsh lost, and returned to academic life. Nowadays in politics Slabbert is sometimes said to be 'too academic', while in the university Welsh is occasionally accused of being 'too political'.

This book is intended primarily to be a work of political analysis and, therefore, 'scholarly'; but we have not hesitated to express our own political convictions. It is unlikely that our book will cause mass conversions to our point of view and/or persuade the South African government to come to the negotiating table. Our more modest ambition is to contribute to the debate on South Africa's future dispensation. We do not expect all our readers to agree with everything we say (although that would be gratifying) and we do not pretend to have found all the answers; but we challenge those who reject our arguments to tell us where we have gone wrong and to offer a more viable set of proposals.

We thank a number of colleagues and friends who helped us by criticizing all or part of the book in manuscript form. They include Rodney Davenport, Bill Foltz, Theodor Hanf, Morris Hirsch, Tom Karis, Arend Lijphart, Eric Nordlinger, Robert Rotberg, Mike Savage and Robert Schrire. The customary exculpation from our errors and shortcomings applies to them with especial force.

We thank Jenny Whyte and Lorna Weisbecker for typing different drafts of the manuscript.

Note on terminology

The usage of correct or acceptable names for the different population groups in South Africa poses difficult problems for authors who wish both to be accurate and to avoid giving offence. In the case of the white groups there is no problem, but in the case of the other groups the terminological issue is a minefield. We have avoided altogether the offensive expression 'non-white', and we have tried wherever possible to avoid the word 'African' for black South African. Indigenous whites have just as much claim as blacks to be regarded as 'Africans'. Accordingly we have used, as far as possible, the term 'black', which now enjoys official approval as the proper designation of those formerly called 'Bantu'. This usage, however, runs into problems when one deals with 'Black Consciousness', whose exponents include Asian and coloured people as well in the blanket category 'black'. The use of 'black' in this more inclusive sense has become widespread. We have not, however, generally used it in this sense except in dealing with Black Consciousness. The context should make our usage clear.

To our children
Riko and Tánia Slabbert
Catherine and Simon Welsh

1 *Introduction: Some options for political development in Southern Africa*

The coup in Lisbon on 25 April 1974 precipitated the end of decolonization, as we have come to know it, with the eventual independence of Moçambique and Angola. In Southern Africa there remained three white minority regimes in control of their respective countries, Rhodesia/Zimbabwe, South West Africa/Namibia and South Africa, for whom the option of colonial withdrawal as a means to resolve the co-existence problem was not available. Yet these countries faced many of the problems of a typically colonial situation: a white minority in control of political power and the economy; unequal urban and rural development; large-scale urban migration and increasing discontent among the majority of the black population, demanding full participation in government and the economy.

External to these countries, international and African developments have simply underscored the tenuousness of the white minority regimes. Big-power strategy with regard to Africa; the action and role of African governments at the United Nations and Organisation of African Unity; the international rejection of racism and anything resembling colonial exploitation, etc. – all these have made it quite clear that exclusive white control over the majority of the population in whatever form or guise will not be tolerated. At the same time developments internal to these countries have brought about similar kinds of pressure. In all three there have been urban black disturbances; political groups have directly challenged the basic assumptions of government policy and low-intensity guerrilla wars have been waged on the borders. The underlying threat of political instability has also affected foreign investors' confidence, which in turn has affected the rate of economic growth and the respective governments' ability to manipulate economic development as a means to buying off black discontent.

There are of course significant differences between these three countries that could have an important effect on how the white/black co-existence problem is resolved. We have in mind aspects such as political sovereignty (in Namibia and Zimbabwe this has been enduringly ambiguous whereas in South Africa this has not been a problem), white-black numerical ratio, differences in degree and kind of industrialization and the availability of external arbiters. Yet despite these differences the basic structural position of the regimes in these countries is the same. At present in Namibia and Zimbabwe the resolution of the conflict is still delicately poised between violent or negotiated change and one's assessment of which will be the final outcome changes almost daily. Whichever way the problem resolves itself in these two countries one thing is no longer an issue, the outcome will not make any provision for exclusive white minority control in the polity or the economy. In South Africa we are nowhere near this stage of development yet but it would be shortsighted in the extreme to argue that South Africa is going to escape the pressures responsible for the Zimbabwian and Namibian situations.

Many analyses have been made of the route and nature of change in South Africa. There have been five-minutes-to-midnight scenarios aplenty, either of the variety where a large-scale racial conflagration is seen as inevitable or where the problems of political and economic transition are tucked away into the residual category of some form of therapeutic revolutionary violence and justified in terms of a romantic utopian ideology. What this book attempts to do is to explore the possibility of peaceful constitutional change against the question: is this a reasonable and viable option available to the white minority regime? A prior question is: given the pressures building up on South Africa, what *are* the options open to a white minority government? Before exploring this question in greater detail perhaps one has to explain this preoccupation with the white minority government. Of late it has become fashionable to argue that whites or more particularly the white government has become irrelevant as far as change is concerned. We want to make it quite clear that we regard such an approach as being based on dangerous illusions. Whatever pressures develop for change in South Africa the government of the day will for the foreseeable future be the primary factor reacting to those pressures and determining the tempo and nature of change internally. In saying this we exclude the possibility of any large-scale foreign intervention be it military or otherwise. This does not exclude the increase in different kinds of external or internal pressure but it does assume that the government has sufficient resources to cope with such pressure in the foreseeable future. We make this point at the outset to emphasize the strategic significance of the white government as a major factor determining the possibility of peaceful change.

Now then, given the recent development in Southern Africa what are the options facing the government in South Africa? As we see it there are basically two general options available: the politics of siege or the politics of negotiation. The difference between them revolves around the problem of unilateral white decision-making. Any form of siege politics has as a defining characteristic the determination of the white group, through its political leadership, to persist with exclusive white control over change. Siege politics necessarily implies the extension of coercive government for its implementation and makes the establishment of consent problematical, if not impossible. In short, with siege politics there is an inbuilt crisis of legitimacy of government. Negotiation politics, on the other hand, is fundamentally concerned with establishing consent and legitimacy. It means that the regime accepts that unilateral white decision-making is untenable and that it attempts to establish a common declaration of intent with blacks in terms of which compromises can be negotiated. Another way of highlighting the differences between siege politics and negotiating politics is that the one is concerned with one-sided conflict regulation, whereas the other is concerned with negotiated conflict regulation, i.e. unilateral political decision-making versus consensual decision-making.

Which of these two the government opts for, when they do so, and for how long, will of course have an important effect on black and international reaction, as well as on whether a violent transformation is seen by more and more as the only way to change the *status quo*. A short outline of these two possibilities in the South African context will make this point clear.

THE POLITICS OF SIEGE

Here we can distinguish between two kinds of siege politics: repressive siege and siege under a modernizing oligarchy.

Repressive siege is similar to what Heribert Adam calls the garrison state.[1] In this case the regime defines its power base as directly threatened and clings to the *status quo* at all costs. Should this become a reality it would necessitate a much more extensive application of coercion than at present as well as a prevention of black advancement generally. Du Toit refers to this option in the following manner:

'This strategy can either function as a *residue* of an earlier stage in the career of the National Party and Afrikaner Nationalism when ideological concerns were still much more central to it and when it did not have to recognize such serious challenges as now in a critical situation. Or it may be seen as a possible *last resort* in some future extremity: the "Masada"-complex or "Garrison-State" model. In either case substantial political change is ruled out: it is either not necessary or no longer possible.'[2]

The length of time that repressive siege could last would depend largely on logistical issues such as the availability of arms and support for the respective groups in conflict and the performance of the economy. The most important consequence of this kind of siege politics is that violence will increasingly be seen as the only means of changing or maintaining the *status quo*.

The cost of repressive siege in political, social, economic and even psychological terms makes it an unlikely option at present. In this respect Adam points out that:

'. . . increased repression for mainly ideological reasons [is] unlikely, because it would mean a return to an irreversibly lost past. Increased repression (mass population transferrals, labour camps, retribution, genocide) for pragmatic reasons would, in a crunch, defeat its purpose in an integrated, interdependant and industrialized economy, where Blacks constitute 80 per cent of the labour force. This does not even take into account the other costs of inside and outside resistance to such a trend.'[3]

Nevertheless, repressive siege as a last resort is an available option to government and should not be completely ignored.

Siege under a modernizing oligarchy is also a variation of siege politics but with a difference. By modernizing oligarchy in this context we mean a group of people within the white minority whose control of the positions of power is more or less self-perpetuating, i.e. they cannot be dislodged by electoral or other means, and who accept the need for change of the *status quo* but only on their own terms. The major difference between this kind of siege politics and repressive siege is that those in power accept that the *status quo* is untenable. They acknowledge, for example, that there has to be 'a move away from racial discrimination', 'that one group should not dominate another', 'that the economy should be opened up on the basis of merit', etc., but maintain that only the white oligarchy is capable of controlling and directing the nature of such changes. It is still siege politics precisely because this claim of the oligarchy is questioned internationally and internally and the power base from which it hopes to bring about these changes is under attack from diverse quarters. In other words the crisis of legitimacy remains.

Siege under a modernizing oligarchy also implies coercive government but coercion is directed primarily at those who challenge the basic assumptions of government policy while allowing for limited black incorporation politically, socially and economically. This is the underlying logic of the Homelands Policy, the new constitutional proposals for coloureds and Asians and more local autonomy for urban black communities. Economically the objective would be to create a 'black urban middle-class' to act as a buffer against black radicalism and activism.

Du Toit succinctly captures the thrust of this option.

'Against this stands the view of the *National Party as the vehicle for political change and accommodation.* Given the need for change in the political exigencies in the current crisis, and given the organizational realities of the present, only the National Party can initiate and control the transitional process. It is recognized that such transition cannot be achieved by coercive measures only, that it is a political process requiring some kind of participation or collaboration from key figures in other sectors of S.A. society. Therefore it is necessary to broaden the base of the National Party in white politics, and to form alliances with appropriate leaderships outside the white group as well. Such incorporation or alliances, however, must be clearly based on the recognition of the hegemony of the National Party *within the framework* as laid down by the Nationalist Government, a framework which is ultimately backed up by its monopoly of coercive force, there is scope for an alliance with leaderships from outside the white group. Such black leaders need not be only the object of government policy; they may gain access to the highest level of executive decision-making. . . . Appropriate élites can be recruited with the help of considerable resources of *patronage* at the disposal of the government, while once installed they can be backed up and protected by coercive force, if necessary. In terms of this strategy the "homelands" policy need not necessarily be aimed at complete decolonization and transfer of control; rather it appears as a form of *indirect rule* which can be extended to Soweto or other urban complexes as well.'[4]

The important thing to appreciate about this option, which is the operative one at the moment and likely to be so for some time, is that social, economic and political change is not denied completely. The changes, such as occur, are, however, erratic and eclectic as the regime oscillates between the desire to modernize and to keep its power base intact. It does not mind certain kinds of opposition as long as it is collaborative and provides a sufficient degree of cooperation to make the system work. This is a cheaper form of siege politics because the costs of control are shared by client groups. However, the crisis of legitimacy is exacerbated in the long run because the very process of selective black incorporation continuously highlights the absence of government by consent. In short the longer South Africa has siege politics under a modernizing oligarchy the less is the likelihood for peaceful change and intergroup accommodation. To justify this rather pessimistic conclusion one has to identify only a few of the consequences of siege politics whether of the repressive or more benign kind.

First, it will lead to increasing racial and ideological polarization. By racial polarization is meant the tendency for white and black increasingly to mobilize political support on the basis of being either white or black. On the white side the emotive appeal will be that whites must stand together because they are under siege; on the black side that they must stand together because this is the only way in which they can effectively present their demands. Ideological polarization means that the economic system will be increasingly questioned and attacked by blacks and defended by whites. At present, research shows that the majority of urban blacks are still committed to some form of free enterprise economy but it also indicates that particularly the younger generation are beginning to question the validity of this system.[5] Their demands are no longer directed to inclusion within an economic and political structure but to the substitution of an entirely different one. To the extent that racial and ideological polarization coincide, i.e. that race and class become synonymous in the minds of the majority of particularly the urban blacks, to that extent the conflict situation becomes less negotiable in South Africa.

Secondly, there will be increasing black solidarity and unity as a result of the government's manipulation of ethnicity. No one can deny that there is a plurality of ethnic groups in South Africa amongst both blacks and whites but, as one urban black leader recently said, 'Ethnicity for the government means that an Afrikaner and a Greek can be a member of one nation but a Zulu and a Xhosa cannot.'

The supreme irony in the government's approach to ethnicity is that the way in which they manipulate it creates a black solidarity which transcends ethnic considerations as a counter-strategy. This increasing black solidarity will become much more amenable to a unified ideological articulation of demands against the prevailing regime.

Thirdly, there will be increasing international isolation and pressure as the crisis of legitimacy sharpens. As was mentioned earlier, the position of white minority regimes in Africa is becoming almost completely untenable. It is a fallacy to expect that once Namibia and Zimbabwe have resolved themselves the South African government will have more 'breathing space'. On the contrary the position of a white modernizing oligarchy will become even more sharply highlighted and an extremely sensitive issue in international and African relations.

THE POLITICS OF NEGOTIATION

Not much need be said about this general option now because in a very real sense the rest of the book is concerned with it. The defining characteristic of the politics of negotiation in the South African context is that the white regime accepts the untenability of unilateral decision-making and attempts to negotiate an alternative constitutional dispensation. In short it attempts to create conditions in which the crisis of legitimacy can be resolved as peacefully as possible.

We think it appropriate to distinguish between two kinds of negotiation politics, namely what we term negotiating capitulation and negotiating for participation. The primary focus of this book is on the latter possibility so a brief discussion of the former is appropriate. Negotiation for capitulation means that those in control of political power draw a clear distinction between problems of 'white survival' and the monopoly and control of political power. Under siege politics these two issues are regarded as more or less synonymous. The circumstances under which the regime would consider this kind of negotiation politics is when its own power base and the economic infrastructure have been considerably weakened and it is caught up in a long-term and inconclusive violent conflict. What is negotiated is not so much an alternative dispensation where different groups, including the white minority, can have some or other form of equitable participation, but the most peaceful and least traumatic transition from white minority control to black government. Insofar as minority group protection becomes an issue in the negotiation it will be for the purposes of transition rather than any long-term entrenchment in an alternative constitution.

This kind of negotiation politics has in effect been taking place in Rhodesia/Zimbabwe over the last few years, but for a number of reasons seems less likely for South Africa in the foreseeable future. A major factor in determining whether negotiation for capitulation is likely is if the 'other side', from the regime's point of view, not only defines the conflict as winnable on its own terms, but if it in fact becomes apparent to the regime that this is so. These two conditions are not remotely present in South Africa at the moment. Another factor of vital significance that distinguishes South Africa in this respect is that it presents the 'end of the line', as it were, for white minority participation in government in Africa. This is the familiar 'nowhere else to go' argument which diminishes the likelihood of negotiation for capitulation.

Our own concern is with negotiating for participation. The major question in this respect is whether an alternative constitutional dispensation for South Africa can be negotiated which would be acceptable to the majority of white and black South Africans, what the conditions of such a dispensation would have to be and what likelihood there is that the regime would initiate such negotiations. We begin with an analysis of the conflict situation in South Africa, then move to a more comparative perspective in which we try to identify the problem of democratic government in other societies with more or less similar situations. Finally we focus our investigation on the South African situation again.

Our mode of analysis is both analytical and normative and we make no excuse for this. We would very much like to see peaceful change come about in South Africa but our desire does not blind us to the enormous difficulties in the way of its coming about. Many of the 'ifs' and 'buts' scattered through our analyses refer to conditions that will have to be realized before such change is remotely possible. We do believe however that these conditions are still realizable otherwise we would not have bothered with an analysis of this kind. Whether these conditions will be realized is a mystery still locked into the struggle of the people of South Africa. But as long as there are options there are possibilities. This work is an analysis of and a plea for one of those options.

A final methodological note to this introduction. The options that have been identified should not be seen as mutually exclusive alternatives. For example a period of repressive siege could result in negotiation for capitulation and after a period of siege under a modernizing oligarchy in which partial democratization takes place there could be negotiation for participation. Similarly there could be a reversal as it were from siege under a modernizing oligarchy to repressive siege or from an initial stage of negotiation for participation to repressive siege. We mention this only to emphasize that these options must be seen as ideal-types constructed to emphasize particular kinds of responses one could expect from the regime under certain circumstances.

It will also become apparent that the white minority regime is given great weight as a factor determining the nature of change. In this we differ from analyses which give primacy to black reaction in labour, urban communities or to insurgency and insurrection. This clearly does not mean that there is not an interactive relationship between government action and black reaction. Of course there is, and this interaction is crucial for the way in which conflict will be resolved. We are of the opinion, however, that for the time being the government can cope with most challenges of this nature to its position of power.

We also suspect that just as there tends to be an inverse relationship between government by coercion and the consent of those governed, so there is an inverse relation between the politics of siege and the politics of negotiation. The longer siege politics lasts, even if it is of the most benign oligarchic kind, the less likely there will be a peaceful resolution of the conflict and the more difficult will be the period of reconstruction afterwards. It is still small comfort that one can tuck away one's pessimism about peaceful constitutional change behind such phrases as 'for the time being' and 'the foreseeable future', but in such imponderables lies the possibility of peaceful change or not.

2 The nature of the conflict

What is the basis of conflict in South Africa? It is easy to say that the basis is colour, or to argue that whenever groups differentiated by colour and culture are incorporated within the boundaries of a single political state conflict is 'inevitable', and further, that the establishment of a racial hierarchy must follow. But this approach begs the question and rests upon unproven assumptions. For example, it is not inevitable that differing groups coming into contact with each other should conflict: conflict depends on the historical circumstances of the contact and its subsequent development.

Contemporary South Africa is notable for the intensity of its racial and ethnic antagonisms. If a future South Africa is to attain a greater degree of internal harmony these conflicts will have to be eliminated or substantially reduced. It is therefore necessary that their character be understood if appropriate measures are to be adopted.

The argument presented here is that racism (defined as the imputation of inferiority to another racial/ethnic group) and racial prejudice is largely to be explained in terms of the conflicts arising between groups. It is not racism or prejudice that causes discrimination and other manifestations of racial antagonism: rather it is a conflict situation that creates these predispositions and the ensuing pattern of discriminatory structures and measures.

For purposes of this analysis we define an ethnic group in the broadest of terms as a group that is bounded off from other comparable groups or population categories in the society by a sense of its difference, which may consist in some combination of a real or mythical ancestry and a common culture and experience. Employed in a context of intergroup relations this definition would cover groups that are physically or racially different as well as those that are culturally different. But the broadness of the definition should not obscure the analytical differences between 'race' and 'ethnic' relations, even if the former may be regarded a special case of the latter.

As Pierre L. van den Berghe points out, where physically distinct or racial groups are involved the form of stratification may evolve into a nearly impermeable caste-like system more easily than where only cultural differences are involved. Physical differences cannot be changed, but people can change their cultures. Thus in the South African case there is a qualitative difference between black/white relations and the relations between Afrikaans- and English-speaking whites. The degrees of enclosure, to use Schermerhorn's phrase, differ considerably. Blacks may not enter the white stratum whose endogamy is enforced by penal sanctions, but Afrikaner and English may, and do, become anglicized or Afrikanerized. However much it may be constrained in actual social practice the individual does, in principle, have some choice in his ethnic affiliation where physical differences are not salient, or where, as in Brazil, physical differences are not decisive in locating people in the social hierarchy.

The uniqueness of South Africa as a racially divided society lies in the extent to which its historically determined lines of conflict have been hardened and reinforced by statutory measures. In addition to the force of customary attitudes, discrimination is given the formidable backing of legal and coercive sanctions. Moreover, the government imposes its own ethno-linguistic categorization upon the black population, dividing them into 'ethnic' groups, and declares the so-called coloured people to be a 'group' in formation, when, in fact, they are little more than a category bounded by their common status as persons who are not white, Asian or black. In other words, they are a residual category, as the definition in the Population Registration Act makes clear.

The extreme emphasis on racial and other distinctions among the different black communities is not replicated in the official view of the white community, which, in spite of its historically serious Afrikaner/English cleavage, is regarded as a single 'white nation'. Clearly the officially recognized lines of racial and ethnic division are a matter of political manipulation rather than of social reality. But it would be wrong to infer from this conclusion that racial or ethnic identities have no real salience, or that their salience will disappear after the formal abolition of racial discrimination.

The disjunction between 'official' and 'actual' groups in South Africa leads to something of a paradox, in that, for all the intensity of intergroup conflict, there can be no precise way of anticipating what precise configuration of groups would crystallize in a social and political context in which group formation was voluntary. A useful framework for understanding the origins of ethnic and racial stratification has been provided by Donald L. Noel, who argues that the three critical variables are ethnocentrism, competition and differential power.[1] If these are present there is a firm basis for predicting the development of an ethnically stratified system. Ethnocentrism may be simply defined as the propensity to evaluate one's own group in more favourable terms than other groups. It need not entail hostility towards those out-groups, but it does contain a predisposition to view them as 'different' or 'strange', from which it is but a short step to regarding them as 'inferior'. Competition refers to the relationship between the interacting groups, both of whom seek similar, scarce resources that are important to the survival of the respective groups. If one of the groups has superior power it will be able to impose its will on the other group and thereby establish a pattern of dominant/ subordinate relationships, a system of ethnic stratification.

Although Noel's theory seeks to explain the origins of slavery and racism in the United States, it has a potentially wider application that would include South Africa. Whites came to South Africa with certain ethnocentric predispositions, entered into competition with the indigenous inhabitants over scarce resources, notably land and cattle, and, by means of their superior coercive power, were able to establish a system of racial stratification with themselves at the apex. A detailed examination of subsequent South African history would show how the same framework would accommodate the incorporation of other groups, such as the blacks and the Asians (imported into Natal as indentured labourers from 1861 onwards), into an established hierarchy of stratification.

At this point, however, certain reservations must be noted. Is ethnocentrism, as argued by Noel, a feature of all autonomous societies as ethnic groups, and is it not to some extent to beg the question if one relies on this proposition to account for the fact that the conflict was established upon ethnic lines? Contrary to the myth, it seems clear that the first white settlers at the Cape entertained strongly hostile views of its indigenous inhabitants even prior to their coming into sustained contact with them. Even more definite is the fact that negative or prejudiced evaluations of the Khoi (so-called 'Hottentots') were present from the very inception of the settlement. One may readily understand that the gulf between the settlers and the natives was a wide one, in terms of language, culture, religion and physical type, including skin colour. From the inception the groups were bounded off from each other by clear demarcations.

In his study of the origins of slavery in the United States Winthrop D. Jordan has shown that the early American colonists, even prior to sustained contacts with the blacks who were to be enslaved, possessed fairly firm negative stereotypes about black people:

'Englishmen found blackness in human beings a peculiar and important point of difference. The Negro's color set him radically *apart* from Englishmen. It also served as a highly visible label identifying the natives of a distant continent which for ages Christians had known as a land of men radically defective in religion.'[2]

Jordan's findings confound any simplistic view that slavery 'caused' prejudice. It may be readily granted that slavery intensified racist feelings out of all proportion to what they had been in the initial stages, but it is equally clear that 'first impressions' were important causal factors in their own right.

We note in passing that 'blackness' itself seems to have had some effect on the genesis of racism. From early times in Christendom, for example, black as a colour had certain adverse connotations like 'ugly', 'dirt', 'sin', 'death' and 'impurity' whereas the colour 'white' represented in each case the opposite. Roger Bastide has traced the development of this colour symbolism in Christianity, and he concludes that 'over and above any historical or economic factors, the roots of segregation are to be found in the idea of contagiousness of sin through colour'.[3] Equally interesting is that the same colour correlations have been found among the Japanese,[4] and among Muslims, for whom by the seventh and eighth centuries the association of blackness with ugliness and an inferior social standing had already been accepted.[5]

These points are worth making in view of the currently fashionable trend to identify racialism solely with slavery and capitalism. There can be no doubt that slavery and subsequent imperialism contributed greatly to racism – non-Marxist scholars readily concede this – but it is arguable whether they *caused* it.[6]

In the development of race relations in South Africa darker skin colours came to be rigidly associated with groups that were perceived as hostile (actually or potentially), 'barbarian', and fit to perform only the lowest of manual and labouring jobs. A dark skin, in other words, became a symbol of one's status as a member of a group that was properly and rightfully dominated. The growth of an ideology of racism (that is, a more-or-less systematized body of doctrine) required another ingredient, and that, ironically enough, was the spread of egalitarian and democratic ideals, often combined with nationalism. If nationalism proclaimed 'the people' sovereign and equal, who, then, were 'the people'? Slavery and racial inequality could only be justified if it could be shown that certain categories were not, because of their inferiority, properly part of 'the people'.

South Africa's system of social stratification reflects its past. The white groups imported slaves, spawned an intermediate 'coloured' group, substantially obliterated another (the Khoisan or so-called 'Bushmen'), conquered and incorporated indigenous African societies and imported the Asians. (Of course the whites themselves were made up of two distinct ethnic groups, and the competition for hegemony between them is an important theme on its own; but in conflict with blacks the whites have displayed a measure of inter-ethnic unity.)

To a substantial extent the racial conflict in South Africa revolves around its institutionalized inequalities of power, wealth, opportunity and status. There are no inherent or intrinsic reasons why groups of differing colours and/or cultures should not be able to live together in harmony: colour (or ethnicity) derives its salience because it symbolizes particular positions in a hierarchy, and it is the hierarchical nature of the society that determines its distributional patterns – who gets what, how and when.

It is clear from these observations that colour as a basis of stratification is closely related to class. Indeed, there is a strong school of Marxist thought which holds that race relations are fundamentally class relations. This issue requires examination, because if race and class are similar there will be obvious implications for the treatment of race conflict, in particular regarding the bargainability or negotiability of such conflict.

In the traditional Marxist view class refers simply to a category of people who stand broadly in the same relationship to the means of production. It is thus an economic category whose indices include occupation, wealth, income and education. An ethnic group is also a category but it may be defined as a group bounded off from others, possessing a sense of its collective identity and resting usually upon a basis of actual or presumed common descent, shared experience and culture. In principle there is no *necessary* connection between ethnicity and class, as an ethnic group may contain quite wide internal class variations. No generalized statements about ethnicity and class are possible because the relationships between them show a considerable range of variation in the social configuration of ethnic groups as among ethnically divided societies of the modern world. Donald L. Horowitz has drawn a distinction between 'vertical' and 'horizontal' ethnic differentiation.[7] In the former case ethnic groups are hierarchically ranked and stratification is synonymous with ethnicity. South Africa, the American South and Burundi would be examples of this type. In the latter case 'parallel ethnic structures exist, each with its own criteria of stratification. Although the question of group superiority is far from moot, the groups are not, in a general social sense, definitively ranked in relation to each other.' Nigeria, Malaysia and

Surinam would be examples of this type.

In South Africa it is obvious that class and race overlap to a significant degree. Most middle-class people are white and most working- or labouring-class people are black. The pattern of income distribution, the ownership of wealth, educational attainments and occupation (the criteria of class membership) follow racially demarcated lines to a large extent. For some Marxists this overlap has been sufficient reason to justify classifying South Africa as a class-stratified society, the argument being that the identification between colour and class is so strong that 'anomalies' such as working-class whites or middle-class blacks remain tied to the class of their more numerous fellow-ethnics. In other words a mental image is created whereby *all* blacks are regarded by whites as lower class because *most* blacks are, in fact, lower class.[8]

Disentangling class and racial or ethnic components in a hierarchy poses both conceptual and methodological problems. In one of the rare empirical investigations of this question John C. Leggett studied working-class communities in Detroit whom he categorized as belonging to the 'mainstream' or 'marginal' working class, the latter being a sub-community of workers belonging to a subordinate racial or ethnic group that is usually proletarianized and highly segregated. The conclusions showed that class consciousness could be combined with racial or ethnic consciousness, but disproved the contention of Marxists 'who point to the presence of class consciousness, but who exclude the significance of the racial factor in accounting for the content and disposition of working-class consciousness'.[9]

Allowing for significant differences, which will be examined below, certain parallels between race and class emerge if one compares the two bases of stratification. Describing early Victorian England, Harrison writes:

'Labouring people in many respects lived in a world of their own, remote from the experience of the literary, articulate middle classes. Increasingly segregated in working class districts of the cities, with a mortality rate twice that of middle class areas, eating different food, wearing different clothes, and observing different social *mores,* the labouring poor seemed to some observers to be almost a separate nation. It was the future Conservative prime minister Benjamin Disraeli, who in 1845 in his novel *Sybil* wrote of the two nations, the rich and the poor. Adventurous social investigators had to discover working class England almost as a foreign land . . . '[10]

Asa Briggs quotes a contemporary observer in 1841:

'It is the unhappiness of most large cities that, instead of inspiring union and sympathy among different "conditions of men", they consist of different ranks, so widely separated indeed as to form different communities. In most large cities there may be said to be two nations, understanding as little of one another, having as little intercourse, as if they lived in different lands.'[11]

Classes could be, and often were, highly segregated from one another, developing distinct sub-cultures and evolving a whole pattern of distinctive class institutions and associations. The threat which the hugely preponderant working classes posed to the security and property of the middle and upper classes was also much discussed, in terms that are reminiscent of discussions among whites in South Africa about the alleged black threat.

In an illuminating study Léon Poliakov has shown how European societies developed myths about their racial origins, which could be incorporated into domestic class-conflicts. The 'Controversy about the two Races' in eighteenth- and nineteenth-century France serves as an example. The nobility argued that they were descended from the ancient and superior Germanic 'race', the Franks, who had conquered the native Gauls. The controversy endured a long time and was characterized by the production of much spurious history – a common feature of all forms of racism. It was not until 1830, when the bourgeoisie were firmly established as the ruling class of France, that the Gallic version of French history prevailed.[12]

It will be clear from the evidence presented above that class and ethnicity overlap and intersect in many cases, but that no generalizations about the relationship may be made as there are widely divergent patterns among the various ethnically divided societies. But the point must be emphasized that the two concepts are analytically distinct, and that ethnicity cannot be reduced in all cases to a matter of class. It may be illuminating to list the points of difference:

(1) The circumstances of class formation in a relatively homogeneous society differ widely from those attendant upon the genesis of ethnic groups.[13] Typically the systems of stratification involving the latter are the results of conquest, the importation of slave or indentured labour, or the juxtaposition of different groups through territorial expansion or annexation.

(2) Classes are usually more open and more permeable than ethnic groups, and hence the possibility of mobility from one class to another is greater. In systems of ethnic stratification where physical and/or cultural differences are sharp the boundaries will be correspondingly clearly demarcated and, where the degree of antagonism is intense, no inter-group mobility will be tolerated in principle, even if a limited

extent of illicit 'passing' occurs.

(3) Ethnic groups may in some circumstances become separatist in their aspiration, and seek to establish their own nation-states. Classes cannot have comparable aspirations – the Marxist notion of a take-over of the state by the working class (or its vanguard) represents an entirely different possibility.

(4) Ethnic groups can contain a full range of classes in either the Marxist or stratification sense. It may well occur that the dominant class within an ethnic group may mobilize the group under the banner of ethnicity as a means of furthering its own class ends.

(5) Typically in a class-stratified society there will be substantial agreement on the norms and values of the society. As Marx put it, 'the ideas of the ruling class are, in every age, the ruling ideas'. In sharply divided systems of ethnic stratification such normative convergence is unlikely. This does not, however, exclude the possibility that the cultural hegemony established by a dominant ethnic group may have a strong acculturative impact on the subordinate groups. There is no fundamental difference, for example, between the values and norms of white and black Americans. (A comparable point may be made in respect of the whites and the coloured people of South Africa, although the latter do not constitute an ethnic group in any proper sense.)

(6) Historically, class conflict has been easier to contain and to regulate through institutionalized peaceful means than ethnic conflict. Socialist parties of the West have universally dropped their radical or revolutionary profiles and accepted reformist stances. Even the Communist parties of France, Italy and Spain have (ostensibly at any rate) become reformist. This is by no means to assert that class conflict has disappeared from even the most affluent societies; merely that it has been amenable to conflict-regulating machinery to such an extent that 'pure' cases of violent class conflict are rare in the contemporary world. As the melancholy record shows, coping with ethnic conflict is much more difficult. In contrast with class, ethnicity is far more volatile and inflammatory, and this, in turn, is because it plumbs deeper levels of the human psyche than class. Where class and ethnic solidarities compete, ethnicity will invariably win. We know of no case, at any rate in modern times, where ethnic solidarity has been eclipsed and superceded by an inter-ethnic class solidarity. It has sometimes been argued that a multi-ethnic working-class solidarity has been prevented by the manipulations of a ruling class fearful of the threat posed to its hegemony. Even where this has occurred, as Percy Cohen points out, it shows how powerful the ethnic element

itself can be.[14] It will not suffice to attribute ethnic divisions in the working class to 'false consciousness', as vulgar Marxists are inclined to do.

Leo Kuper offers a succinct statement of the differences between class and race as the underlying bases of social stratification:

'Classes constitute a system of social relationships and a hierarchical order. In Marxist theory, they are defined by relationships to the economic order; the political, educational and associational inequalities being superimposed on the economic differentiation. Since classes arise out of the economic order, economic change is presumably the crucial variable. Races, on the other hand, do not constitute a hierarchical order *per se.* There is no intrinsic reason why races should constitute categories in social relationships, nor are hierarchical relations inherent in racial differences. Races only become social categories, and race relations only become hierarchical through the manner in which racial difference is elaborated as a principle of organisation and association in the political and other institutions. It is these associated factors which give race an independent significance. Economic position is only one of the associated factors, and not necessarily the most crucial.'[15]

Kuper's assertion that race has an independent significance may be taken as the nub of the scholarly debate about race relations. Some Marxists would deny that race has any significance, or allow it only a limited significance. Thus Frederick A. Johnstone's analysis of the gold-mining industry is based upon an approach that rejects the concept of a 'race relations' and employs instead 'a quasi-Marxist, quasi-structuralist' approach that interprets 'race relations' in class terms and analyses the system of racial domination as 'a product of the system of production of which it formed a part, and as determined in its specific forms, functions and nature by this system'.[16]

Johnstone's argument is that the South African working class came to be made up of two groups of workers subject to quite different relations of production with the property-owning class – a group of ultra exploitable (black) workers and a group of politically free (white) workers.[17] He explains the development of the job colour bar in mining as follows:

'The extension of the exploitability of the majority of workers, by the racially discriminatory forced labour system of the employers, extended the structural insecurity of the proletarianised but politically free and less exploitable (white) group of workers, leading the latter to institute an extensive system of employment protection, and determining that it, too, should take the specific form of racial discrimination. It was thus a case of one system of class colour bars – the exploitation colour bars of the dominant (owning) class – generating another – the employment colour bars of the politically free section of the economically dependent (working) class, including the job colour bar of the white mine workers. It was the involvement of the employers – notably the mining capitalists – in racial discrimination which generated the involvement of the white workers – notably the white mine workers – in racial discrimination.'[18]

Various comments arise out of these hypotheses. First, it is historically debatable whether it was the mining capitalists who *initiated* the white workers' involvement in racial discrimination. Johnstone is concerned with a short period of the mining industry's history, the years leading up to 1922, but some have traced the claim of white mine-workers to racially preferential treatment to the early days of Kimberley diamond fields prior to the emergence of large-scale enterprises. Thus a Diamond Diggers' Protection Society was formed in 1870 essentially to protect white diggers from black and coloured competition.[19] There can be little doubt that suspicion of the mine-owners' intentions intensified the white miners' fear of black competition but it did not create it. These miners were part of, or if they were immigrants they entered into, a society whose racial lines of cleavage had already been firmly laid down. A sense of their 'due' racial status and an aversion to the cruder forms of manual labour did not have to be wrought in them by the machinations of capitalists. If this is so, is it then still tenable to hold that race was irrelevant or secondary? The point is surely that however intrinsically lacking in significance race may have been in the early days of the establishment of a multiracial society (and even this contention is dubious, as the earlier analysis shows), it acquired a significance independent of other variables. Subsequent issues of conflict were slotted into an existing structure of conflict. The same point is made by Katharine West: 'Whatever their origins, once aroused, ethnic hostilities assume a life of their own and can be expected to continue despite the elimination of the economic and political inequalities that may have caused the original conflict.'[20] To hold this view is not, as Johnstone accuses theorists of the plural-society concept of being, to be guilty of 'ethnological determinism'.[21] Merely it is to say that racial domination cannot be explained solely as a product of the system of production.

Secondly, there are problems for a Marxist analysis posed by the existence of a politically significant white working class: if the working class is divided into politically free (white) and ultra-exploitable unfree (black) segments how does one reconcile this with an explanation derived from the relations of production unless race operated at some time as an independent factor? (A similar issue arises in early American history: why was it that, although there were both white and negro servants of comparable socio-economic status, it was only the negroes that were subsequently enslaved?) Johnstone does not explain how white workers came to exert so much political influence in spite of their 'extreme structural insecurity'.[22] If race is irrelevant and the distribution of power is a function of different groups' relations to the productive system, then, logically, neither segment of the working class should have the countervailing power effectively to challenge the property owners – and yet that is precisely what the white workers (through the Labour Party in alliance with the National Party) did in 1924. Power to shape the major institutions of society is derived from several sources: it is not just the derivative of economic power (and we do not impute so crude a view to Johnstone). Clearly the ownership of property is one such source, but we would argue that in the context of South Africa it has not been decisive. A stronger case could be made for holding that the determining or ultimate sources of power were coercive or military and political.[23]

Another Marxist interpretation of conflict in South Africa, by H.J. and R.E. Simons, differs from Johnstone's at some critical points. They argue that race was an independently significant factor:

'South Africa uniquely demonstrates that a dominant racial minority can perpetuate social rigidities and feudalistic traits on an advanced and expanding industrial base . . . civic status is determined at birth and for life by colour rather than class, by genealogy rather than function; a person can move up or down the social scale within his primary colour group, but he cannot transfer to another such group; functional categories cut across the colour line, but members of one race cannot combine freely with co-functionaries of another race.'[24] The authors, in holding that the racial factor was significant, are not claiming any kind of racial determinism. They emphasize that the elaboration of race into a principle of social organization stems from 'contrived factors' that blighted the vision of 'eventual solidarity among workers of all races against capitalism'. Unlike Johnstone, whose analysis places the responsibility for racial discrimination on property owners, the Simonses hold that 'white Labourism has been a primary cause of policies that incite racial hostility, isolate colour groups and dissolve class consciousness in colour consciousness'.[25]

Neither of these approaches conclusively resolves the problems posed to Marxism by the absence of an interracial working-class solidarity. The thrust of Marxist sociology accords primacy to class as a focus of allegiance and an instrument of change. Marx, however, was careful not to suggest that the formation of class solidarity and class consciousness were inevitable. He was aware of the problems that ethnic division caused for class solidarity but there can be little doubt that he underestimated the tenacity with which ethnicity and nationalism would endure in spite of objectively common class situations that transcend ethnic or racial divisions.[26] The experience of states like Russia, China and Yugoslavia that are ostensibly based on Marxist principles and view ethnic issues as fundamentally ones of class, strengthens this view, for in each case ethnic minorities have been a persistent source of tension. In the case of Yugoslavia ethnic conflict threatens the integrity of the state; in Russia ethnic dissent among non-Russian minorities, who number nearly 50 per cent of the total Soviet population, has explosive potentials; and in China, where minorities comprise a mere 6 per cent of the population, policy has see-sawed back and forth since 1949 in the face of non-Han resistance to being integrated into a 'homogeneous proletarian culture'.[27]

Part of the analytical problem for Marxists has been their extraordinary reluctance or inability to develop a sociology of class that is more attuned to the conditions of contemporary societies. One of the difficulties, for example, in criticizing Johnstone's work is that nowhere does it contain a systematic analysis of class and class formation – which is a singular omission in an analysis that elevates class to a central position.

In Johnstone's case, despite his repudiation of crude economic determinism, his Marxist assumptions incline him to underestimate non-economic factors. As the quotations above show, the core of his argument is that the power of the property owners, accruing to them from ownership, enabled them to shape the fundamental discriminatory pattern of industry. But the actions of the white workers show that factors other than class are also significant and, indeed, can outweigh class power. These other factors are status and power, and with their introduction into the analysis the Weberian concept of stratification has been reached. Weber's theory is that inequality has different dimensions – class, status, and power – which interact with one another and whose various combinations determine the pattern of stratification in any given society. It may often be the case, as Weber acknowledges, that a substantial degree of overlapping occurs so that a particular class is dominant in terms of ownership, power and status; but there may also be inconsistencies as, for example, when a particular group may not be dominant in terms of class or status, but is dominant in terms of political power, perhaps because of its preponderant numbers. The case of Afrikaners *vis à vis* English-speaking whites in South Africa is close to this possibility. The point has been concisely stated by Frank Parkin:

'The most obvious and clear-cut example of a major inconsistency between the different dimensions of inequality is that occurring in multi-racial societies. The system of social honour (status) based on ethnic or racial differences is analytically, and often empirically, distinct from that based on the division of labour. Consequently, status positions associated with ethnic ranking are not necessarily in alignment with occupational or class positions. The negative social honour attaching to black minorities in Britain and America, or to the Jews in continental Europe, cannot be explained in class terms.'[28]

There is a strong tendency for some neo-Marxist writers to isolate class as the critical variable in all situations of ethnic conflict, and to impute to 'capitalist needs' a major share of the blame for institutionalized racial discrimination. This view goes too far and cannot accommodate all of the evidence. In a trenchant critique of analyses of ethnicity that focus solely or largely on economic causes Walker Connor concludes that

'the theory of relative economic deprivation offers an unsatisfactory explanation for ethnonational dissension. The growing tendency of peoples to resent and resist being ruled by those deemed aliens appears to operate quite independently of the economic variable. Rich and poor states, and rich and poor nations, have been rather indiscriminately susceptible to the ethnonational virus. Economically static and economically fluid environments have both witnessed increased ethnonational dissension.

'Is this, then, to deny any role to economic considerations? Not at all. As evidenced by the great emphasis that is placed upon economic deprivation (real or imaginary) in ethnonational propaganda, economic arguments can act as a catalyst or exacerbator of national tensions. But this is something quite different than acknowledging economic deprivation as a necessary precondition of ethnonational conflict. Deprivation is but one of several possible catalysts.'[29]

Whatever may be thought of capitalism as an economic system, its association with ethnicity and racial discrimination in a number of situations is contingent, and cannot be ascribed to the operation of malign forces that are inherent in it. Such reasoning has become influential among scholars examining the roots of segregation in South Africa. In criticizing this view Ronald Hyam examines the growth of segregationist policies and institutions in the first decade of twentieth century South Africa and he concludes:

'There is a strong tendency in some quarters to see these policies (and logically, even Union itself) as a capitalist plot to produce for South Africa cheap labour and a specific attempt to formulate a native policy appropriate to the conditions of capitalist economic growth. Apart from the fact that the British government disliked "capitalists", and certainly was never manipulated by them, such a view is too narrow. It sees South Africa in far too isolated a context, and it underestimates the extent to which racial discrimination for its own (or at least non-economic) sake was a motive political force at the turn of the century.'[30]

The analysis presented thus far has attempted to show that ethnic conflict stems fundamentally from inequality in the distribution of social advantage. In arguing against a purely class analysis the aim has not been to reject the view that economic inequalities are important – clearly they are of vital importance – but rather to widen the scope of this perspective, and to suggest that other kinds of inequalities are also important and that to designate the collectivities engaged in the conflict as classes is analytically inappropriate. In brief, ethnic conflict is very much concerned with the struggle between 'haves' and 'have-nots', but the components and dynamic processes of 'having' and 'not having' transcend class and class conflict. They also make the struggle more intractable.

The structure of conflict in South Africa is based on colour, which may be taken as a summation of the various factors that have been discussed in the preceding section.

In South Africa the legal measure which formally compels racial and ethnic 'group membership' is the Population Registration Act of 1951. In terms of it every individual is classified as either white, coloured or black. Within the coloured and black categories more detailed subdivisions occur. Such classification is of cardinal importance to the life chances of the individual concerned because the Population Registration Act forms the basis for a whole range of consequential legislative measures which structure opportunities and privileges on a racial or ethnic basis. Measures such as: the Prohibition of Mixed Marriages Act, which prevents interracial marriages; Section 16 of the Immorality Act, which prohibits sexual intercourse between persons of different racial groups; the Group Areas Act, which allocates geographical areas on a racial or ethnic basis; the Separate Amenities Act, which determines which public facilities may be used by which race group, etc. Without the Population Registration Act these measures could not be implemented but in terms of it it is possible to determine where people may eat, sleep, live and work on a racial or ethnic basis.

It is our conviction that a measure such as the Population Registration Act lends a clear racial overtone to the conflict situation in South Africa. Despite the official ideology of the government which pays lip service to the 'plural nature' of South African society and its 'diversity of cultures', opportunities and life chances are structured on a purely racial basis by measures such as the Population Registration Act. It should therefore not surprise anyone that blacks react with suspicion towards government concern with ethnicity and that those classified as coloured are beginning to seek common cause with black consciousness movements. Within these movements there is a deliberate downplaying and even rejection of ethnicity as a factor in the South African situation.

It is important to highlight the significance of the Population Registration Act because it complicates the nature of the conflict situation in South Africa. For as long as white domination persists ethnicity will be less salient as a feature in the political arena. In fact there will increasingly be a strategic black solidarity against white domination. However, we believe it would be very shortsighted to ignore the possibility of ethnic competition and conflict once white domination has been ended. Therefore, in trying to find ways of resolving the conflict in an evolutionary and relatively peaceful manner, one has to consider not only white fears and black frustration and aggression, but also the potential for ethnic conflict once racial domination is no longer a feature of South African society. The underlying question to be kept in mind is: what kind of constitutional structure will to the greatest extent prevent racial and/or ethnic mobilization? Is it one that ignores race and ethnicity as political issues or deliberately takes them into account?

Fundamental power over the entire society rests in the hands of a white oligarchy; legal status and the rights that ensue from it are determined for individuals by the ascriptive criterion of colour. Historically, other configurations of conflict were important. Until comparatively recent times most whites considered the ethnic conflict between Afrikaner and English to be the most salient. This conflict had important ramifications that affected the conflict between white and black.[3] But to an increasing extent the conflict has taken on a binary character, as the fundamental polarization of society into white and black emerges into sharp focus.

This development does not mean that ethnic conflict within the white group has been eliminated; rather it has been muted even more than it historically was by the rise of black opposition to white domination. Nor does it mean that the black groups are without conflict in their relationships with one another – clearly the intermediate legal and civic statuses of the Asian and coloured categories (and the widespread sense of superiority over blacks within them) have inhibited the development of complete black solidarity. But there is an unmistakable trend for the common perception of white oppression to generate a sense of black identity that transcends the differences among the black groups.

Conflict between groups stems from the aims of rival groups to secure the same scarce material and non-material resources. If the resources were not scarce there would be no occasion for conflict over their attainment; and if the respective groups desired wholly different resources there would similarly be no occasion for conflict. (This situation has been approximated in real life by the case of the Tungus and Cossacks of Siberia, who live in an interdependent, symbiotic co-existence but do not conflict with or seek to dominate one another because they do not compete for land or natural resources.)[32]

The ability or capacity of a group to engage in conflict relations will depend on its power-resources and the extent to which it can mobilize them.[33] It will be recalled from the earlier discussion that where one group has superior power-resources and mobilizational capacities over the other(s) it will be able to establish and institutionalize a system of stratification. Power-resources vary in their tangibility; they include: the numbers of people constituting the group; coercive military and police power; superior technological know-how and other more advanced educational skills; control over the economic institutions of the society, wealth and income; political power, including the right to vote and the ability to determine or influence the political decision-making process. Obviously the exercise of these power-resources requires that there exists among the group or its leaders the will to exercise power and, crucially, the capacity to mobilize the resources for deployment in the group's interest. Here less tangible resources enter the picture: the quality of leadership and its ability to organize the group effectively; the development of an ideology that legitimates the group's exercise of power.

Ethnicity itself may be taken as an example of the latter phenomenon. It may be both a rallying cry for group mobilization and a legitimation of the group's dominant position or a defence mechanism against oppression by a dominant group.[34] Herbert Blumer's analysis of race prejudice as a sense of group position relates to these propositions. He argues that racial prejudice in a dominant group is usually characterized by four basic types of feeling: (1) a feeling of superiority; (2) a feeling that the subordinate race is intrinsically different and alien; (3) a feeling that as the dominant group it is entitled to either exclusive or prior rights, privileges or advantages in many important areas of life; and (4) a fear and suspicion that the subordinate race harbours designs on the prerogatives of the dominant race.[35]

Clearly one form of power can generate other forms:[36] the consolidation of a dominant group's position may be a lengthy process in historical time. Moreover, the cohesiveness and solidarity of the group may vary under different circumstances, one important variable being the extent to which its members perceive that they are being threatened *as a group*. It must be emphasized that in this kind of power-group analysis one is not concerned solely with the resources and mobilizational capacity of the dominant group. Exactly the same kind of inventory must be drawn up for the dominated groups: what kinds of power-resources do they possess and to what extent can they mobilize them? It may well be that a dominated group has potential power-resources whose mobilization is frustrated by the tactics of the dominant group. For example, South African blacks may be said to possess considerable potential resources in the form of their numerical preponderancy and the dependence of the economy on their labour. But to a large extent the full exercise of these power-resources is prevented or inhibited by the policies and the rival power of the dominant group.

In taking initiatives or, generally, in engaging in action, the moves of either dominant or dominated groups will be based upon their assessments of their respective resources and mobilizational capacities.[37] This underlying process may be likened to an economic cost/benefit analysis; and it may be based upon incomplete or invalid information.

Inter-group conflicts in divided societies tend to take on a regularized or institutionalized structure: they become patterned and, to a greater or lesser extent, certain 'rules-of-the-game', procedures and conventions may become established.[36] These will be conditioned to a considerable extent by the ideologies, cultural predispositions and other attitudinal attributes of the rival groups. It may be that the dominant group will seek to create institutions designed to regulate and contain the conflict: the effectiveness of such institutions will obviously depend on a number of factors that will have to be specified.

It must be emphasized that in presenting this power/conflict framework of analysis there is no suggestion that the configuration of conflict in any particular society need be static. The issues of conflict may change; the intensity with which groups push their demands may vary; and it is not inconceivable that groups may 'change sides' as when, for example, a threatened dominant group seeks to bolster its position by incorporating or co-opting a previously subordinate group. (It is this kind of power-play which lies at the heart of the South African government's constitutional proposals: by bringing in the Asian and coloured groups on the side of the whites they are trying to build a stronger power-base among non-blacks.) A further consideration is that this power/conflict model implies no acceptance of the legitimacy of the structures and institutions established by the dominant group for its own instrumental and manipulative uses. Dominated groups may well seek to mobilize their resources for the complete overthrow of a system. As Anatol Rapoport says:

'A revolt of slaves against their status as slaves cannot be "settled" by a compromise whereby the slaves are accorded better treatment, or whatever. Once the *structure of the system* becomes the real issue, offers of this sort will be seen only as attempts to preserve the structure and will be rejected as long as the revolt can be sustained.'[39]

This kind of issue leads to the heart of the matter: the extent to which issues are negotiable or bargainable, which will be extensively discussed in a subsequent chapter.

Much of the foregoing discussion has been premised on the assumption that the collectivities involved in the power conflict are clearly bounded from one another by readily identifiable characteristics. Ethnic conflict involving groups with different colours clearly has such boundaries, and the increasing intensity of the conflict will increasingly pressurize individuals and categories to align themselves unambiguously with one side in the conflict.[40] The exponents of Black Consciousness, for example, are invoking a contrived black ethnicity as an instrument of power because they believe that it is easier to mobilize on this relatively simple and emotionally appealing basis and because they believe that an interracial movement directed against apartheid would unnecessarily obscure the real basis of the conflict, which they see as colour. Polarization, in other words, generates a need for sharply defined sides.

The power/conflict model focuses largely on the divisive forces in society and it therefore runs into the danger of ignoring or underplaying the forces that hold the society together. Societies cannot be understood solely in terms of conflict: conflict, ironically, presupposes some degree of social interaction and perhaps even co-operation. Nor would it suffice to say that the cohesiveness of South African society is dependent solely on coercion and terror. Clearly these latter factors are important and are the ultimate guarantors of the social structure but, as Max Gluckman and others have pointed out, there are cross-linkages between the colour groups that provide an additional source of cohesion. In his famous article on 'The Bonds in the Colour Bar' Gluckman showed how black and white did not interact with one another as monolithic, antagonistic blocs. Both groups contained significant internal divisions whose existence facilitated the growth of cross-linkages between the colour groups and thereby inhibited the development of intense conflict along a single axis. Gluckman writes:

'There emerged in Zululand a social system containing Blacks and Whites which had a cohesion of its own, arising from the common participation of Zulu and Whites in economic and other activities in which they became more and more dependent on one another. . . . The system contained many sources of dispute and friction, but these arose largely out of new forms of cooperation between the colour groups.'[41]

Economic interdependence, the generation of common material needs, the widespread acceptance among blacks of Christianity and education, embryonic common class-perceptions as between black and white middle-class people, and a myriad of interpersonal ties of friendship, patron-client relationships and common interests have all served to mitigate the sharpness of conflict. Heribert Adam has raised the possibility that the Nationalist leadership in South Africa, in the interests of its own preservation, might seek to capitalize on these trends and try to prevent an explosive conflict by fostering a rising black middle class with a stake in the maintenance of the status quo, thereby transforming South Africa from a race society into a class society.[42]

It remains true, however, that racial polarization is increasing. Nationalist policy has deliberately eliminated many of the cross-linkages, and in more recent times Black Consciousness has rejected the interracial co-operation and contact that occurred in a number of spheres. Even so, the trend towards polarization must not be overstated. There are contradictory forces at work. The overall process is complex and subtle. If one examines the cohesiveness of groups as an issue, one finds that the intensification of conflict produces different, even contradictory responses among members of the same colour group. For example, the Black Consciousness movement rejects in principle any involvement by blacks in state-sponsored political institutions such as homeland governments. It seeks to maximize black solidarity as a countervailing power to white power. Yet significant numbers of blacks have co-operated with these institutions, not because they accept the underlying policy but because they see in them a means of obtaining leverage (or power-resources) within the overall political system. Appreciable numbers are employed in the civil services and others have been the recipients of loans from the various development corporations. In other words, a comparatively large 'client class' has been generated by separate development. The significance for our argument is that one effect of these processes is to turn conflict in on the black communities themselves, thereby reducing their potential thrust and solidarity. Broadly comparable phenomena are found in South West Africa/Namibia and Zimbabwe-Rhodesia, where white-sponsored independence programmes have exacerbated cleavages among the black populations.

No *a priori* assumptions can be made about the implications of these trends for future efforts at conflict resolution. On the one hand, it may be that the absence of a monolithic solidarity among the rival groups could facilitate a political settlement because inter-group linkages and alliances between segments or classes of the groups will be easier to forge, thereby reducing the intensity of pressure along a single (racial) axis. On the other hand, the intensity of feeling generated by division within the black communities could create even more serious tension by creating a political situation in which rival black groups seek to maximize support by vying with one another in making extreme demands.

The problem of conflict in South Africa is that the lines of cleavage are mutually reinforcing. Even if race and class are analytically distinct they overlap to a considerable extent and there is a strong tendency for them to be fused in black perceptions. Conflict resolution would be easier if class, status and race could be detached from one another – a proposition that will be further explored in the chapter dealing with the institutional mechanics of conflict resolution.

It will be clear from the argument of this chapter that the easing of racial tension in South Africa will require structural changes. We have tried to demonstrate that the conflict is about the various kinds of inequalities that are institutionalized in the society. Exhortations by people of goodwill, politicians (even Nationalist ones nowadays) and others to the effect that racial prejudice is 'a bad thing' serve little purpose if the structures that generate racism are left untouched. It must be recognized that the dominant white group has real fears. Without necessarily passing any moral judgement on them, it is true that they are beneficiaries of a highly unequal exploitative system. They fear the loss of privileges, the possible expropriation of property, and being swamped by a huge black majority. Ignoring their own repressive, undemocratic practices, they fear the instability and 'chaos' which they believe would follow from black participation in a democratic system of government: Idi Amin becomes the symbol of black majority rule.

Racial conflict is fundamentally about the allocation of resources (material and non-material). There is a strong tendency, on both sides, for this conflict to be viewed in zero-sum terms – what you get I lose. The problem of conflict resolution will be to orient people's perceptions away from this view, and to induce them to think in terms of joint efforts to attain common or superordinate goals whose realization will make *all* groups better off.

3 *The politics of divided societies*

A considerable amount of pessimism has been caused by the widespread degeneration or collapse of democratic government in ethnically divided societies. To list the numerous cases is to recite a litany of conflict, strife, authoritarianism and violence, including several instances of civil war where the fabric of civil society has been torn apart. It has been estimated that of all domestic violence in the world between 1961 and 1965, between 25 and 30 per cent had its origins in ethnic conflict; and another estimate puts the figure for fatalities in ethnic violence between 1945 and 1970 at over 10 million.[1]

The ethnically divided society might be termed the norm in the contemporary world. Walker Connor has calculated that all but fourteen of today's states contain at least one significant minority, and half of this small group of states are characterized by irredentist situations where the dominant ethnic group extends beyond the state's borders.[2] He has also shown that among the 132 states examined, twenty-five (18,9 per cent) contained an ethnic group accounting for more than 90 per cent of the state's total population; in a further twenty-five the largest groups accounted for between 75 and 89 per cent of the population; in thirty-one states (23,5 per cent) the largest ethnic groups represent 50 to 74 per cent of the total population; and in thirty-nine states (29,5 per cent) the largest groups are smaller than half of the state's total population. Moreover, in fifty-three cases (40,2 per cent) the population is distributed among more than five significant groups.[3]

The political difficulties that ethnic conflicts cause have been a source of comfort to the South African government, which argues that the inability of 'integrated' or 'common' societies to sustain democratic systems of government is a legitimation of its policies. Its spokesmen and propaganda services (including radio and television) cite, with evident satisfaction, the numerous manifestations of ethnic conflict, and some of their more sophisticated productions contain elaborate expositions of the case for the 'impossibility' of the multiethnic state.[4] One does not have to accept these propagandistic arguments (and, even less, the implications for policy that are drawn) to accept that ethnic division does pose serious problems for statecraft, and that, in particular, South Africa, with its complex configuration of groups, will have no easy way out of its dilemmas.

Part of the problem is that the democratic model of society, a norm that commands world-wide support in theory (even Russia claims to be democratic), was developed in the relatively homogeneous societies of the West, and exported by them, largely through the instrumentality of colonialism, to much of the Third World. Colonialism was an inherently undemocratic relationship and the anti-colonial revolt was, in one respect, born of the anomaly whereby democratic societies practised democracy at home and authoritarianism abroad. But the Lockean tradition of democratic thought posited the individual citizen as the right-possessing actor in the democratic process: it did not contemplate situations in which highly structured groups mediated between the individual and the state and became, in effect, the most salient political units.

Of course, one may point out now, with the benefit of hindsight, that the emphasis on individualism was misplaced to begin with: groups have been involved ever since the origins of representative forms of government; and one may further point out that the societies of the West were not all that homogeneous. In post-revolutionary France, for example, 'drastic measures, amounting to outright terrorism in the case of Alsace, were taken', to achieve language unity in the face of extensive language heterogeneity – so extensive, in fact, that the majority of French citizens were unable to speak French or spoke it with difficulty.[5] Moreover, Irish, Scots and Welsh nationalisms, Breton and Basque separatism, and other comparable phenomena in established democratic societies, indicate that however submerged or latent ethnic cleavages may appear to be, certain circumstances may activate them.

It is a striking aspect of ethnic conflict that it is not confined to any one type or category of state. It is found in the established Western democracies, like Belgium, Canada and the United Kingdom; in communist states like Russia, Yugoslavia, Rumania and China; and, almost ubiquitously, in the numerous states that have emerged out of the colonial revolution after 1945. Variables like the degree of economic development, levels of education, the kind of political system and length of exposure to its norms, appear to count for little in explaining the incidence and severity of ethnic conflict.

Clearly ethnicity was a phenomenon encountered long before its rise to particular prominence in the 1960s and 1970s: its force had been felt in the Austro-Hungarian Empire in the latter part of the nineteenth and early twentieth centuries; Switzerland had experienced civil war along ethnic lines in 1847; Ireland had been a pressing problem for Britain since at least the rebellion of 1798; and conflict was endemic in those societies where settler ruled native, as in Algeria, Kenya, South Africa, Indonesia or Rhodesia. Yet the assumption was widespread in the era of decolonization that ethnic differences (often referred to as 'tribalism') were not serious obstacles to 'nation-building'. As Walker Connor has pointed out, the anticipation that 'modernization' would lead to a decline of attachments to the ethnic group and a corresponding identification with the nation-state, had not been fulfilled.[6] Indeed, not only has it not been fulfilled, but the salience of ethnicity has been heightened.

The optimism about the prospects for 'nation-building' rested, in turn, on an optimism about the plasticity of human society, which is an important ingredient of both liberalism and Marxism – the dominant ideological forces of the period after World War II. In the aftermath of Nazism, racism became universally execrated, and along with this went a tendency to regard ethnicity as something only marginally less deplorable. Diverse social groupings could be moulded into cohesive populations; 'tribal' cultures were doomed to extinction; and 'modernity' would replace 'tradition'. Much of this thinking was based on facile extrapolations from what was assumed to have been the Western experience of nation-building. Moreover, it struck resonant chords in the minds of many African political leaders: to them acknowledgement of the strength of ethnicity seemed to be a confirmation of Africans' 'backwardness' and their inability to work modern systems of democratic government. More importantly, they believed that political structures which, through federalism or other institutional devices, sought to protect ethnic groupings would fatally weaken the independent new state by making it vulnerable to separatist demands and by giving ethnicity a power-base that would perpetuate it.

It was not universally true that colonial nationalist movements had transcended the ethnic divisions of the colonial society. In a number of cases, like Nigeria and Uganda, and elsewhere, as in British Guiana, Malaya and Cyprus, even a common opposition to colonial rule had not been able to create or sustain an interethnic nationalist front in the pre-independence period. This meant that the negotiations leading up to independence were often characterized by protracted struggles over which group was to assume overall control or what safeguards could be erected for minorities.

As we have indicated, the optimism of earlier decades has given way to pessimism, at least in the minds of many scholars who study ethnic phenomena. An exposition of this point of view, stated in theoretical terms, has been presented by Alvin Rabushka and Kenneth A. Shepsle, whose paradigm of politics in plural societies is as follows: the formation, *ceteris paribus,* of a broad-based multi-ethnic coalition during the formative period, typically the period of anti-colonial nationalism; its survival through the post-independence period, fostered by ambiguous pronouncements on divisive ethnic issues, and the generation of demand for national issues; the emergence of ambitious politicians (political entrepreneurs) whose quest for the perquisites of political office provokes appeals to ethnic passions; the consequent resurrection of ethnicity as the salient dimension of political competition; the development of a politics of outbidding; the disappearance of brokerage institutions and the ethnicization of public goods; the ineffectuality of moderate elements; and, finally, the decline of democratic competition, a result of electoral machinations and political violence. The authors conclude that western democracy 'cannot be sustained under conditions of intense, salient preferences because outcomes are valued more than procedural norms. The plural society, constrained by the preferences of its citizens, does not provide fertile soil for democratic values or stability.'[7]

Although we will criticize this paradigm in the following chapter, there can be no gainsaying its cogency and explanatory force. Democracy *is* exceedingly difficult to establish and maintain under circumstances of deep division. We have to acknowledge that John Stuart Mill was substantially correct when he wrote in 1861 that 'it is in general a necessary condition of free institutions that the boundaries of governments should coincide in the main with those of nationalities'; and Lord Acton, who wrote in 1862, appears substantially wrong when he defended the multi-national state arguing, 'That intolerance of social freedom which is natural to absolutism is sure to find a corrective in the national diversities, which no other force could so efficiently provide. The co-existence of several nations under the same state is a test as well as the best security of its freedoms.'

Pessimism alone will not suffice. Given the frequency of its occurrence in the contemporary world, ethnic conflict must somehow be coped with unless violence is to become endemic over large parts of the world, and societies or subgroups within societies are to stagnate or labour under repressive rule. It should be recalled, moreover, that the rise of nationalism and ethnicity is a comparatively recent development in human history, dating on any widescale occurrence only from 1789. The ethnic attachment has not been a universal condition of man's existence. We may recall, too, that for centuries Europe was wracked by religious conflict which subsequently abated, or at least was able to be peacefully regulated. Ethnicity *may* be a relatively transitory phenomenon, but this is cold comfort for those who have to endure the miseries and insecurity of life in deeply divided societies.

In principle there is no reason why ethnic conflict cannot be understood and its dynamics comprehended within a framework of analysis. A by-product of the upsurge in ethnic conflict has been the proliferation of scholarly accounts of ethnicity, both theoretical and case-studies, spanning several academic disciplines. To understand is, at least, to be in a better position to regulate and control. The observer may often think that the actors in ethnic conflict behave 'irrationally', and the evidence of possibility that people take leave of their senses on a wide scale is compelling. The following comment on Northern Ireland suggests this:

'It is as important for the Catholic working-class to feel persecuted as it is for the Protestants to feel at risk from the enemy within and the Catholic hordes waiting over the border. This is what provides each side with the sense of community which is felt to be the only real security available . . . virtually everyone in Ulster feels himself under threat and reacts accordingly. There is no inclination for reason or compromise simply because the most urgent need is to combat a threat which may seem small or non-existent to outsiders but looms obliteratingly over those locked into the situation.'[8]

Yet the invoking of ethnicity is a perfectly rational action in multi-ethnic societies where groups are engaged in a struggle for power. The introduction of democratic politics, with its egalitarian connotations (albeit more honoured in the breach than in the observance), together with a greatly widened politicization of decision-making in 'old' as well as 'new' states, have all contributed to the growth of ethnicity as a focus of mobilization. Political leaders have felt impelled to secure power-bases for themselves, and in many cases ethnic affiliation presented the most easily exploitable social fissure. In many of the new states of Africa, for example, ethno-linguistic groups or clusters could be mobilized as power-blocs, or had been so mobilized during the colonial era. The Ibo of Nigeria were a cultural cluster of autonomous village-based groups. The development of a sense of Ibo-hood came only with the social, economic and political changes introduced by colonial rule. The social structure of the Kikuyu was comparable. Crawford Young writes:

'The Kikuyu have emerged since independence as the dominant

cultural grouping in Kenya; their self-awareness took shape in the context of intense deprivation and has been consolidated in circumstances of unprecedented opportunities for collective advance made possible by the configuration of ethnic politics since independence.'[9]

Much the same kind of analysis can be made of Afrikaner nationalism. There was no real sense of Afrikaner national identity until the last quarter of the nineteenth century. It developed as a response to British imperialism and, in the twentieth century, it was employed as an instrument of political mobilization that could, and subsequently did, gain control of the political system (see pp. 80–1).

Numerous comparable examples may be cited from other ethnically divided societies. The point to be emphasized is that ethnicity is a relational concept; it emerges only when groups are involved in competitive or conflict relations. It is not, in the African cases, simply a matter of 'tribalism', but much more an instrument of group mobilization in societies where, typically, the impact of colonial rule, economic development, education and missionary activity has been uneven, and groups seek either to maintain their privileges or to gain further political resources for the purpose of overcoming their relative deprivation. Much of the underlying basis of ethnic conflict in Nigeria can be understood in terms of these factors. The same is true of ethnicity in the American context, where immigrant groups tended to cleave together for purposes of security and in order to enhance their bargaining power within the wider society. As a recent analysis puts it, 'It is the unequal distribution of power, especially between racial groups, and to a lesser degree between ethnic groups, that is the critical dimension of interethnic competition and of hierarchical arrangements between the races'.[10]

It may be pointed out here that there is nothing inevitable about a group's developing a sense of ethnic identity. Not all groups in South Africa have done so: English-speaking whites have not become in any significant sense an ethnic group (although, of course, they share fully in a wider white racial identity); neither have the coloured people, who are a residual category of people and groups of diverse origins that are not 'white'. Both of these categories are minorities in the numerical sense and both have seen their best interests as being served by alliances with other groups or segments of them. Thus, historically the English have, mostly, looked to a section of non-Nationalist Afrikaners as allies in the struggle for power; a few have sought allies across the colour line.[11] Most coloured people have similarly regarded themselves as being identified with the whites rather than with blacks, although significant numbers of younger people are now increasingly identifying themselves with the new (and essentially ethnic) Black Consciousness movement. The point is that neither the English nor the coloured people can hope to attain significant power by themselves and therefore it is not in their interest to emphasize their ethnic separateness.[12]

As was argued in the preceding chapter, the bases of ethnic group formation may lie in a number of factors such as race, culture, language, religion or a combination of these. Ethnic groups may even seek to widen their differences from others by deliberately fostering a distinctive feature such as an indigenous language, even if it means rescuing it from partial disuse: Gaelic in Ireland is a case in point. Alternatively, ethnic identities may survive even when extensive cultural assimilation has occurred. As Milton M. Gordon's analysis of ethnicity in America demonstrated, despite massive acculturation to Anglo-Saxon norms, the structural separation of ethnic groups still remained.[13]

These points underline the fact that far-reaching social change and the extensive development of ties of interdependence among ethnic groups does not diminish the salience of ethnicity; in fact it may well increase it as more intense competitive and conflicting interaction occurs in, for example, an urban setting, and the respective groups seek to retain or gain power-resources. In an analysis of Nigeria, Robert Melson and Howard Wolpe have argued that 'modernization, far from destroying communalism, in time both reinforces communal conflict and creates the conditions for the formation of entirely new communal groups'. The effect of modernization is to generate demands for similar resources: 'It is by making men "more alike", in the sense of possessing the same wants, that modernization tends to promote conflict.'[14]

As the power of government has become more and more centralized, even in federations, and the state's role in the allocative process has become of prime importance, so the conflict between ethnic groups has focused on the goal of attaining supreme political power. The strategy and aims of ethnic groups will depend on their actual and potential resources, most crucially on their numbers, and their physical location within the society. In societies like Malaysia and Guyana, where the numerical proportions of rival groups are of critical importance, the ruling groups will cling on to power with a desperation that is born of the conviction that politics is a zero-sum game in which you are in power or out of power. In Lebanon the numerical size of the different Christian and Muslim groups was an equally sensitive issue, to the extent that no census has been taken since 1932 lest a new one should show, as is commonly supposed to be the case, that the total non-Christian population now exceeds the Christian.

In Malaysia, Malay political domination is entrenched in the bargain struck between the leaders of the Malay, Chinese and Indian communities in 1957. Even though the Malays constitute a bare 50 per cent of the total population they are the 'natives of the soil' and accordingly regard themselves as having the right to political hegemony. In Guyana, neither the African nor the East Indian communities are 'native' to the country, being the descendants of slaves and imported indentured labourers respectively. Recent estimates indicate that the Africans number 36 per cent of the population and the East Indians 51 per cent.[15] Communal passions split the society in the early 1960s and impeded the movement towards independence. When deadlock was reached between the rival movements in the independence negotiations, proportional representation was imposed and in the elections of 1964 James Burnham's Peoples National Congress, the African party, managed to oust Cheddi Jagan's Peoples Progressive Party, the East Indian party, by entering into a coalition with the United Force, a small party led by Portuguese businessmen, who mustered sufficient votes to tip the scales against Jagan.

In circumstances where proportional representation mirrors very accurately the racial breakdown of the electorate, and where the East Indian population is increasing more rapidly than the African, Burnham looked for means of boosting his support; in 1968 his government enacted legislation that enfranchised non-resident Guyanese, who numbered over 60 000 and constituted one-sixth of the electorate.[16] In the election in the same year over 93 per cent of the overseas votes and over 50 per cent of the domestic votes went to Burnham's party, giving him a comfortable majority. It is quite clear, however, that a considerable amount of fraudulence was involved in inflating his support.[17]

Of course there are a number of cases where an ethnic group, because of its size, cannot hope to attain supreme power. All it can try to do is to protect itself against unqualified majoritarianism, that is to say, the unbridled power of a (democratically) elected majority. Ethnic minorities in this situation, if they are regionally concentrated, may press for regional autonomy, federalism, or even, in extreme cases, partition. The Tamils of Sri Lanka, who number 11 per cent of the total population (another category of Tamils, the Indian Tamils, account for a further 10,6 per cent of the population but, because they are denied citizenship, have no franchise rights), are concentrated in the north-east of the island and have sought unsuccessfully to secure regional autonomy.[18] The Catholics of Northern Ireland, who amount to 35 per cent of the population, have been similarly steam-rollered by the Protestant majority who, although their majority in Northern Ireland is not in real doubt, fear their incorporation into a united Ireland in which they would be outnumbered four to one.

A comparable situation exists for the Turks of Cyprus, who number fewer than 20 per cent of the total population. From 1964 onwards a substantial number of Turks from isolated villages and the Turkish quarters of ethnically mixed villages moved to areas that were subsequently consolidated into Turkish enclaves, with the intention of creating at least a partial geographical basis for a federal structure.[19] In 1974 Cyprus was invaded by Turkey and the island was subjected to forcible partition.

In the case of Canada Quebec separatism is another manifestation of minority rejection of majoritarianism. French Canadians constitute approximately 28 per cent of the total Canadian population and the large majority of them live in Quebec, whose population contains also an English-speaking minority of 1,2 million or 20 per cent of the total Quebec population.[20]

Although a degree of inter-ethnic accommodation has prevailed in Canada for more than a hundred years, the so-called 'Quiet Revolution' in Quebec during the 1960s presaged demands for a special status or even independence for Quebec. These demands emanate from the widespread feeling among Quebecois that they will not attain their rightful degree of autonomy unless they are *maitre chez-nous,* i.e. they are not prepared to submit to majoritarianism, even where it has been circumscribed by federal arrangements and the range of other institutional devices that have characterized the Canadian political system's attempt to accommodate ethnic diversity.

The four cases of ethnic minorities sketched above point to an important hypothesis which we shall develop in chapter 4. It is the proposition that democracy in a deeply divided society is not served by unqualified majoritarianism. The relevance of the examples for a future democratic South Africa is that the ratio of blacks to non-blacks would be comparable to the population ratios in each of the examples. It is important to note that even if these minorities are, in numerical terms, small, they nevertheless possess power-resources. Milton M. Gordon has put forward the hypothesis that

'the optimal situation in a democratic-egalitarian pluralistic society . . . is one in which the minority group has an *intermediate degree of power* – less than that of the majority, so that it cannot disrupt the society completely, but enough so that it can levy strategic influence to protect its rights – "cause trouble", so to speak, in areas of discriminatory treatment, and in which it is supported by "outside" power in the face of a violent threat by the majority on its existence and legitimate aspirations.'[21]

The former Canadian prime minister, Pierre Trudeau, has made the same point more cryptically: 'In terms of realpolitik, French and English are equal in Canada because each of these linguistic groups has the power to break the country.'[22] Obviously, neither Gordon's nor Trudeau's comments may be taken as suggesting that this kind of power configuration is a sufficient condition for a democratic political system. The suggestion is rather that it may be a basis on which steps towards establishing such a system may be taken.

A more favourable configuration is where no single group in a multi-ethnic society is in a position to dominate the others. Arend Lijphart has argued that 'if all subcultures are minorities, their leaders will tend to be more willing to compromise and less tempted to dominate the other groups than where two subcultures are equally strong or when one subculture enjoys a clear hegemony'.[23] Thus, ethnicity has not been a serious issue in Tanzania because no single group predominates; and in India where language, caste and religion have generated 'a fantastic panoply of subcultures, each of which is a relatively small minority', extreme diversity has been a source of strength for democratic government.[24]

The case of ethnicity in Yugoslavia may be cited as an intermediate one where, although two groups, the Serbs (39,7 per cent) and the Croats (22,1 per cent), are bigger than any other groups, they are counterbalanced by other groups, none exceeding 10 per cent of the total population, who account for nearly 40 per cent.[25] During the inter-war period the Serbs were dominant; and the ethnic issue in Titoist Yugoslavia has to a large extent revolved around Croat allegations of 'Great Serb chauvinism'.[26] Since 1972 League of Communist policy has been to decentralize political and economic power to the federal republics and autonomous provinces, each of which contains the major concentration of the various groups. Moreover, considerable (and largely successful) efforts have been made to ensure that each ethnic group is fairly represented in the key institutions of Yugoslav society. Much of the ethnic conflict today appears to stem from one of the classic problems of federalism, namely the economic inequalities among regions that, as in Yugoslavia's case, are structured along ethnic lines.[27]

We turn now to a discussion of whether constitutions are a significant factor in mitigating or exacerbating ethnic conflict. From the examples mentioned so far one may deduce that ethnic conflict occurs in states that are democratic or undemocratic, federal or unitary; which may lead one to draw the conclusion that constitutions or the type of political system involved in fact count for very little as a variable in explaining the severity or otherwise of ethnic conflict. A strong argument can be made for the point of view that constitutions are mere reflections of the society. In a much-quoted remark that reflects this perspective William S. Livingstone said that 'the essence of federalism lies not in the institutional or constitutional structure but in the society itself. Federal government is a device by which the federal qualities of the society are articulated and protected.'[28] Much of modern political science similarly relegates study of the formal provisions of constitutions to a marginal role, and in the quest for understanding of what makes democratic government viable, constitutions have received very little attention.

Consideration of these issues is important in the quest for appropriate models for the political system of South Africa, because it may well be that any constitutional design for a democratic government will be a fruitless exercise in the context of ethnic passions whose force is so great as to be able to rip through the delicate fabric of constitutionalism. As Rabushka and Shepsle noted, in ethnically inflamed societies outcomes are valued more than procedural norms (see above, p. 34), and constitutions are to a very large extent to do with procedural norms. It is hardly surprising, therefore, that studies of ethnic politics are concerned more with behaviour and social structures than with political institutions. The thrust of our own analysis and proposals also inclines in this direction.

There is an obvious and trite sense in which constitutions do reflect 'society' in as much as they are often the outcome of pacts, bargains or compromises reached by the major political forces in society, whose power-bases are rooted in the socio-economic structure. If the constitution is congruent with these forces, and can adapt itself to changing power-balances, it may put down roots of legitimacy and develop a 'living force' of its own. Perhaps the most notable examples of this phenomenon are the British and United States constitutions, whose hallowed provisions and practices do have a marked effect on the shaping of political life. Carl J. Friedrich, who represents an older perspective in political science, writes:

'If constitution-making . . . is seen as a continuous process, it evidently is a meaningful and significant part of modern democratic government. In this light the mocking attitude of some political scientists toward "institutional" concern, in contrast to their own "behavioral" approach is rather misleading, since behavior and institutions are not mutually exclusive or antithetical terms referring to radically divergent realities. Quite to the contrary, institutions consist in established, repetitive behavior. . . .'[29]

In the modern post-colonial world many constitutions have come and gone. Poverty, underdevelopment and acute ethnic cleavages have imposed intolerable strains on constitutionalism, and its fate in many Third-World states has been rapid abandonment. Nevertheless, constitution-making has been taken seriously, as the many protracted constitutional conferences presided over by departing colonial powers suggest. In the new states constitutions 'serve as a kind of surrogate tradition where no national political traditions could yet exist.'[30] In circumstances where habits, conventions and political cultures have not yet crystallized, the strong tendency has been for constitution-makers to try to prescribe in minute detail what political behaviour shall be, and little is left to the spontaneous growth of conventions.

Our main concern in the context of constitutional engineering is with the capacity or otherwise of constitutional safeguards to curb ethnic domination or discrimination and to protect minorities. A critical aspect of this question has been the widespread reluctance of nationalist leaders to accept fetters on their power, or, where they have acquiesced in them, to abide by the constitutional restraints. S.A. de Smith writes:

'The very suggestion that a majority party is not to be trusted to act fairly or to keep its own supporters in order is liable to evoke deep resentment; the emotional revulsion against those who insist on regarding themselves as a peculiar people may be heightened by recollections of their flaunting of undue advantage in the recent past and by awareness of their continuing superiority in wealth and education. In face of these facts, constitutional proposals which single out a communal minority for a preferred position in the new order will seldom be considered objectively on their merits.'[31]

De Smith, who has had considerable experience in drafting constitutions, lists nine types of safeguard against the abuse of majority power:

(1) a written constitution with the requirement of special procedures for the amendment of particular clauses of the constitution, and the judicial review of legislation;

(2) the legitimacy of organized dissent by the official recognition of the Leader of the Opposition;

(3) the organization of the electoral system and the allocation of seats to give representation to minorities;

(4) a second chamber for minority and regional interests and traditional elements;

(5) special institutional mechanisms to obstruct discriminatory legislation;

(6) attempts to screen sensitive areas of public administration from political control – delimitation of constituencies and the conduct of elections, the administration of justice, the process of prosecutions, the civil service and police, and the audit of public accounts;

(7) the protection of traditional rulers;

(8) bills of rights;

(9) federalism.[32]

The insertion of some (or all) of these safeguards into a constitution will certainly create the formal means for protecting minorities, but the problem remains, as the quotation from De Smith indicates, that their very presence may be counterproductive insofar as they serve as a continuing irritant to the majority. Moreover, formal restraints on governmental power tend to make constitutions rigid and, as the jurist Salmond warned, 'a constitution that will not bend will sooner or later break'.[33]

The arguments presented above are not intended to provide justifications for the proposition that exercises in constitution-making for divided societies are futile. The aim is rather to suggest that constitutions are not sufficient conditions for the regulation of conflict in such societies: they have to be complemented and underpinned by a range of other formal and informal devices and institutions that focus directly on the conflict. Even more important are the attitudes of the politicians, civil servants, judicial officers and others who operate the machinery established by the constitution. To the extent that these groups believe that conflict-regulation by democratic means is desirable, the constitution will become protected by a democratic political culture. This last proposition, of course, begs the question of how it comes about that democratic values become accepted and internalized by political leaders, even when they are sharply divided by ideological differences. There is no easy answer to this, except to say that where democratic methods work and the allocative process is seen to be equitable, then the support for democracy may develop a real basis in the society. It is in this that constitutions have importance and are not necessarily the mere creatures of society.[34] As J.A. Laponce has said:

'[Constitutions] have no other value than that attributed to them, but, even when ignored or scoffed at, they preserve, if only in a verbal way, an ideal, a rule that may possibly be given life again. Thus, even though a right written into a constitution may have neither judicial nor political sanction, it still is not devoid of usefulness. The moral value, as limited as it might be, is never negligible.'[35]

Moreover, as will be argued in subsequent chapters, there are institutions like the executive, and how it is structured and composed, and the electoral system and its effect on the party system, which may have a direct bearing on the course of the conflict and, therefore, are not irrelevant variables. The executive is the locus of effective power in modern government, and the representation of minority ethnic groups in the executive or its accessibility to them, will be a material factor in their protection; parties are usually the major vehicles of political power-resources, and accordingly they are of importance in the politics of ethnic conflict: are parties inter-ethnic in their composition, or are they ethnically based? What effect does the kind of electoral system have on the shape of the party system and, in turn, on the structure of conflict?

Such questions are of critical importance to the political process in ethnically divided societies: where the divisions run deep the party system will reflect the divisions. Even if, as in the cases of Canada and Belgium, the party system was established in times before the heightened and pre-eminent salience of ethnicity, it will come to reflect this new pattern of conflict.[36] Over the past decade Belgium's traditional major parties, which reflected earlier religious and ideological conflicts, have been divided into ethnic wings, and purely ethnic parties have made gains. In Canada, the process has not advanced so far, but in Quebec in 1976 the *Parti Quebecois* ousted the Liberals from their traditional domination on a secessionist platform.

In situations of deep ethnic cleavage, then, the prospects for viable inter-ethnic parties based upon class, function or region are poor. There have been numerous attempts to create such 'bridging' parties but we know of no single case where an inter-ethnic party has succeeded in fending off or ousting ethnically based rivals. (A near-precedent occurred in the Mauritius elections of December 1976 when the inter-ethnic Marxist *Mouvement Militant Mauricien* nearly succeeded in defeating the governing parties, which are mostly ethnically based.[37])

Given the intense feelings that ethnicity evokes, its impact on parties and party systems should come as no surprise. Parties, after all, are groups founded upon aggregations of common interests, and if the promotion of ethnic group interests are paramount, then the ethnic-rootedness of parties follows nearly automatically.

It is not only through party competition that the politics of ethnicity is manifest. Key institutions of the state like the civil service, the armed forces and the police are very likely to become embroiled in the ethnic conflict as the rival groups seek to secure preference for their members or allege that such preference is being accorded to their rivals. Ideally, these institutions should be above politics, but this is seldom attained, even in societies that are not wracked by ethnic conflict. It is not only a question of employment that is at issue, although this is of critical importance, especially in poorer countries where the civil service is the major employer;[38] it is also a question of the equity with which ethnic groups feel that they will be treated, and the security that they will enjoy. Typically, the ethnic composition of civil services, armies and police forces, is unbalanced in the sense that some groups, by virtue of their longer exposure to modern education, have secured a pre-eminence in the civil service or, for other reasons, they dominate the armed forces, who may then be seen as being assimilated to the power-resources of the dominant group. As Cynthia Enloe has observed, it is often the case in ethnically divided societies that 'the ethnic imbalances in the state security forces were more than simply a reflection of the communal problem; they were an active factor exacerbating the problem.'[39]

There are no easy ways out of these problems. Common sense and equity would suggest that the representation of each ethnic group in the bureaucracy and the armed services should be more or less in accord with its proportionate size in the total population, even if this means to some extent sacrificing merit as a criterion of employment or promotion. It is also important, difficult though this may be, to try to insulate the civil service and the armed forces from manipulation by politicians.

The survey in this chapter has demonstrated that it is exceedingly difficult to create and maintain democratic political systems in circumstances of ethnic division. To achieve the goal of greater democracy in South Africa seems an insuperable task. Moreover, all of the societies cited have had their revolution of democratization: however undemocratic the outcomes have often been, the principles of equality and the right to participate in government for all citizens have been accepted, even if only temporarily. South Africa still has to pass this hurdle, and then only can she face all the other formidable hurdles that have formed the substance of this chapter.

It may seem that the pessimistic point of view has overwhelming evidence in its favour; yet there are a number of societies in which democratic systems have survived in circumstances of deep division, and other cases where earnest efforts have been made to re-establish democracy after very serious breakdowns. Ethnicity is being less universally regarded as a transient phenomenon that would be eroded away by the inexorable processes of 'nation-building'.

The widespread reluctance of African nationalists in most parts of Africa to acknowledge ethnicity is, at least in some states, being modified by a more prudent and sober view of how best to cope with it.[40] Both Sudan and Nigeria have emerged from devastating civil wars that arose out of ethnic and regional issues, and are now reconstructing their political systems in ways that may offer better prospects for regulating conflict. South Africa, of course, is a very different society from either Sudan or Nigeria but certain lessons can be learnt, and therefore brief examinations of both cases may be instructive and may also help to persuade black South Africans that the proposals offered in this book derive at least in part from the political experience of other African states.

Sudan straddles the divide between the Arab north and black Africa.[41] Its population of over sixteen million consists of an Arab majority in the north and an African minority numbering approximately three million who live in the south. The war between the north and south, which endured for over twelve years until 1972, originated in the southerners' refusal to accept Arab domination and Arabization. Southern politicians had wished for a federal solution, and threatened secession if this were not guaranteed. The war cost a half-million southerners' lives, caused devastation and dislocation on a wide scale, and led to the flight of over one million as refugees.

The war ended mainly because the struggle reached deadlock, with neither side able to achieve a decisive victory. In terms of the Addis Ababa Agreement signed in 1972 the opposing sides agreed upon a compromise that preserved the unity of Sudan and a common citizenship, but gave extensive powers to the southern region. Defence, foreign affairs, nationality issues, currency, foreign trade, and communications were reserved for the central government, while all other governmental functions were left to the regional government. Other provisions of the Agreement gave the southern regional government substantial veto powers over central government legislation which, in its opinion, adversely affects the welfare, interests, and rights of the southern region.[42]

In addition to these institutional measures southerners were appointed to ministerial posts in the central government and to other high posts. Some 6 000 of the southern guerrilla forces, the so-called Anyanya, were incorporated into the national army of the south and overall command was given to Joseph Lagu, the former leader of the southern forces, and an instrumental figure in the reconciliation of the warring sides.

Sudan remains a one-party state, ruled by President Ja'afar Nimeiri's Sudan Socialist Union; but within this context Sudanese political life has manifested remarkably open and democratic qualities. The aim of the party is to bring in under its umbrella the proponents of all political persuasions, and in the national and regional elections held in February 1978, a substantial number of non-SSU candidates were allowed to contest seats under the SSU banner, subject to their being granted 'certificates of non-objection'.[43]

The Sudanese example of reconciliation and national reconstruction is instructive, even if its durability over a longer period and beyond the present set of leaders remains to be tested. It shows how self-interest could lead to an accommodation between previously warring groups, and how crucially important the role of the rival leaders was in reaching and maintaining a settlement.

The case of Nigeria differs fundamentally from that of Sudan in that there was no doubt that the breakaway Biafran state was defeated, though not pulverized, by the federal Nigerian army. This was not a 'no-win' situation, but the federal authorities did display a good deal of magnanimity in bringing the secessionist state back into the Nigerian fold.

After a long period under different military regimes a united Nigeria is due to return to civilian rule in 1979. Its new constitution has been described as the 'result of a hard won consensus of agreement among forty-nine qualified and experienced Nigerians covering the whole spectrum of political views'.[44] Another observer has analysed the recommendations of the constitutional drafting committee under various headings, which include:

(1) an unambiguous commitment to a federal system;

(2) the elimination of 'cut-throat' political competition based on a system or rule of 'winner-takes-all', characteristic of Nigeria's political past;

(3) the de-emphasizing of institutionalized opposition and the development of 'consensus politics' and government based on community of all interests;

(4) the decentralization of power;

(5) the evolution of a free and fair electoral system to ensure adequate representation at the centre;

(6) the depoliticization of the census (for long a thorny issue in Nigerian politics);

(7) the formation of 'genuine and truly national parties'.[45]

In terms of the new draft constitution Nigeria is divided into nineteen states. Regardless of size each state is to have equal representation in the federal Senate. The major aim in this respect, as in other provisions of the constitution, is an attempt to thwart the possibility of large-scale ethnic mobilization and to ensure that smaller ethnic groups have effective representation. Complex procedures are to govern the amendment of the constitution, the creation of new federal states and boundary adjustments. Section 9(3) of the constitution requires for such changes the affirmative vote of a four-fifths majority of all members of both of the federal Houses of Parliament and an affirmative resolution from two-thirds of the Houses of Assembly of all the states.

Even more striking as efforts to institutionalize maximum consensus are sections 125 and 126, which provide the framework for the election of the president. For our purposes it is not necessary to explore the details of these provisions, which are complex (and may, in any case, have been slightly amended by the time the constitution comes into force). The principle thrust is clear enough: the winning candidate must not only have the highest number of votes, but those votes must be broadly spread throughout the majority of the nineteen states. It will be impossible for a candidate to win if he runs on an ethnic ticket or as a 'northerner' or 'southerner'.[46]

A number of other provisions reflect the concern to neutralize ethnicity. Section 14(3) states:

'The composition of the Government of the Federation or any of its agencies and the conduct of its affairs shall be carried out in such a manner as to reflect the federal character of Nigeria and the need to promote national unity thereby ensuring that there shall be no predominance of persons from a few States or from a few ethnic or other sectional groups in that government or other sectional groups in that government or in any of its agencies.'

Discrimination on a variety of grounds, including religious, ethnic or linguistic ties is prohibited, and it is laid down as the states' 'duty' to 'encourage intermarriage among persons from different places of origin, or of different religious, ethnic or linguistic association or ties'; and to 'promote or encourage the formation of associations that cut across ethnic, linguistic, religious or other sectional barriers'. (Section 15)

Ministerial appointments are to be made in accordance with Section 14(3) (quoted above), with the proviso that the president shall appoint at least one minister from each state, who shall be an indigene of such state. (Section 135[3]). A similar principle of proportionality is to govern presidential appointments to the public service and the composition of the federal armed forces.

The constitution makes it virtually impossible for ethnically exclusive political parties to arise by providing that parties must be open to all citizens, regardless of place of origin, sex, religion, or ethnic grouping, and, further, by requiring that the members of the executive committee or governing body of a party shall be deemed to reflect the federal character of Nigeria 'only if the members thereof belong to different states not being less in number than two-thirds of all the States comprising the Federation'. (Section 203[2][b])

We have quoted Nigeria's draft constitution in some detail because its spirit is very similar to the spirit in which our own proposals have been framed. In both Nigeria and Sudan it is clear that simple majoritarianism has been rejected as a political principle, and in both countries substantially consociational principles have been adopted. Sudan frankly recognizes the ethnic/regional division and incorporates it into the political system. Nigeria's recognition of the ethnic factor is indirect in that it is seen as a danger to be neutralized by making it virtually impossible to mobilize under an ethnic banner.

4 *The possibility of democratic government in divided societies*

A short answer to the proposition that democracy is not possible in divided societies might be to point out that there are, in fact, a number of cases where that proposition is not true. For example, the following societies are characterized by ethnic divisions but may be classified as democracies: Belgium, Botswana, Canada, Fiji, India, Israel, Jamaica, Malaysia, Gambia, Mexico, Mauritius, Senegal, Singapore, Sri Lanka, Surinam, Trinidad and Tobago, Switzerland and the United States of America. Of course, there will be immediate objections to a number of the states included in this list and we would acknowledge its crudeness as a categorization. Belgium and Canada are hardly good examples of democracy's ability to cope with ethnicity, but the point is that in neither case has democracy been abandoned in spite of severe ethnic conflicts. India's case for inclusion might be considered dubious: democracy in the years of Mrs Indira Ghandi's premiership became deeply flawed, and its restoration is too recent an occurrence to enable a judgement to be passed on its durability. Nevertheless, India's vastness, diversity and gigantic problems make the toppling of the Congress Party by democratic means a remarkable achievement.

Malaysia and Sri Lanka are also questionable cases. The former state will be considered in more detail below, but Sri Lanka's treatment of its Tamil minority undeniably flaws its competitive democratic system which has regularly enabled a change of government to take place through the ballot box. To be sure, the changes have occurred within a context of Sinhalese majority domination, and Tamil parties have been insufficiently strong to give them much leverage as potential coalition partners for either of the major Sinhalese parties, who in any case may have rejected such partnership because it could have 'tainted' them in the eyes of Sinhalese voters.[1] Writing in 1967 Robert N. Kearney concluded:

'Despite the spiraling of communal tensions and emotions inflamed by the language issue, the political gulf has not approached a total break. Bargaining between Sinhalese and Tamil political leaders has occurred almost continuously. To a considerable extent, the communal struggle has been fought out within the common institution of Parliament, where spokesmen of both communities argue their causes within the same chambers, according to the same rules of procedure, and, although with declining frequency, often in the common language of English. Since 1958 communal rivalry has not deteriorated into mob violence.'[2]

By 1977, however, Tamil demands had escalated into a drive for a separate Tamil state, and in the aftermath of the election in that year communal violence broke out and claimed 140 lives. Drastic legislative steps were taken to curb a terrorist organization spawned by the separatist movement. A new constitution was promulgated in 1978, and, although limited concessions were made to the Tamil language, no provision was made for any degree of decentralization or autonomy for the northern and eastern provinces, where most Tamils live.

Sri Lanka's ethnic problems remain unsolved, and its claim to be regarded as 'democratic' has become increasingly tenuous. It is, rather, a striking example of the dangers of unlimited majoritarianism in a divided society.

The description of Mauritius as a democracy is problematic: prior to December 1976 there had been no general election since 1967, a state of emergency, with extensive curbing of political liberties, having been imposed in 1971. The restrictions were lifted in November 1976 and a vigorously fought election was held in the following month. Although democracy may not yet be established, it has been said that the roots of liberalism in Mauritius are strong.[3]

Surinam's eligibility for inclusion may be disputed as, although it has complete internal self-government, its status is that of a dominion within the tripartite Kingdom of the Netherlands. In spite of its division into three major ethnic groups Surinam has maintained a democratic political system, akin to the Dutch model, since 1954.[4] It forms an interesting contrast to its neighbour Guyana, whose undemocratic practices were mentioned in the preceding chapter. Guyana, it may be said, does not, *prima facie,* qualify for categorization as a democracy, but a recent observer has noted that freedom of speech, association and assembly seem fairly well preserved, and while the freedom of the press has been greatly weakened it has not been eliminated. 'Whereas many of the basic qualities of liberal democracy no longer exist, the government has not achieved or perhaps even attempted the degree of control of economy or society that characterizes totalitarian systems.'[5] It may be wondered whether Burnham needed to resort to the measures that he employed, as there are grounds for believing that his party would have won a free election quite comfortably without them. After the controversial 1973 election Jagan and his party decided to boycott parliament but he is reported as still believing that they might return to power by democratic means.[6]

However many reservations there may be, these cases suggest that the Rabushka/Shepsle paradigm of politics in plural societies is open to question. In his detailed comparative study of the politics of cultural pluralism Crawford Young reaches a different conclusion:

'Latent pluralism is not always activated by competitive elections; in Latin America, at those places and times where free elections have occurred, the potential cleavages of race and ethnicity have never been discovered. In the Philippines, despite the fact that ethnicity there lay rather closer to social consciousness than in Latin America, the bipolar party competition which has obtained for much of this century served to inhibit politization of linguistic identity. The fluid factionalism which underlay the apparent bipolarity offered no structural possibility for cultural perception. This system had other defects which contributed to its demise in 1972, but cultural pluralism had no part in it. India is another vindication of the positive role democratic elections can play in a plural setting. Although cultural factors play an important part in Indian elections, they create an arena of bargaining and communal compromise which has been critical to the vitality of India. . . . In the Pakistan case, West Pakistan élites could simply not have gotten away with the inequitable distribution of national resources had open elections been permitted in the early years of the republic. For these reasons, we cannot accept the Rabushka-Shepsle hypothesis that democratic politics are incompatible with cultural pluralism.'[7]

It is not enough to present paradigms that are over-deterministic in their implications and ignore the possibility that politics and political leadership are independent variables that may act as a counterpoise to the potentially destructive effects of ethnic and other serious forms of cleavage. Young's analysis incorporates a number of case studies which demonstrate the situational character of ethnicity; that is, it is a response evoked by certain situations, and the possible variations in its intensity. It is not, in other words, a quality that is fixed and immutable, although, to be sure, in situations of extreme polarization its elasticity will be limited.

Coping with the political problems of deeply divided societies has been the field of another school of political scientists who have devised the concept of consociational democracy to account for those cases where a specific type of democratic political system has survived in spite of deep social cleavages. Analysis and theory-building around this model has been complemented by the work of Eric. A. Nordlinger on conflict-regulation in deeply divided societies. The classic consociational democracies are four smaller European states, Austria, Belgium, the Netherlands and Switzerland, whose social structures are characterized by severe and potentially disruptive fragmentation along the lines of religion, language and ideology. In each case the political élites, despite their intense rivalry, have recognized the explosive potentials of conflict and have sought deliberately to take steps to establish and institutionalize mechanisms for coping with the conflict.

At this stage we must emphasize that we are making no claims for the exportability of the consociational technique to South Africa. It is obvious that the circumstances of the four classic consociations are widely different from those of South Africa, and the applicability of the techniques to conflicts involving race and associated inequalities of considerable dimensions is a moot point that will have to be examined in the light of the evidence. The critical question seems to be whether the conflicts that have been accommodated by consociational techniques are comparable in their intensity (actual and potential) and negotiability to those of South Africa. We may explore this question by looking at the nature of the conflict in each case.

In his analysis of Austria after World War I William T. Bluhm remarks that 'economically and culturally the new state was a loose bundle of centrifugal forces' and that 'it was a state that nobody wanted'.[8] Its boundaries had been imposed by its conquerors, and the population was characterized by sharp divisions of culture, religion, class and even language that made its fragmentation comparable to that of many of today's developing countries.[9] Even before 1919 Austrian public life had crystallized into three highly antagonistic blocs, representing the main divisions of society: the Catholic conservatives, the Social Democrats, and secular middle-class nationalists. Each of these blocs, or *Lager,* 'tried to become the centre of all loyalties of its followers, and the struggle for the votes of the people turned into a struggle for their souls'.[10] The *Lager* sought to encompass the totality of their followers' interests, generating in the process a network of organizations not unlike that of Afrikaner nationalism. The new state lacked support from strong centripetal forces and its embryonic parliamentary system was soon subjected to the strains of unregulated religious, class and ideological conflicts whose intensity was such as to cause each of the major groups to form its own private army. In the later twenties violence became continuous and finally in 1934 the constitutional regime was suspended and Austria was placed under authoritarian-corporatist rule until the *Anschluss* in 1938.[11]

The *Lager* survived through the war, but in 1945 the attempt was made again to establish a democratic political system, and this time it was successful. The reasons for this success will be discussed below, but the point made here is that conflict remained at an intense level. In a study of a community in Austria G. Bingham Powell writes:

'All issues and problems assume a partisan flavor; the atmosphere of mistrust and estrangement makes the polity a tinderbox. The processes of bargaining and accommodation, which make possible a viable political life, labor under severe difficulties in such an atmosphere. When divisions over concrete issues coincide with the enmity of the major groups, the additional burden of psychological antagonism may overwhelm the system.'[12]

Contemporary Belgium is noted for its severe ethnic conflict, but for much of its past history the more significant lines of cleavage have been religious and ideological. Until roughly 1960 conflict in Belgium stemmed mostly from relations among the three historic blocs, representing the Catholics, Liberals, and Socialists. It is in coping with this pattern of conflict that accommodationist practices were created, which succeeded in regulating the conflict through peaceable means. Belgium experienced no civil war or sustained violence. But the issue of public support for denominational schools created considerable strains, including a measure of mob violence, in the years after 1879 and again during the 1950s.[13] Linguistic issues were not absent during the period prior to 1960, but they were not the most intense. It is only in the 1960s that language became the dominant issue, threatening the fundamental structure of the state. Kenneth McRae suggests that the tone of linguistic conflict is far sharper than the religious-ideological one. 'Religious-ideological debate may be sharp, even hostile, but the differences are long-established, understood, accepted and tolerated, if not always treated with respect. Linguistic differences are bitter, intolerant, and reveal little reciprocal understanding.'[14] The crucial question facing Belgium is whether the accommodationist techniques that were successful in coping with the earlier pattern of conflict will be successful with linguistic conflict. The changes in the Belgian constitution, designed to meet the problem, are discussed below.

Corresponding broadly to the *Lager* of Austria and the 'spiritual families' of Belgium are the *zuilen* of the Netherlands. *Zuilen* are, literally, pillars, but Arend Lijphart employs the term 'bloc'.[15] Dutch society consists of three main blocs, the Catholic, orthodox Calvinist, and the secular. Both the Calvinist and the secular blocs are, in turn, subdivided, and may be regarded as separate blocs. The secular bloc, for example, is more accurately seen as a Liberal bloc, consisting of the secular upper middle and middle classes, and a Socialist bloc consisting of the secular lower middle and lower classes.[16] The extent of the cleavage in Dutch society may be gauged from the following indices: the blocs are regionally based, although not isolated from one another; political parties are 'the virtually exclusive representatives of relatively small class and religious segments of the population and receive very little backing from any other segments'; Dutch society lacks an overall consensus, as consensus exists rather within the blocs; and 'the blocs live side by side as distinctly separate subcultural communities, each with its own political and social institutions and with interaction and communication across bloc boundaries kept to a minimum. Is this one nation or . . . several nations inhabiting the same country?'[17] Around 1910 three issues had generated much tension and the political situation looked 'quite serious': the demand for universal suffrage, industrial relations, and the school issue, involving Protestant and Catholic claims to state support for denominational schools.[18] Although each of these issues had potentially explosive possibilities, no explosion occurred as timely steps were taken to defuse the conflict.

Switzerland is divided along linguistic, religious and class lines. In 1970, 74,5 per cent of the population were German-speaking, 20,1 per cent were French-speaking, 4 per cent were Italian-speaking and 1 per cent Romance-speaking.[19] Protestants account for 57 per cent of the population and Catholics 41,4 per cent. In both cases these proportions have remained stable over a long period of time. All except six of the cantons have large German-speaking majorities, which indicates that linguistically the population is cantonally concentrated. It is important to note that religious affiliation does not coincide with language; the cantons are nearly evenly divided between those with Catholic and Protestant majorities respectively.[20]

In Swiss history, whose unique contours have shaped its established pattern of accommodation, religious conflict has traditionally been more serious than linguistic conflict. The tranquillity of contemporary Switzerland should not make us overlook the numerous episodes of sharp conflict between the time of the origin of the Swiss Confederacy in 1291 and 1847; in the latter year seven conservative Catholic cantons resisted liberal reforms initiated by the national movement and constituted themselves as the *Sonderbund,* whose rebellion was crushed by federal troops.[21] Linguistic issues, although never absent, were subordinated to religious ones. Thus 'the French Swiss of one canton, it is said, feel no greater solidarity with the French Swiss of other cantons than with German or Italian Swiss'.[22] The political parties also reflect the priority of religious, class and economic conflicts. At the federal level linguistic considerations are almost completely eclipsed by these other conflicts, although friction may occur at the cantonal level, particularly in the bilingual cantons.[23] An example of the latter phenomenon occurs in the Jura region of Bern canton where a strong separatist movement has developed among the French-speaking Catholic minority who occupy the less developed rural parts of the region, involving, in the 1960s, a degree of terrorism and mob violence.[24]

Clearly, in each of the four societies briefly considered above, the potentials for violence have been high, and in some cases the potentiality has been realized. Religious differences, for example, are notable for their inflammatory qualities. One may think back to the religious wars of Europe, the great Hindu–Muslim divide in the Indian sub-continent, the civil war in Sudan, and the sectarian conflict of Northern Ireland, to appreciate that religious conflict can be peculiarly intractable. It is not usually a matter of religion *per se* that sustains the conflict. 'Religious communities become politicized in conflict situations where the real issues are frequently social, political and economic. Religion derives its chief importance from its function as a symbol of group identity and self-esteem.'[25] Similarly, language differences may generate intense conflict, a proposition that can be easily confirmed by even a cursory comparative survey. In Belgium the ability of its accommodationist practices to cope with the language conflict remains to be seen; Switzerland was fortunate enough to attain a linguistic equilibrium 'at a time before language was made a symbol of rampant nationalism'.[26]

Merely to state the issues of conflict, however, is to deal with only part of the problem. The intensity of an issue of conflict depends upon a number of variables, including the historical context of the society, its structure of conflict, and, in particular, the relationship of the issue to other issues of conflict, which may be reinforcing or cross-cutting in their effect. We leave this point for subsequent discussion.

The critical factor in the consociational model is the ability of the rival political élites to recognize that they have more to gain from a measure of co-operation with one another than they have to lose from the continuation of unrestrained conflict that would imperil the existence of the system. In the Austrian case Bluhm writes:

'Co-operation flowed largely from a mutual contractarian spirit produced by mutual experience of the "state of nature" which culminated in a readiness to suspend the ideological disagreements that all recognised as extant. Each party displayed a "pragmatism" of dissensus, willingness to conclude agreements in a pragmatic manner, to reach compromises for the solution of pressing common problems, while remaining conscious of deep differences in principle, different visions of the good society.'[27]

The emergence of the contractarian spirit had been fostered by Austria's experience of war and the post-war threat of division and Soviet domination. Leaders of all parties had suffered common persecution at the hands of the Nazis, and this heightened their respect for one another.[28] All of these factors promoted a sense of the need to engage in at least some limited form of co-operation if Austria were to survive.

Belgium's accommodationist practices stem from the Catholic and Liberal leaders' agreement in 1827–8 on a 'union of oppositions' to the Dutch King William's rule. It was, according to Lorwin, 'an unusual effort of tolerance and comprehension', aimed at securing their country against foreign domination.[29] This compromise laid the basis for conflict regulation in the parliamentary system that was established after the attainment of independence. Martin O. Heisler writes:

'The two groups formed parliamentary and eventually electoral parties and competed vigorously for political power during that time. They alternated in government and opposition. Yet their competition was limited by the realization that, if their fundamental value-differences were allowed to come into unlimited conflict, the small, weak new state's existence would be jeopardized. The élites agreed to disagree within limits; and differences were often negotiated by the political leaders of the two factions.'[30]

The same approach to conflict regulation enabled the Belgian system to cope with the rise of the Socialist Party in the last decades of the nineteenth century and the acute class conflicts which mobilisation of the working classes generated. Seeing a violent threat to the continuation of the system, the established leadership co-opted the Socialist leadership and thereby blunted their militancy. 'Co-optation brought the Socialist leadership into the policy-making arena. It provided access to power. But it also bound the Socialists to the existing regime.'[31]

Of the Netherlands Lijphart writes:

'The basic prerequisites for the success of such a system of political accommodation are a clear recognition by the élite of the gravity of the problems confronting the system and the constant peril of disintegrative tendencies. . .'[32]

A decisive moment in the establishment of the consociational system came in the years after 1910 when, as was noted above, the tensions of Dutch society reached a serious pitch. From 1913 onwards sustained efforts were made to settle the conflicts and in 1917 the *Pacificatie,* or peaceful settlement, was reached. Lijphart describes the *Pacificatie* as a 'crucial episode' and he singles out three main features of the settlement that were subsequently incorporated into the on-going process of accommodation: first, the pre-eminent role of the political leaders in recognizing problems and transcending their ideological differences in reaching agreements; secondly, the participation of the leaders of *all* blocs in the settlement; and thirdly, the importance of the principle of proportionality in the settlement[33] – a principle that will be discussed below. The settlement of the schools question in Belgium strikingly parallels the Dutch settlement: in 1958 the heads of the three main parties negotiated the 'school pact' by which it was hoped to defuse the issue for at least a twelve-year period. This, too, may have been a 'crucial episode' in validating the traditional accommodationist approach, but it came much later in time, and moreover, only when the issues of Belgian politics were about to change to another axis. Indeed, it has been argued that the emergence of the linguistic conflict to pre-eminent salience occurred partly because of the preceding successful accommodation of the religious and class cleavages.[34]

Switzerland's accommodationist practices, as has been indicated, arose out of its long history in which the decisive factor was the mutually perceived need of the cantons to cleave together for defensive purposes. There is, in modern times at any rate, no decisive moment at which rival élites came together and deliberately entered into a settlement, except perhaps in the aftermath of the Sonderbund war, when the victorious Liberals rather than pulverizing the defeated Catholic cantons, made concessions to them in the interests of creating a modern nation-state. Eric A. Nordlinger writes of Switzerland:

'The Swiss confederation originated in the mutual desire of heterogeneous communities to preserve their individual independence through a mutual security arrangement. Three centuries later that goal continued to influence the behaviour of Swiss élites. A major motivation behind the Protestant offer of concessions to the Catholic cantons after the Sonderbund War was the realisation that a country surrounded by more powerful neighbours required a unified and centrally controlled national army. And to insure this unity and central direction conciliation of the Catholic cantons seemed the optimum strategy.'[35]

It will be clear from the brief accounts sketched above that a critical variable in the politics of accommodation in each of the societies considered above is the ability and capacity of the rival political élites to transcend even bitter cleavages in the interests of maintaining the integrity of the society. Élite behaviour thus fulfils a pivotal role in the consociational model. Moreover, in each case, apart from its internal conflicts, the consociations were being, or had been, subjected to external threats, which served as a unifying force.[36]

In an analysis of the motives that lead political élites to seek an accommodation of conflict Nordlinger lists four such motives, at least one or more of which must be present if conflict regulation is to be attempted: (1) an external threat; (2) the belief that intense conflict and its actual or possible consequences will detract from the economic well-being of the leaders' segment or conflict group; (3) the acquisition or retention of political power; and (4) the avoidance of bloodshed and suffering within their own segments. The conditions under which these motives are likely to appear vary: thus, according to Nordlinger, smaller powers are likely to place a heavy emphasis upon internal unity in the face of external threat; where there is a sizeable commercial class dedicated to the pursuit of economic values, economic motives are likely to be highly salient; the desire for a share in political power is most likely to be foremost when no conflict group can command a majority and none seems likely to do so; and the avoidance of bloodshed will be a motive when the possibility of violent strife seems likely.[37]

Apart from a particular set of motivations and the abilities and capacities of political élites, the consociational model posits the employment of several techniques or devices that both express and underpin the fundamental mutual recognition of the need for accommodation. At the élite level, this implies the formation of a cartel of élites, through which the disruptive possibilities of unrestrained, adversarial political competition may be managed. In the Austrian case the instrument through which this was achieved was the 'Grand Coalition'. Bluhm writes:

'Parliamentary elections could not serve as consensus-building or declaring processes. They tallied instead the strength of opposing armies. If the existence of opposing armies was not to result in catastrophic conflict, if they *had* to be brought to agreement, this could only be by a procedure resembling a continuous treaty or contract negotiation, a constant conclave of their chiefs, resolving issues through compromise and unanimous decision – a "Grand Coalition".'[38]

In accordance with this principle and its contractarian spirit the Conservatives, although winning an overall majority in the elections of 1945, formed a coalition government with the Socialists, and instituted proportionality in the distribution of ministries and in the top echelons of the bureaucracy. In key ministries, for example, a Conservative minister would be paired with a Socialist undersecretary. This device served the two-fold function of inducing both parties to co-operate and enabling critical opposition to occur within the Grand Coalition through the practice of *Bereichsopposition* in which each coalition partner acted as a critic of the departments controlled by the other.[39] In effect the coalition partners exercised a mutual veto over each other. The coalition was renegotiated after each election, and lasted for twenty years until 1966 when it was mutually decided that parliamentary democracy had become sufficiently rooted to allow a single-party alternating pattern of government to become the norm.

In the Dutch case Lijphart describes the institutionalized accommodationist practices as 'summit diplomacy', in which representatives of the rival blocs meet in secret conclave: 'Parliamentary approval represents no more than the final stage of the accommodation process. . . . What is held up for public view on the floor of the chambers is the result of the interbloc negotiations which now merely requires ratification.'[40]

A crucial feature of the consociational model is the limitation placed upon majoritarianism. In the Netherlands, for example, great efforts are made to reach a compromise that is acceptable to all or most of the blocs, and decisions are not taken on the basis of simple majority votes. Lijphart writes:

'On issues considered vital by any bloc, no decision can be made without either their concurrence or at least substantial concessions to them. The veto power is not absolute. No single group can block action completely, but its wishes will be considered seriously and accommodated as much as possible. In short, the rule is majoritarianism tempered by the spirit of concurrent majority.'[41]

In the Swiss case, majoritarianism is avoided and instead the principle of amicable agreement underlies the decision-making process in the political system. Steiner writes: 'If we survey the history of Switzerland since the oath of federation in 1291, we can see a clear tendency toward the regulation of political conflict by compromise rather than by authoritarian decisions or by majority rule.' In line with this historical development the Swiss Federal Council, which is the apex of the semi-parliamentary system and corresponds very broadly to a cabinet, is composed on a proportional basis, which, since 1959, has included all the major parties in accordance with the 2 : 2 : 2 : 1 formula, and hence is representative of all the religious, linguistic, economic, and regional interests. The members of the federal council are chosen jointly by the two federal chambers and they do not agree upon a common programme in advance. As all important interests are represented within the council, the process of collective decision-making requires that differences be negotiated, which has the effect of ensuring that each decision is a nationally acceptable compromise. Steiner's findings lead him to the key hypothesis that: in a political system with strong subcultural segmentation, the more often political decisions are made by amicable agreement, the more probable is a low level of intersubcultural hostility.[43]

Recent constitutional developments in Belgium reflect another device which is designed to cope with serious conflict. In 1962 Belgium was divided into linguistic zones, and in 1970 further changes required that the number of Flemish- and French-speaking members of the cabinet should be equal, and, while the prime minister might be from either group, he is supposed to be bilingual. Furthermore, the two houses of parliament have each been divided into two language groups or cultural councils, each having legislative powers for their own region in cultural, educational and linguistic matters. Although the cultural councils have legislative powers, they have no power to levy taxes, their budgets being determined by the national parliament. Moreover, it remains unclear what the parameters of the councils' spheres of competence are.[44] A further constitutional provision makes it a requirement that the boundaries of the linguistic zones may be altered only by an act of parliament passed by a majority vote of each linguistic group of both houses, provided that a majority of both members of each group are present.[45]

It must be emphasized that the introduction of these essentially consociational techniques – proportionality, concurrent majority requirement, and devolution to cultural groups – has not yet been shown to succeed, although they are the outcome of a long process of negotiation in which all salient groups were involved, in the tradition of Belgian consociationalism.

The emphasis on inter-élite negotiation and accommodation in consociational politics has direct implications for the style in which politics is conducted. The secrecy requirement, mentioned in the Dutch case, suggests a limitation on the flow of potentially inflammatory information to the wider society, and the consequent damping down of what might otherwise be volatile political debate. Another related device is the endeavour to depoliticize issues and thereby neutralize their disruptive potential. Nordlinger lists this as a conflict-regulating practice whereby the rival élites agree to lift out of the ambit of competitive politics certain issues and areas of public policy which impinge upon the respective groups' interests and values.[46] Lijphart shows how in the Netherlands sensitive issues can be neutralized by being presented in complex technical terms that are incomprehensible to most people! Another significant depoliticizing institution is the Social and Economic Council, which, although mostly an advisory body, is in practice a highly influential body whose technical advice carries great weight. It is composed on a proportional basis and represents an ongoing forum for the accommodation of inter-bloc interests.[47]

The autonomous role of the political élites carries further implications for their relationships with their rank-and-file followers. As Lijphart says of the Dutch blocs, 'Élite domination is the pattern everywhere'; and, in turn, the institutionalization of accommodation practices consolidated the blocs by helping them to become more firmly entrenched in their control over their parties, schools and other segmented associations.[48] The requirement of a significant measure of autonomy for the élites necessarily implies that the leadership must be secure in its backing by their followers. If bargains are to be struck and adhered to there must be no chance that the leaders will be repudiated by their followers or replaced by more extreme leaders from the same group. The crucial importance of leadership, its calibre, flexibility and negotiating skill in particular, is stressed by all the writers on consociationalism. Nordlinger writes:

'In each case of conflict regulation it was the conflict group leaders who took the initiative in working out the various conflict-regulating practices, who put them into operation, and who did so at least partly with the goal in mind of arriving at a conflict-regulating outcome. Furthermore, it is obvious that they, and they alone, were in a position to do so. Clearly the conflict group members (or non-élites) are too numerous, too scattered, too fragmented, too weak, and too unskilled to be able to work out and operate any of the six conflict-regulating practices.'[49]

It will have been apparent from the preceding discussion that the operation of consociational democracies is premised on the fact of strong group attachments that mediate between the individual citizen and the political system. The groups are, so to speak, the coins of currency, and the tenacity of their hold over their members may be very strong.[50] Elections produce little variation in results in view of the inter-group equilibrium that is established and the boundary-maintenance that is enforced. Clearly such a basis for a democratic political system departs radically from any Lockean notions of 'individualism' and, so the consociational theorists maintain, from the assumption that democracy requires a more or less homogeneous social base. According to Lijphart,

'Consociational theory differs from other theories of integration not only in its refutation of the thesis that cultural fragmentation necessarily leads to conflict, but also in its insistence that distinctive lines of cleavage among subcultures may actually help rather than hinder peaceful relations among them. Because good social fences may make good political neighbours, a kind of voluntary *apartheid* policy may be the most appropriate solution for a divided society. Political autonomy for the different subcultures is a crucially important element of a consociational system, because it reduces contacts, and hence strain and hostility, among the subcultures at the mass level.'[51]

Further points need to be made before the question of consociationalism's applicability to racial conflict may be considered. First, the extent to which any society is consociational may be placed on a continuum: it may be more or less in conformity with the consociational model. Canada may be said to have consociational elements in its political system, while the absence of truly serious cleavage has led Brian Barry, for example, to question whether Switzerland can be appropriately described as consociational.[52] Israel, Fiji, Sudan and Nigeria have marked consociational features. Moreover, consociationalism may serve as a building block on the way to a more cohesive society. It is not, in other words, necessarily a permanent configuration of group alignments and, as the process of *ontzuiling* in the Netherlands shows, it may subsequently give way.

Secondly, and crucial to the question of consociationalism's exportability, are the factors that have been conducive to its viability in the European context.[53] Two of these factors have been noted: external threats to the country and smallness in power and population. The other factors are: (1) a multiple balance of power among the rival groups. If the groups are more or less evenly balanced and none is sufficiently powerful to make a bid for hegemonic power, there will be a greater inducement to seek an accommodation; (2) acceptability of the grand-coalition or élite cartel form of government as a normative model. By this Lijphart means a coalescent or co-operative style of politics rather than what S.E. Finer has usefully described as 'adversary politics';[54] (3) some degree of national solidarity: however narrow its base there must be some common concern and will to maintain the system and prevent greater fragmentation and instability; and (4) distinct lines of cleavage: according to Lijphart, 'Rival subcultures may coexist peacefully if there is little contact between them and consequently few occasions for conflict';[55] and elsewhere he states that distinct lines of cleavage are important because they are likely to be associated with a high degree of internal political cohesion of the groups, which is vital to the success of a consociational democracy's operation since it depends upon the ability of the élites simultaneously to co-operate with one another and keep their followers in line.[56]

We return now to the important question of how deep, in fact, are the cleavages that have been transcended in the consociations considered so far. As was mentioned above, Barry has suggested that Switzerland is not characterized by deep cleavages and therefore, while it employs certain consociational devices, it is not properly speaking a full consociation; and the thrust of his further criticism is to doubt that Austria's experience supports the proposition that consociational methods were really a necessary condition of stable democracy, at least in Austria, given the favourable political and economic circumstances of post-1945 Western Europe, which were far more auspicious for democracy than the circumstances of the inter-war period.[57]

This criticism is pertinent, but it raises the problem of the counterfactual condition: how does one know what *might* have happened if, instead of solution X, solution Y had been adopted. There is no easy correlation between the distances or gaps separating conflict groups along various dimensions and the intensity of conflict. As Simmel has shown, the closer groups are together the more intense their conflict may be. Moreover, the crucial factors in determining a conflict's intensity are not so much the 'objective' facts or issues but what the parties believe to be facts. The point about the Austrian case is surely that in 1945 it *was* believed by all the significant actors that the 'grand coalition' and proportionality principles *were* necessary to cope with conflict, and, had they not been instituted, unmanageable conflict may have erupted as a result of something like a self-fulfilling prophecy. Again, after the experience of consociational techniques, key actors appear to have believed that they had been necessary. Bluhm quotes Alfred Malita, a former president of the Austrian National Assembly, as saying that the twenty-year coalition had 'created out of a sheer will to cooperate a habit of democratic politics, a democratic tradition'.[58]

But what does seem correct is Barry's wider point that the economic prosperity of Western Europe greatly facilitated the maintenance of democratic politics. As he notes, it is one of the best-established generalizations in political science that a prosperous country is more likely to be stable than one with high unemployment, and stagnant or falling production. A plausible corollary of this is that the management of conflict is made easier by relative plenitude of resources. As Young has observed, 'the bitter edge of struggle is removed when the national institutions can manage distributive politics in such a way that something palpable is available for all'.[59]

It is important to note that in each of the four consociations considered the axes of cleavage cut across one another, rather than reinforce one another cumulatively. Thus, in the case of Switzerland, the lines of language, religion and class did not coincide but cut across one another – except, significantly, in the conflict-prone region of Jura. Steiner's conclusion is that the 'cross-cutting of political parties with other groups seems to keep the parties from differing strongly in their demands on the political system'.[60] In the Dutch case the axes of religion and class cut across each other at right angles. Lijphart writes:

'There are class differences and divergent economic interests in the Catholic bloc, and the heterogeneous class composition of the party requires the reconciliation of these interests within the party. The party leaders are under constant cross-pressures from the different wings of the party, which predispose them to moderation and compromises both in intraparty and interparty relations. It is impossible to account for Holland's stable democracy without references to this crucial political role of the religious parties, particularly the Catholic party.'[61]

It is true that though the cross-cutting cleavage hypothesis is a debatable one, and Nordlinger argues that it is unproven,[62] the evidence does suggest that in the four consociations its plausibility is considerable. Conversely it is equally plausible to assume that in a society like South Africa, where the racial and class cleavages are to a large extent mutually reinforcing, conflict will be more intense.

A further area of unresolved debate about consociationalism turns on its historic roots in each case. Hans Daalder has argued that in the Swiss and Dutch cases the adoption of consociational techniques was preceded by a long historical tradition of predisposing factors:

'In the Netherlands and Switzerland, traditions of pluralism and political accommodation long preceded the processes of political modernization. Against Lijphart's views of consociational democracy as the outcome of a desire on the part of élites to counteract the potential threat of political divisions, one might put the reverse thesis: earlier consociational practices facilitated the peaceful transition towards newer forms of pluralist political organization in these two countries. Consociationalism, in this view, is not a response to the perils of subcultural splits, but the prior reason why subcultural divisions never did become perilous.'[63]

Elsewhere Daalder makes the further implication that 'if consociationalism presupposes the earlier existence of a special élite culture rather than intelligent choice by particular élites at a critical juncture of a nation's history, its transfer to other societies is likely to meet with greater difficulty'.[64]

Clearly these are plausible observations, but they do not seem to us to undermine the theory of consociationalism; rather to require its modification and elaboration to incorporate historical variables as well. To demonstrate the importance of the historical predispositions is not necessarily to diminish the importance of the actual techniques as means of coping with conflict.

Those associated with the consociational school have been properly cautious in estimating the extent to which consociationalism might be invoked to cope with racial and ethnic conflict. Lijphart, in emphatically repudiating apartheid, declares that it would be improper to extrapolate from the Dutch experience any conclusions on racial conflict;[65] but elsewhere he writes in a cautiously hopeful vein.

The non-European experience of consociationalism has been mixed: in Malaysia, a deeply flawed democratic system has survived; a conscious effort to establish a consociational system in Cyprus failed; a reasonably successful consociational democracy in the Lebanon was swept away by the civil war; and the experience of Surinam has not been fully tested. But before these examples are taken as evidence of the model's unexportability each of these cases should be briefly examined.

Malaysia is dominated by its tripartite ethnic division of Malays, Chinese and Indians who, in the heartland of Malaya, account for 50, 37 and 11 per cent of the population respectively. The cleavages between the Malay and Chinese communities are especially sharp, and do not appear to have been generated by the experience of colonialism and capitalism.[66] In addition to mutually unflattering racial stereotypes the economic imbalance between the two communities is considerable, the average per capita income for Chinese being two-and-a-half times that of Malays.[67]

Malaya (as it then was) received its independence in 1957 but its politics prior to that had been dominated by ethnically based parties. By the early 1950s the respective ethnic groups' political leaders, recognizing that ethnicity was an ineradicable force and, moreover, a powerful instrument of mass mobilization, began increasingly to appreciate that an intercommunal alliance might reap considerable benefits. Accordingly in 1952 a multi-ethnic alliance was worked out between the United Malay National Organization, the Malayan-Chinese Association and the Malay-Indian Congress. The Alliance easily became the dominant force, took the country into independence, and remains in power today.

In brief the bargain struck between the two major communities rests upon recognition of the Malays as the 'natives' of the country and, hence, their entitlement to political supremacy, the exclusive use of Malay symbols as national ones, Malay as the national language and, subsequently, preferential treatment designed to overcome their economic backwardness. In return the Chinese are accorded rights of citizenship and a security which smaller and more vulnerable Chinese minorities elsewhere in South-east Asia have lacked.[68]

By the time of independence, Von Vorys writes,

'the Alliance was developing a method of its own in settling intercommunal issues. There were no projects of survey research to determine popular views, nor any bureaucratic procedures. The heads of the communal parties worked things out privately, informally, and secretly. Not that the members of this Directorate always agreed. On the contrary, the Malays and Chinese within the Alliance councils could not have presented their views more vigorously nor bargained harder. But, the leadership of UMNO, MCA, and MIC agreed that to carry on negotiations in public on such communally sensitive issues as citizenship and Malay privileges would trap them in a rigid pattern and place the communities on a path of polarization which would inevitably lead to confrontation and communal violence.'[69]

In the sense that one does not know what other kind of system had any chance of succeeding, the Alliance formula worked adequately into the late 1960s. The country survived its widening into Malaysia and the rapid extrusion of Singapore, but the inter-ethnic alliance was an uneasy one, and its relatively conservative leadership, constrained by the delicate balance, became increasingly alienated from their respective grass-roots supporters. The implementation of steps to make Malay the effective official language was too slow for more extremist Malays, while the policy, although agreed to by the Directorate, alienated many Chinese.[70]

Serious ethnic violence erupted in May 1969 after a general election in which UMNO lost ground to more militant Malay ethnic parties. UMNO's response was to take steps to entrench the special status of Malays more deeply and, by means of the New Economic Plan, to boost the Malays' position in the economy. Although the basic Alliance formula was retained, the umbrella was widened to admit other parties and renamed the National Front. Altogether ten parties fought under the National Front banner in the 1978 general election and together they won 132 of the 154 seats in parliament, with UMNO winning 71 of these. The hegemony of the UMNO-dominated National Front appears invulnerable, and Malaysia can be categorized therefore as a single-party dominant system.[71]

The national ideology, *Rukunegara,* gives highly preferential rights to the *bumiputras,* that is, Malays and other indigenous peoples. Malay is the sole official language, and it will be used throughout the schools by 1980. *Bumiputras* receive highly privileged access to the civil service, preferential treatment in loans, employment, and access to universities. A target of 30 per cent share-ownership and management by *bumiputras* in commerce and industry has been set for attainment in 1990. This strategy, which is essentially a form of affirmative action, was premised on the hope that economic growth would permit redistribution without being unduly unfair to non-Malays. The results of the policy have been disappointing. Fewer Malays than expected have benefited, and there has been no rapid growth of a Malayan entrepreneurial class. Moreover, the slowness of the 'trickle effect' through to the poorer classes of the Malay community has aggrieved them, while the Chinese and Indian communities have become increasingly frustrated and resentful of the restraints placed upon them.

Recent reports indicate that the prime minister, Datuk Hussein Onn, is committed to maintaining the delicate ethnic balance on which the Malaysian system rests, and that he is determined not to allow non-Malay discontents to get out of hand or to condone Malay abuse of their advantaged position. He has successfully fought off Malay extremists, but the longer-term threat remains.

In an attempt to depoliticize the modified Alliance contract it was decided in 1970 to prohibit any questioning of *Rukunegara,* even in Parliament. At the same time discussion of any issues touching communal sensitivities was forbidden.[73]

Malaysia, then, veers strongly towards the non-democratic end of the political spectrum; but its achievement in remaining a relatively open society for nearly 20 years in the face of serious cleavages should not be underestimated. Milton J. Esman has characterized the basis of Malaysian politics as 'precarious mutual deterrence or unstable equilibrium':

'Since each community is in a position both to defend itself and to inflict unacceptable damage on the other, there are strong incentives, particularly among leadership elements, to pursue policies of peaceful, if competitive, coexistence and mutual, if competitive accommodation.

Neither community, notwithstanding the fantasies of their more chauvinistic members, is strong enough to expel or to destroy the other without risking heavy punishment to itself, nor do the patterns of settlement make geographic partition a possibility.'[74]

The case of Fiji may seem excessively remote from the concern of a book dealing with South Africa's future, but we mention it to show, as with our other examples, that reasonably democratic systems may survive in inauspicious environments where rival leaders have a will to make them work, and where simple majoritarian notions of democracy are avoided. The Fijian example illustrates also that serious conflict may be defused if the parties to the conflict recognize that it is in their interest to reach an accommodation.

There are echoes of the Malaysian situation in Fiji, whose population, scattered over 800 islands, consists of over half-a-million people, 52 per cent of whom are Indians of non-indigenous descent. The most important political fact about Fiji is that native Fijians are outnumbered. It is not surprising that they resisted any moves towards Fijian independence which, they believed, would lead to permanent Indian domination. The Indian leaders, whose community chafed under the virtual monopolization of land by the Fijians, pressed for a common roll franchise, arguing that non-racial parties based on common interests would arise and make racial considerations irrelevant.[75]

In a constitutional advance in 1965 communal voting rolls were established and, with the aid of a generous allocation of seats to the European community, Fijian dominance was assured. Colonial officials were reported as saying that they had pushed the Fijian and Indian communities as far as possible and that 'no compromise was possible between the European-Fijian demand for no constitutional advance and the Indian demand for rapid progress that would have angered a large part of the population'.[76]

Racial tensions ran high in 1968 when the Indian-dominated Federation Party made striking gains in by-elections. Fijian demonstrators, aroused to new heights of bitterness, demanded the repatriation of the Indians. With the threat of serious violence running high, leaders in both communities recognized the danger of unrestrained conflict and measures were taken to defuse it. Speaking of this time at a later date Ratu Mara, the Fijian leader, referred to the

'. . . days when we sailed so close to the rocks, . . . we came so near to the edge of the abyss that we could see with unmistakable clearness the dangers that lay there if we did not change course. So we changed course. . . . Let us not forget too easily those dangerous days, lest we recklessly find ourselves back in the same position.'[77]

The amenability of the Federation Party to interracial co-operation was facilitated by S.M. Koya's becoming leader. Koya recognized the paramount need for peace, and in April 1970 he and Mara reached agreement on retaining the franchise system that was weighted in favour of the Fijians. The close personal relationship established between the two leaders spread downwards into their respective parties, and enabled Fiji to attain independence in October 1970.[78] A highly complex electoral system was created, whereby each voter had four votes, one of which had to be cast for a candidate of his own racial group, while the other three had to be cast for national seats divided among candidates of the three racial groups.

The fragility of the system was demonstrated in 1977 when the Indian-dominated Fijian National Federation Party won the general election, largely because a significant minority of anti-Indian Fijian nationalists deserted their traditional Alliance Party, thereby splitting the native Fijian vote. Indian voters, many of whom had supported the multiracial Alliance (modelled on the Malaysian Alliance), shifted their allegiance to the N.F.P. in the face of anti-Indian sentiment in the Alliance and the open racialism of the Fijian National Party, which advocated a policy of 'Fiji for the Fijians'. Because of the narrowness of its victory and serious internal strife the N.F.P. was unable to form a government and after five months new elections were held that gave the Alliance a convincing victory.[79]

It will be obvious even from this very cursory account that the durability of democracy in Fiji remains in some doubt. The critical importance of leadership in reaching an accommodation is underlined in Fiji's case, but whether the particular leaders can maintain the accommodationist pattern in the face of the politics of racial outbidding by extremist rivals is open to question. Nevertheless, the system has survived nine years and optimists might reasonably argue that accommodationist practices, if they are reasonably successful, can become embedded in the political culture and thereby help to sustain a democratic system.

Whatever doubts may be expressed about the viability of Fiji's political system, there can be little doubt that in the Fijian situation only some form of consociational or semi-consociational system had any chance of success. But, at the same time, it must be clearly recognized that it is no panacea, and that even after relatively lengthy periods of successful working consociational systems may collapse. Lebanon is a case in point but perhaps what is surprising about it is not so much that its consociational system collapsed under the impact of civil war, but that from 1943 until 1975, with the exception of a breakdown in

1958, it supported a remarkably open system of government; and, had it not been for extraneous factors, it may yet have survived.

Lebanon is situated near the vortex of Arab/non-Arab conflicts and great power rivalries in the Middle East. As mentioned earlier (see p. 37), the myth on which Lebanon's system of proportionalism rests is the census of 1932, which showed that the Christians outnumbered Muslims in the ratio of six to five. Common opposition to French rule enabled Bechara al Khoury, leader of the Maronite (Christian) sect, and the Sunnite (Muslim) leader Riad Sulh, to reach an agreement, in the form of the National Pact of 1943. The Pact, which has been the underlying basis of Lebanese politics, provided for Lebanon's national independence and attempted to secure a formula for its role as a denominationally mixed society in a predominantly Arab region. The Pact also formalized the practice of allocating political offices proportionately on a sectarian basis. In addition, parliamentary seats were allocated on the same basis, 54 seats and 45 seats being reserved for Christians and non-Christians respectively. By established custom the President was a Maronite and the Prime Minister a Sunnite. Careful attention was paid to sectarian considerations in the formation of cabinets and key ministries were reserved for particular sects.[80] As far as possible an attempt was made to secure parity between Christian and Muslim in the cabinet, and after the 1972 election eleven out of the fourteen parliamentary blocs had at least one representative in the cabinet.[81]

Although the effective representation of all sects in the cabinet provided a forum for intersectarian negotiation and lent a measure of cohesion to the society, there were grievances among some Muslim sects about their under-representation, and complaints about over-representation of Christians in the top military and security posts and in the higher echelons of the bureaucracy. Fundamentally these objections stemmed from a widespread feeling among Muslims that the ratio based upon the 1932 census was obsolete, in that a new census would almost certainly show an overall Muslim majority.[82]

The Lebanese system clearly rested on a precarious balance: it was disrupted by serious violence in 1958, but was quickly restored on a 'no victor, no vanquished' basis and renewed efforts were made to share power on the basis of a broad intersectarian consensus.[83] Yet, in spite of its achievements, Lebanon's consociational system was deeply flawed. Its Maronite-dominated élite cartel was resistant to changes in Muslim representation both in the cabinet and in parliament, and class cleavages had the effect of exacerbating Christian-Muslim cleavages.[84] Perhaps the political system could have the appropriate adjustments, but in the face of Lebanon's involvement in wider Middle East rivalries it was rendered helpless.

The war of 1975 was sparked off by the presence in Lebanon of some 300 000 Palestinian refugees, mainly Muslim, whom the Lebanese government found exceedingly difficult to control. The fundamental causes were more complex in that the clashes between the Palestinian guerrillas and the (inadequate) Lebanese security forces strengthened domestic cleavages, already being exacerbated by Muslim resentments at Christian political and economic supremacy. The conflicts finally merged in 'a single comprehensive hostility between Christians and Muslims'.[85]

Cyprus's involvement in Greek-Turkish rivalry may also have prevented whatever slender chance its constitution had of providing an accommodation for its seriously conflicted ethnic groups. This is hard to estimate. S.A. de Smith describes the constitution under which Cyprus became independent in 1960 as 'the most rigid, detailed and complicated in the world', and 'so encumbered with prohibitions as to be almost unworkable'.[86] It was premised on the bi-ethnic composition of Cyprus: 78 per cent Greek and 18 per cent Turkish, but the numerical proportions employed in parliamentary representation, the administration, and coercive forces were weighted in favour of the Turks. For representation in parliament, in the council of ministers and in the civil service the quota was to be 70 : 30 Greek to Turk; in the army, police and gendarmerie it was 60 : 40. The President was to be a Greek Cypriot and the Vice-President a Turkish Cypriot, and they were to have the right to appoint the council of ministers and also a power of veto over decisions of the council in the fields of foreign affairs, defence and security. The legislature was elected by separate ethnic voters' rolls, and separate ethnic majorities were required for the enactment of legislation concerning the electoral law and laws in respect of municipalities, taxes and duties. In addition, the Greeks and Turks of the legislature could elect from among themselves communal chambers to deal with communal matters. The constitution also made provision for bi-ethnic representation on the Supreme Constitutional Court, which served as the final authority in constitutional disputes. The basic articles of the constitution were entrenched and 'cannot, in any way, be amended, whether by way of variation, addition or repeal'.[87]

The constitution was explicitly designed to prevent the exercise of simple majoritarianism over a minority; but it went further than that and created the conditions for completely ham-stringing the political process to the extent that on no issue of significance to the Turkish community could the Greek majority prevail.[88] A recent analysis concludes:

'The constitutional framework of the Republic of Cyprus was designed to contain the ethnic conflict by satisfying some of the most basic requirements of the two Cypriot Communities by ruling out both union [i.e. *Enosis* with Greece] and partition. Beyond this however the Cypriot constitution . . . did not contribute anything toward a substantive resolution of past or potential inter-communal conflict. Its intricate formulas and cumbersome structures were precisely designed to freeze and perpetuate the ethnic division. Instead of encouraging cooperation it institutionalised separatist tendencies. . . . The public life of Cyprus was oriented by the very spirit of the constitution toward ethnic antagonism instead of toward democratic development of socially based party politics. Constitutional experts everywhere concurred that the Cyprus constitution despite its ingenuity was practically unworkable. In real life, efficient government proved impossible and controversies quickly arose. The danger points centered on the question of the army's composition (that is, at what level should the units be ethnically integrated), the passage of tax legislation, the establishment of separate municipalities, and the implementation of the 70 : 30 ratio in the composition of the civil service.'[89]

The weighting of the constitution in favour of the Turks alienated the Greek majority, but by the same token it led the Turks to demand that it be enforced punctiliously.[90] Neither side displayed the cooperative attitudes and the will that can perhaps make even the most improbable constitutional instrument viable. Unlike Lebanon, relations between the top leaders were cool and formal at their infrequent meetings.[91] Nevertheless, there were some glimmerings of hope in the early 1970s that, in the face of paralysis, the rival leaders were beginning to appreciate the need for a genuine accommodation. The invasion by Turkey in 1974 and the forcible partition of the island, of course, put an end to that.

The experience of Cyprus has a number of implications for political engineers in other deeply divided societies. It raises the question of whether constitutional safeguards for minorities can be effective; or, to put the same question in different words, whether formal abridgements of majoritarian power will not do more to alienate the majority than provide for the security of the minority? Cyprus, we suggest, shows that the line between proper safeguards and undue privilege is a fine one.

Surinam's attempt to apply consociational principles has been briefly alluded to. Christopher Bagley's account shows the clear influence of the Dutch prototype, whereby the separate racial and religious blocs, none of which constitutes an overall majority of the population, are incorporated into the social and legal structure on the basis of formal equality:

'There appears in fact to be a conscious ethic of "verbroedering", an explicit acceptance of the ethnical principle that ethnic groups ought to co-operate in the running of society. In line with this very Dutch ethic is a system of proportional representation which means that no party can rule without the support of the other parties, and a more or less permanent coalition – as in the Netherlands – is the result.'[92]

Again following the Dutch model, relations among the political élites take the form of summit diplomacy carried on in secret: 'The House of Assembly is presented with decisions on which it comments, and votes according to the wishes of the party leaders.'[93]

Implicit in the thrust of this chapter's argument has been the proposition that group identities, be they religious, ethnic or ideological, cannot be wished out of existence. Any hope that the democratization of a deeply divided society will have an automatic 'non-racial' outcome is a chimera, as is the hope that a common sense of national identity will emerge. Divided societies, by definition, lack this common commitment to shared symbols, and the extent of a common consensus may be narrow – or even non-existent. A further implication is that what is commonly understood as democracy in the Anglo-Saxon or Anglo-Saxon-influenced world will have to be significantly modified in its application to deeply divided societies. Democracy entails universal adult suffrage, but not necessarily simple majoritarianism. This fine analytical distinction must be carefully noted, because mere 'head-counting' and the enforcement of a numerical majority will can have profoundly undemocratic outcomes in divided societies. As Nordlinger has observed:

'Pure majoritarianism along with highly stable electoral patterns would relegate the minority to the status of Calhoun's "permanent minority". In the context of a severe conflict there would then be the distinct danger of Tocqueville's "overbearing majority" and what Calhoun labelled "absolute government". Moreover, in deeply divided societies a "permanent minority" – whether it be small or large – is not likely to reconcile itself to permanent impotence. Unlike the minority in the democratic model, which is accorded a reasonable chance of becoming tomorrow's majority, a "permanent minority" is unlikely to accept highly unpalatable governmental decisions or procedural rules which invest the majority with the authority to impose its will upon the minority.'[94]

Smock and Smock make the same point in their book on the politics of plural societies:

'A group, whether communal or political, that feels permanently excluded from political power has little incentive to play according to the rules of the game. . . . Participation, or the hope of it, tends to vest politicians and the communities they represent with a stake in the system and with its concomitant responsibilities.'[95]

To the extent that a divided society can ensure that none of its constituent groups feels unfairly excluded from a meaningful share in power, and does not feel continuously that its identity (should it have one) and security are threatened, it may be possible for a democratic system to be established. But, as is apparent in the case-studies cited, the vitally important ingredient for any system of government to work is that the rival groups have the will to make it do so, and that they appreciate that they have more to gain from a measure of co-operation with one another than they have to lose by perpetuating a destructive conflict.

If group identities are strong, conflict is likely to be exacerbated by strong-arm tactics of trying to steamroller them out of existence. Where they exist they have to be coped with and accommodated, and it seems clear from the comparative evidence that that can be achieved only if groups are accorded a real security, while, at the same time, inducements are offered to them to develop a wider loyalty to the state that is not necessarily inconsistent with their narrower group loyalty.

The extent to which groups develop a loyalty to the wider society and a belief in the legitimacy of its political institutions will largely depend on the equity with which the system functions. If its operation is such as to entrench a particular group's relative deprivation then that group is likely to become more alienated; conversely, a previously dominant minority cannot expect its privileges of wealth, income and status to be protected in the name of safeguards for minorities.

Various instruments for the securing of an intergroup accommodation have been alluded to in this chapter. Smock and Smock suggest that the following mechanisms, possibly written into the constitution, would provide an institutional basis for such an accommodation: (1) the distribution of political and administrative offices to the major communal groups proportionately; (2) the allocation of economic resources and amenities equitably; (3) the establishment of channels of communication with groups in order to allow them to articulate their demands; (4) the maintenance of institutional forums in which the representatives of the various groups can meet for discussion and bargaining; and (5) the adoption of an electoral system that reduces incentives for communal appeals and increases the pressures for co-operation.[96] In the same work they suggest that a coalition approach to parliamentary politics may have sufficient merit to warrant the adoption of a constitutional provision requiring that all parties that win more than a certain minimum of parliamentary seats should be invited to join the government.[97]

All of these seem to us to be sensible suggestions that incorporate the advantage of seeking to reorient the political process away from winner-takes-all conceptions of, and the adversary style in, politics. It may be objected that efforts to damp down competition will diminish the quality of democracy; but if the price of unrestrained, adversary politics is the collapse of democracy then surely a measure of mutually agreed restraint is worthwhile. No assumption must be made that in seeking to regulate conflict the sources of conflict must be ignored or swept under the carpet: groups locked in conflict are hardly likely to be amenable to conflict-regulating machinery if they feel that their interests or legitimate grievances are being pushed aside for the cause of maintaining a spurious peace.

It will be obvious that none of the techniques and institutions discussed in this chapter can ensure the entrenchment of democratic government. They may be necessary conditions, but they are by no means sufficient conditions. Moreover, it must be pointed out that any political system which eschews simple majoritarianism pays a price in terms of the efficiency and swiftness of the political process. If the rules of the game require that maximum consensus be obtained, at least on certain categories of legislation, it stands to reason that the process whereby such consensus is obtained may be protracted in time; there may also be temptations to avoid certain issues for fear of the intense conflict they might evoke.

These points are the central weaknesses in the consociational style of government, and they account also for its inevitable conservative bias. Lebanon displayed these characteristics, and they contributed to the collapse. But the question may be raised, what other democratic form of government could have succeeded there for as long as that did?

5 *The evolution of South Africa's constitutional and political structure*

The roots of South Africa's current impasse lie deep in its history. The problem of reaching an accommodation with the black population has been postponed for generations. Indeed, given the white supremacist convictions that have animated successive South African governments, an accommodation that was based upon any conception of racial equality was hardly even thought of, except as a disaster to be avoided.

In this chapter we give a brief overview of the forces that have shaped South Africa's political institutions, and we try to show how inappropriate these institutions are for achieving a genuinely democratic political system in a multiracial society. Our purpose is a constructive one, because the past has valuable lessons for the future, and no society is so much the captive of its traditions that it cannot transcend them. The South Africa Act of 1909 emanated from a compact among the political leaders of the four colonies that were to constitute the Union of South Africa. In those times the 'racial' issue was mostly perceived by whites as referring to relations between Boer and Briton, and the making of the constitution turned largely around the problem of achieving a political accommodation between them. The relations between black and white were not ignored, of course, but they were accorded a lower priority. As James Bryce had put it in 1897:

'Although the relations of the white race to the black constitute the gravest of the difficulties which confront South Africa, this difficulty is not the nearest one. More urgent, if less serious, is the other race problem – that of adjusting the rights and claims of the Dutch and the English.'[1]

In all of the uniting colonies racial oligarchies were firmly established. The defeated Trekker republics had been assured by their conquerors that black political rights would not be forced upon them; Natal had pioneered a harsh form of racial segregation, and its representatives were to take the hardest line of all on the issue of black rights at the National Convention of 1908–9; while in the Cape, although there was a non-racial franchise and black and coloured voters made up nearly 15 per cent of the electorate, there was widespread agreement that the admission of blacks to equal political rights should in no way be construed as an opening to a subsequent black majority. Indeed the Cape's foremost statesman and a contender for the first premiership of South Africa, John X. Merriman, expressed his dislike of the African vote and defended its retention merely for its 'safety-valve' functions.

The compromise reached at the National Convention permitted each of the colonies to retain its own franchise arrangements, but the Cape gave up the right (which had been hypothetical until then) of a black to become a member of either House of Parliament. The clauses dealing with the franchise and those dealing with the equality of English and Dutch as official languages were entrenched in the constitution, being amenable to amendment only by a two-thirds majority of both Houses sitting together at the third reading.

Substantially the settlement of the colour issue was avoided by the Convention. Although the need for a common 'native policy' was one of the chief motives for unification and a basis for one had been set out by the South African Intercolonial Native Affairs Commission of 1903–5, any attempt to resolve it would have wrecked the Convention. The priority was to establish a framework for amicable relations between the white groups, and even this had been difficult to achieve as the debates on language rights had shown.

The Convention generated a somewhat misleading impression of amity between the whites. Conciliation was in the air, and it led delegates to make some predictions which, in the light of subsequent history, were astonishingly naive. Merriman, for example, in refuting the case for a federation, cited the case of Canada where 'local jealousies and differences of race and religion had prevented the achievement of a union other than imperfect'. He claimed:

'Happily for us in South Africa we had not the same obstacles to face. In religion there was no dividing line for the great bulk of the European population belonged to the Protestant Churches. In race the people were essentially the same and experience proved to us that the race difference was superficial and would disappear.'[2]

Similarly Smuts argued that South Africa's problems were easier to solve than Canada's or Australia's. 'Canada was divided by race, religion and interest, Australia was economically divided, while in South Africa we already had a Customs Union and other close connections.'[3] Other observers, like Lord Brand, were more cautious, although he optimistically suggested that there would be opportunities in the future for parties to form themselves on lines which would blur and perhaps eventually obliterate the 'racial' cleavage. But he added, 'Pessimists no doubt will say, it must be admitted with some plausibility, that nothing will split the Dutch, or unite the British.'[4]

Considerations of potential ethnic power were never far below the surface. Many English anticipated that continued immigration would tip the demographic scales in their favour and make South Africa irrevocably 'British', and staunch Afrikaner nationalists could calculate that without such immigration and with the exclusion of black voting power, Afrikanerdom could dominate the political system. The broad middle ground of conciliationists, like Botha and Smuts, hoped that tolerance would bring ethnic peace and facilitate the merger of the two white groups into a single stream.

Looking back at South Africa's political and constitutional development after 1910 one asks the question whether the original constitution and its republican successor of 1961 could have been satisfactory instruments for securing racial and ethnic harmony? Obviously black demands could not have been met: they were ignored from the outset, their rights were steadily eroded, and their mounting claims for inclusion were stoutly resisted. But even in the limited context of Afrikaner/English relations how satisfactory was the constitution as a framework for regulating and mitigating ethnic conflict?

Some have argued that the adoption of a federal constitution in 1909 might have augured better for South Africa. The Cape's non-racial system could have been more securely entrenched and it could have set an example to the rest of the country. The possibility is an imponderable and, besides, a federation could also have entrenched racial discrimination in those provinces where it was practised. To some extent federation had this effect in the Southern states of the U.S.A., where the clamour for 'states' rights' was essentially a defence of racial discrimination.

The makers of Union established a strongly centralized unitary form of government deliberately, it being argued (notably by Smuts) that South Africa's problems required 'uniform treatment and firm handling'. Federation was rejected because it allegedly fragmented power, enabled corruption to flourish, and placed undue power in the hands of unrepresentative bodies such as the courts. Sops were given to the federal idea in the form of provincial councils (which Brand anticipated would become 'the haven of mediocrity') and the provision for equal representation of the provinces in the Senate, a body that would be subordinate to the House of Assembly, a house of review and 'a place where ministers may make graceful concessions which they have refused elsewhere.'[5]

The constitution reflected the British or Westminster tradition, with its emphasis on the sovereignty of Parliament and the relatively untrammelled power of the executive. No provision was made for a bill of rights and nor were the courts vested with any powers of review, save, as it transpired, in respect of the entrenched clauses.

Much has been said in recent times of South Africa's Westminster model of government and its inappropriateness for a multiracial society. It should be noted that the South African version has traditionally lacked two crucial attributes of the Westminster system, namely its context of democratic government under the rule of law, and the protection of civil liberties.

Another important institution that was established was the electoral system, based on single-member constituencies and the plurality or 'first-past-the-post' principle. The Convention considered proportional representation but rejected it. Lord Brand commented:

'Those who had advocated proportional representation had seen in it a valuable means of softening racial antagonisms. It is unfortunate that the British minority scattered throughout the country districts, and to a less extent the Dutch in the towns, will now be deprived of all hope of proper representation. . . . The line between town and country is in itself too strongly marked, it is intensified by race prejudice. Proportional representation might gradually have broken down these barriers with the most fortunate results to the country.'[6]

The contentious issue was the weight to be accorded to votes, and finally the system adopted favoured the rural constituencies by allowing them to be 'unloaded' to the extent of 15 per cent below the electoral quota, while urban constituencies could be conversely 'loaded' by the same amount.

The combined effect of these constitutional provisions was to establish a framework within which a single group could capture supreme power that was concentrated in a single decisive site: parliament was sovereign, and the electoral system, rather than inhibiting the consolidation of communal voting blocs (as proportional representation might have done), allowed a 'winner-takes-all' outcome.

In South African party politics the major source of party affiliation has been language. Although party and ethnic group have never precisely coincided, it was ethnic issues between whites that formed much of the stuff of parliamentary politics until into the 1950s.[7] The sanguine hopes mentioned above were not realized. The story of white politics and parties is really the story of how Afrikaner nationalism, despite obstacles and vicissitudes, could ultimately capture control of the political system and subject the entire society to its domination. The point we wish to emphasize is that the nature of the constitution facilitated this capture or, to put the point less strongly, at least did not provide much of a curb. The further point, which is a lesson for the future, is that unqualified majoritarianism, which we have had in parliamentary politics, can result in domination by the numerically preponderant group over the other, even where that other group is comparatively large and significant in economic terms.

It was a question of political arithmetic that explains the abolition of the Cape's non-racial voting system. The historic paranoia of Afrikaner nationalism has been the belief that the minority English group together with their non-Nationalist Afrikaner allies would seek to compensate for their numerical deficiencies by using black and coloured votes against the Nationalists. It was these fears that led Hertzog in the 1920s to table his 'Native Bills' at the core of which was the removal of Cape blacks from the common roll. (By 1920 black and coloured voters constituted over 20 per cent of the Cape electorate, but this percentage was slashed to less than 10 by the enfranchisement of white women and the abolition of qualifications for white voters in 1930 and 1931 respectively.)

The removal of coloured voters from the common roll in the 1950s was an even clearer manifestation of the same drive: in 1948 the Nationalists won the election, in alliance with the Afrikaner Party, with a majority of five. In the provincial council elections of the following year the United Party won back the seats of Paarl and Bredasdorp with the aid, so the Nationalists supposed, of newly registered coloured voters.[8] The omens for the 1953 election were clear, especially if it were recalled that the number of qualified potential coloured voters was estimated to be three times the number actually registered. Compulsory registration of voters had been introduced in 1945 but did not apply to coloured voters. When a new voters' roll was compiled in May 1946 coloured voters were not automatically transferred to it, but were required to re-register, resulting in a substantial decline in their numbers to a mere 7,3 per cent of the Cape electorate.[9]

The Separate Representation of Voters Bill was introduced into parliament in 1951 and was enacted as ordinary legislation with simple majorities in both Houses. The legislation was rejected by the Appellate Division of the Supreme Court on grounds of its not having complied with the special legislative procedures required in terms of the Union Constitution for amendment of the entrenched clauses. The government's response to its defeat at the hands of the courts was to enact, again by simple majorities, the High Court of Parliament Act of 1952. In terms of this legislation both Houses of Parliament were to be transformed into a 'High Court' for the purpose of reviewing any judgment of the Appellate Division that had invalidated an Act of Parliament.

Predictably the High Court proceeded to overrule the Appellate Division's decision, and declared that the entrenched clauses of the constitution were no longer binding. The High Court's decision was challenged in the courts and declared invalid by the Appellate Division.

Further efforts were made by the government in 1953 and 1954 to obtain the requisite majorities, but these failed. Finally, the government resorted to extreme measures in 1955: legislation was passed to increase the quorum in the Appellate Division from four to five, and five further judges were appointed to the court. It was further provided that in cases involving the validity of Acts of Parliament a quorum of eleven was required, judgment requiring the concurrence of at least six of the judges.[10] (It is quite probable that this measure was resorted to as an alternative to dismissing judges, a course that was apparently being considered in governmental circles.[11])

The next and conclusive measure was the enlargement of the Senate in such a way as to ensure that the government could obtain its two-thirds majority. The removal of coloured voters from the common roll was effected in 1956, and the validating legislation withdrew any entrenchment of voting rights. In the present constitution only the clauses guaranteeing the equality of the official languages are entrenched. Of the constitutional crisis Alexander Brady has written:

'The Nationalists were determined to apply the majoritarian principle in achieving their ends, which in a democracy of such cultural and ethnical diversity must generate deep tensions. In defence they asserted that their concern was merely to establish the sovereignty of parliament as it existed at Westminster. In South Africa the sovereignty of parliament raises for democracy more difficult issues than it does in Britain, where a federal temperament, if not a federal law, operates within the state. In the Union the exclusive sentiments of Afrikaner nationalism has sharply divided the European people, and here parliament's sovereignty exercised in the interests of one cultural section could result in tyranny. Hence the more the Nationalists exalted the idea of a flexible constitution amendable by a parliamentary majority, the more anxious became the English-speaking South Africans.'[12]

One may pose the question here of what might have happened if the Cape common roll franchise had not been abolished by the measures of 1936 and 1956. Although the provincial distribution of seats was determined on the basis of the number of white voters only, one can surmise that a solid anti-Nationalist bloc of voters would have grown, preventing the Nationalists from attaining power in 1948 and strengthening the black and coloured opposition to discrimination all over the country. But this is pure conjecture. Nationalist speculation has it that if the Nationalists had been ousted from power in 1953 by an increased coloured vote there could have been civil war and the end of parliamentary government.

The retraction of the parliamentary franchise in South Africa is the obverse of what has occurred in other political systems, where a ruling party has sought to broaden the base of its electoral support by enfranchising new strata of the population, as in the second British Reform Act of 1867 when Disraeli tried to strengthen the Tories by extending the franchise to part of the urban working class. The same kind of electoral considerations have prevailed in South Africa but with the opposite effect. Moreover anti-Nationalist parties hesitated to mobilize black electoral support, when it was still possible to do so, lest this result in a white backlash that was politically more damaging than the black votes were beneficial.

The fate of the entrenched franchise clauses has led many to the conclusion that constitutional safeguards are worthless: a sufficiently determined government can smash through mere paper guarantees and, if need be, subvert the entire constitution. It may be true that in the final analysis the only safeguards in a constitution lie in its overall acceptability to the large majority of the people who are bound by its provisions. But constitutional safeguards can delay, obstruct, and, to some extent, deter even ruthless ruling parties and force them to take what could be politically embarrassing or damaging steps. Political power is always potentially dangerous, and if constitutional safeguards and instruments like a bill of rights can contribute to the checking of power and the growth of a respect for constitutionalism (which means essentially limited government) then they are clearly worthwhile.

Centralized and nearly total power has enabled the Nationalists to strip away the rights of blacks and entrench and expand the power of the South African racial oligarchy. Even the separate or communal representation (by whites) accorded to black and coloured voters was abolished. Directly and indirectly (through its weaknesses) the South African constitution has facilitated this process. The ground rules for the conduct of political activity, which form part of the constitution, have been elaborated to entrench the Nationalists' impregnability. The Prohibition of Political Interference Act of 1967, for example, makes it difficult if not impossible for a multiracial political alliance to emerge; and the restrictions on freedom of association combined with draconian security legislation make it exceedingly difficult for opposition forces to mobilize their political resources and challenge the system. Ideally constitutions ought to create a framework for what is loosely called government by consent, but South Africa's constitution, by enshrining racial discrimination and minority rule, has led to a situation where government by coercion is a more accurate description. The South African experience, moreover, has abundantly verified the proposition that where groups are excluded from an effective share in political power they will be discriminated against.

Parliament, in these circumstances, has become a wholly ineffective body. Of course it is true that in many parliamentary systems the same allegation has been made. With the widening of the scope of governmental activity and the centralization of power in the cabinet, real power has shifted decisively away from parliament. With a stable majority votes of confidence are not in doubt.

The same phenomenon occurs in aggravated form in South Africa. Only once has parliament caused the downfall of a government and that was in September 1939 on the issue of South Africa's entry into war. (It is a moot point whether, if parliament had been dissolved and an election called, Hertzog would not have won.) South Africa has become a classic case of 'crystallized politics' which A.J. Milnor has defined as:

'the result of a group of voters which has developed as a unit, sharply divided from the rest of the social system and unable either to communicate with it or to understand its wants and needs. Its representatives are not forced to compromise, because they are a majority of the legislature. They are never defeated because as long as the channels of political communication remain open and fair, they cannot lose . . . '[13]

In an analysis of these issues in general, and in particular of the massive security powers which the present government has assumed, W.H.B. Dean has written that

'the self-conceived function of the South African parliament is simply to provide support for a government which had obtained a majority of seats in parliament at a general election. . . . the sole function of the legislature is to provide the executive with the legislation the executive considers necessary to give effect to its policy. The idea of the legislature controlling, or even bringing down the government, through mechanisms such as cabinet responsibility and the use of questions, has little or no role to play.'

The author goes on to assert that the government's responsiveness to popular pressure is maintained through the National Party, which has supplanted parliament as the link between the electorate and the executive.[14]

These considerations underline a point made above: if the basis of voter choice has been substantially along ethnic lines, and if one ethnic group can mobilize and unite its members who are in the majority demographically within the enfranchised strata, then the effect will be to ensure them a perpetual parliamentary majority and total control of the political system because it operates on a simple majoritarian or 'zero-sum' principle. We believe that if truly democratic politics are to be established in any plural society this principle has to be rejected, and ways found of avoiding the 'crystallized' situation and ensuring some form of power-sharing.

We would note here the effect of the electoral system in inflating the size of the Nationalists' majorities. A recent study has estimated that in the 1948 election the National Party obtained the votes of only 31,6 per cent of the electorate, while in the 1970 election (in which they sustained some losses) the figure was 40 per cent.[15] It has been estimated that in the election of 1974 the Nationalists won 70 per cent of the seats with 54 per cent of the votes cast. These significant distortions, as well as the tendency to 'crystallized politics', might be avoided if some form of proportional representation were to be adopted.

A further consequence of crystallization has been the remarkable solidarity of cabinets after 1948: there have only been three cases where ministers have either resigned on principle (Mr T. Gerdener) or were forced to resign (Dr A. Hertzog and Dr C.P. Mulder). This is not because we are blessed with undue proportions of super-efficient politicians, but fundamentally it stems from the drive for maintaining ethnic unity. To resign on principle means entering the political wilderness; to sack the inefficient, corrupt, senile, or the dissident is thought to display a lack of inner cohesion which could be exploited by one's opponents. This is not to say that certain ministers have not been eased out in curious circumstances, but inefficient or otherwise inadequate people have in a number of cases been tolerated for far too long.

The omnipotence of the South African executive has enabled it to react to challenges in a manner that borders on arrogance. No government in any modern parliamentary system (democratic or otherwise) has lasted in power for as long as the National Party government of South Africa has succeeded in doing. The corrosive effect of this situation is nowhere more clearly to be seen than in the tendency of members of the governing party to identify that party with the State. Effectively South Africa has followed the common African trend towards the single-party or single-party-dominant system in which the political leadership is inclined to conflate the interests of party and State.

In recent times the most striking example of the abuse of executive power in South Africa has occurred in the events surrounding the Department of Information. At the time of writing many of the unauthorized, illegal activities of the (now disbanded) Department were still being revealed. The minister responsible, Dr C.P. Mulder, was forced to resign from the cabinet, but serious charges have been made regarding the complicity of the members of the government. The issue of cabinet responsibility remains moot.

For our purposes it is not necessary to dwell upon the Information scandal and its possible ramifications and repercussions. But even on the basis of what is presently known it can be described as the manifestation of a far-reaching perversion of the parliamentary system resulting from the vesting of unaccountable power in the hands of bureaucrats.

The possibility of a highly centralized system was inherent in the South African constitution from its very inception. The provincial councils were a compromise arrangement, and their functioning down the years has shown them to be among the least satisfactory of representative institutions in the South African system. Constitutionally they have always been subject to the overriding veto of the central government, which, in addition, has steadily whittled away provincial powers. Nearly all of the revenue for provincial expenditures is derived from the central government's allocations, which means that the provinces now have little or no independent tax base. A further important source of central government influence over the provincial councils derives from the central government's appointment of the provincial administrators, who are the key officials in the provincial system.[16]

Earlier hopes that the provincial councils would not be run on party political lines were not realized and, with Nationalists now controlling all of the councils except for Natal, they offer little or no resistance to the process of centralization. Leading Nationalist provincial officials have been content to see the provinces as simply instruments of the centre, and they have acquiesced in the removal of provincial powers.

The process of centralization has seriously affected 'white' local authorities as well. All local authority by-laws are subject to provincial approval. Similarly the provincial authorities oversee local authority financial matters, and, in the case of capital programmes the approval of the central government's treasury is required.[17]

The expansion of central government control in matters of race has been the major factor in the diminution of local authority powers. In a speech in 1956 Dr H.F. Verwoerd, then minister of native affairs, declared bluntly that the State laid down policy and 'the local authorities are the agents of the State with respect to the execution of such policy'.[18]

Since Union in 1910 local authorities had shared responsibility for urban African administration but, beginning in the 1950s, the Nationalists moved steadily to clip their wings. They believed that some of the larger municipalities, like Johannesburg, which were controlled by anti-Nationalists, were deliberately thwarting the implementation of apartheid. The process of removing local authority powers in this sphere proceeded to its logical culmination in 1971 when, in terms of the Bantu Affairs Administration Act, provision was made for the establishment of boards that were to control all aspects of African affairs in the common area outside of the homelands. Although local authorities have representation on the boards they are essentially instruments of the central government, and their directors are carefully chosen to ensure their reliability in implementing the government's policy.

In other respects, too, local authorities have had to yield to pressure from the centre. Statutes like the Group Areas Act (enacted in 1950 and subsequently much amended) have revolutionized the residential configuration of towns and villages, often against the wishes of the local authorities. A further serious invasion of local authority autonomy occurred when in 1972 coloured municipal voters in the Cape were deprived of their franchise rights and were given instead rights of participation in exclusively coloured management committees in declared coloured areas.

Historically the law and law-enforcement agencies have been one of the major instruments in South Africa for the implementation of racial policies. It is in this context that one must examine the place of the courts in the constitutional and political framework. In the absence of a bill of rights and other machinery for the exercise of judicial review (other than in the limited sphere of the entrenched clauses) the courts have been inherently incapable of providing much of a check on the growth of authoritarianism. The powers of politicians and officials have vastly increased, while the legal remedies available to the victims of power abuse have declined.

In recent times the government has to an increasing extent deliberately excluded the courts from reviewing administrative action. This has occurred most egregiously in the field of security legislation where the effect has been to extinguish *habeas corpus* as a right available to those detained without trial. In several cases where the courts have been able to find loopholes and mitigate the harshness or inequity of laws the government has moved rapidly to plug the loophole by amending the legislation to exclude the courts.

Complementing these factors has been the general passivity of the judiciary itself. For the most part judges have been inclined to shy away from political issues that might lead them into conflict with the executive. C.J.R. Dugard, in an analysis of the influence of legal positivism, describes the judiciary as a body 'which views its task in the field of statutory interpretation as a purely mechanical one . . . content to leave all policy matters to Parliament . . . [and] seemingly immune to value judgments'.[19] In the critical area of the enforcement of security laws the courts have been inclined to manifest executive-mindedness. Numerous allegations have been levelled against the authorities concerning the use of third-degree methods to extract incriminating information from political detainees. Overwhelmingly the courts have chosen to believe police denials of brutality rather than to accept detainees' allegations. A.S. Mathews has written:

'None of the detention laws now in force in South Africa specifically directs that evidence obtained from a solitary confinement detainee shall be admissable in court. Where the circumstance of the confinement and interrogation points towards coercion the judges could readily admit expert evidence concerning the effect of interrogation in solitary confinement on a witness and declare the evidence inadmissable if there is any doubt about its voluntary nature. Up to now there appears to have been a judicial reluctance to grapple with this issue.'[20]

The makers of Union were concerned to guard against the operation of political factors in judicial appointments. In arguing against a federal system Smuts warned that it placed undue power in the hands of judges, whose appointments might therefore be manipulated by politicians. The choice of a unitary system seems to have made little difference, for, however difficult it may be to prove conclusively, there can be little doubt that political factors have played a part in appointments – and non-appointments – to the South African bench.[21] This consideration points to the need for drawing up a new constitution to neutralize this factor by substantially diluting the role of the executive in making judicial appointments.

Our review of the constitution has underlined its weaknesses and its inherently unsatisfactory character for a multiracial society. Even within the limited confines of white politics it has been unsuitable for coping with ethnic conflict. In its 'winner-takes-all' provisions the constitution has been a useful instrument for Afrikaner nationalism, facilitating its grasp of near-total power and bestowing upon it great powers of patronage and possibilities of leverage. It is one of the ironies of South African political experience that the flexibility of its constitution has fostered the rigidity of its politics.

6 *Possibilities for a democratic South Africa*

If any single theme has predominated thus far it is that the attaining and sustaining of a democratic form of government in South Africa is going to be an enormously difficult task. Nevertheless, it is one that must be attempted in spite of all the odds. It is difficult to envisage future circumstances in which there is a mass expulsion and/or emigration of whites and perhaps of other non-African minorities as well. This kind of doomsday thinking is premised on the assumption that guerrilla forces, operating from without and within South Africa's borders, can overthrow the established South African regime by violence.[1] We know of no comparable precedent in modern history for such a revolution: nor do we believe that those who talk easily of violence can have any conception of what a South African war would exact in terms of the toll of human life and the devastation of society.

To abhor violence, however, is not to deny that it has already come to South Africa: we are already in the early stages of a war which, if not checked, will show an unbounded ferocity comparable with the Algerian war of 1954–62. Nor would we deny that the social structure of South Africa is characterized by a marked degree of structural violence. Racial discrimination stunts and warps the lives and being of the people who are its victims, and may lead them to degenerate into the hopelessness and despair that is born of poverty, powerlessness and frustration.

The record of so-called 'white settler societies' in achieving peaceful accommodations with their indigenous majorities is not an encouraging one. Algeria, in the heyday of French rule, had a white population of one million, over 10 per cent of the population; today it has practically none; the significant settler populations of Angola and Moçambique have also been reduced drastically; and in Zimbabwe-Rhodesia, where a haemorrhaging guerrilla war has been waged for the past six years, costing already nearly 10 000 lives, the future of the small white minority remains in doubt, despite the measure of accord reached by the internal settlement. In Kenya, scarred by the violence of 'Mau-Mau' in the 1950s, and in Zambia, appreciable white minorities exist, but only in the vulnerable position of a powerlessness that is commensurate with their size relative to that of the African majorities. Neither society, however, could properly be termed democratic. Only Botswana merits this description. Although it is a model of good race relations, its white population is too small to be regarded as anything like a potential threat to the established regime.

Leo Kuper commences a brave analysis of the possibilities of peaceful democratization in white settler societies with the following sentences:

'White settler societies are notoriously repressive and undemocratic, indeed, among systems of race relations, they are the very embodiment of racial domination and discrimination. We often assume that transformation of their political structures must be violent, and in revolutionary perspectives, the Algerian war represents the prototype of liberation from white domination. It seems impossible to conceive of *internal* social processes in white settler societies which might *contribute* to evolutionary change from racial conflict and oppression toward consensus and democratic participation.'[2]

South Africa obviously differs in critical respects from any other African case: it is a sovereign, independent state and is so acknowledged by even its most hostile foes; and its non-black minorities account for nearly 30 per cent of the total South African population, including Bophuthatswana and Transkei. J.L. Sadie's population projections for the year 2000 suggest that without immigration the non-black minorities will number approximately 25 per cent of the total population.[3] These proportions are well above the threshold, in simple numerical terms, that enables a minority group to 'cause trouble' (see pp. 39–40). Of course this statement is based upon the crude and possibly unfounded assumption that the basis of future conflict is going to be on a simple black/non-black polarity, and, in turn on the assumption that these categories will cohere into groups. Whatever the future course of events in South Africa and their outcome, it seems to us highly unlikely that South Africa will cease being a multiracial society. Even in the event of a total black victory by force (which we consider improbable), a substantial number of non-blacks will remain in the society, but it is highly unlikely that they will be accommodated in a democratic system. In any consideration of what kind of political system might be appropriate for a democratic South Africa the crucial factor is how, if at all, fundamental change will come about. Revolutionary violence and counter-violence on a wide scale and of lengthy duration, it need hardly be said, does not create a promising basis on which to establish democratic government; if it could be averted and negotiations for a new political settlement be initiated, there would be a significantly better chance that an acceptable kind of political framework could be set up.

At the moment South Africa shows ominous signs of becoming locked into a spiral of violence. A war psychosis is being generated, and the potentiality of a 'garrison state' is being created. More and more blacks, especially of the younger generation in the towns, have lost any hope that violence can be avoided, and, moreover, they see in violence, following Fanon's writings, a necessary means of purging black minds of the psychological residues of white domination. It would be realistic to assume that violence will not abate; to an increasing extent there will be guerrilla incursions, urban uprisings and urban terrorism. For the time being, however, all of these forms of violent opposition are unlikely to make much of a dent in white South Africa's security; but if they were combined with increasing international hostility, including the real possibility of economic sanctions and aid to the guerrilla forces, that security may turn out to be an illusion.[4] The Soweto disturbances of 1976 and their aftermath may prove to have been a watershed in the hardening of black resistance to separate development, because those events showed the existence of young blacks whose alienation has gone so far that they are unafraid of dying for the cause of ending racial oppression.

It may be that neither white nor black in South Africa would have the resources to achieve a total victory over the other, in the event of civil war. It may not deter either side from conflict. As Lewis Coser has observed:

'If the adversary's strength could be measured prior to engaging in conflict, antagonistic interests might be adjusted without such conflict; but where no means for prior adjustment exists, only actual struggle may afford the exact knowledge of comparative strength. Since power can often be appraised only in its actual exercise, accommodation may frequently be reached only after the contenders have measured their respective strengths in conflict.'[5]

It might occur, on the other hand, that a 'no-win' situation of deadlock could be reached, in which both sides realize the devastating damage they can inflict upon each other, at which stage negotiations for peace and a new dispensation may begin. Anthony Oberschall has written: 'Whether conciliation will be sought depends on the costs and benefits that both sides expect from a negotiated agreement weighed against the costs and benefits of continued confrontation.'[6] It stands to reason that the sooner the conflict can be terminated, the greater the chance of salvaging some measure of interracial goodwill from the disaster.

In the present and likely future circumstances of South Africa one cannot expect that conflict can be eliminated. Conflict is ubiquitous in all societies, and all one may hope for is that institutions may be devised that will regulate and contain it peacefully, and that the cutting edge of the issues of conflict may be sufficiently blunted to enable a durable accommodation to be reached. We need to remind ourselves that the problems of human relationships, unlike problems in mathematics, are not amenable to 'solutions'. A solution of the problem of racial conflict may be unattainable, but it may be possible to reduce its intensity and thereby cope with it.

It was argued in chapter 2 that the salience of race was derived not so much from any intrinsic qualities pertaining to race itself, but from the structured and institutionalized inequalities associated with it. A necessary condition of dealing with racial conflict will be the establishment of a political dispensation that is acceptable to all groups, but it will not be a sufficient condition. Inequalities throughout the society, such as in the distribution of income and wealth, in access to education and in the broad sphere of social interaction (where white assumptions of black inferiority are galling in the extreme to blacks), will have to be reduced if the steam is to be taken out of the racial conflict. There is no facile suggestion here that these inequalities can be easily or rapidly overcome. But what is crucially important is that they should be tackled as a matter of national priority by the concerted efforts of all racial groups.

There is little need in this work to dwell upon the failure of separate development as a viable policy for accommodating racial conflict in South Africa. Its shortcomings have been exhaustively catalogued and analysed in a plethora of literature, some of which is cited in the bibliography. Fundamentally, separate development seeks to separate politically groups that are economically interdependent, and in the name of preserving group identity it perpetuates a system of racial privilege. The black homelands, of which Transkei and Bophuthatswana are formally independent (although internationally unrecognized), are incapable of sustaining their *de jure* populations; and this situation is unlikely to change. In 1975 blacks in the urban areas of 'white' South Africa (also known as the 'common area') outnumbered whites by nearly two to one. The projection for the year 2000 is that the ratio will be nearly three to one.[7] The official policy that urban blacks are 'temporary sojourners' who must seek their political self-determination through their respective homelands remains unchanged and, indeed, the government has announced its intentions of pressing homelands citizenship onto the entire African population until, in principle at least, the number of Africans who are South African citizens is reduced to zero. As the Minister of Bantu Administration and Development put it:

'There must be no illusions about this, because if our policy is taken to its full logical conclusion as far as the Black people are concerned, there will not be one Black man with South African citizenship.'[8]

In spite of this, the government recognizes that it is unable to dispense with the black population of the common areas, and in the urban areas (outside of the Western Cape) blacks, regardless of their homeland citizenship, who qualify under section ten of the Bantu (Urban Areas) Act for residence rights, are being permitted to own houses on 99-year leases. Moreover, the government is seeking to confer more powers of autonomy on Soweto and has also eased certain other restrictions, notably on the freedom of black entrepreneurs in the towns.

The policy, in other words, is full of contradictions; but the point to be emphasized is that far from reducing racial conflict by reducing contacts, separate development has aggravated racial tension. The granting of independence to Bophuthatswana and Transkei has made little difference to the core problem of South Africa and that is white insistence upon the maintenance of racial hegemony. Their bargaining power or leverage in the South African political economy is limited by their overwhelming dependence on South Africa. Transkei's budget for 1977–8, for instance, relied upon a direct grant from South Africa for over 70 per cent of its revenue, and a further 6 per cent was to be raised by borrowing from the South African capital market.[9] It remains entirely unclear how Transkei will survive economically the recent rupture in diplomatic relations with its patron.

Their rejection as citizens has been deeply resented by many Africans not so much because of what the deprivation materially involves, but more because of its symbolic affirmation of their status in the society; similarly the issue of land, although materially of much greater significance, has equally important symbolic connotations: it was largely on this issue that Chief Kaiser Matanzima of Transkei formally broke diplomatic ties with the Republic, and nearly all of the other homeland leaders, who preside over fragmented and unconnected bits and pieces of territory, have voiced objections on the score of land. It may be noted here that the Nationalist government has repeatedly refused to release more land to blacks than the amount stipulated in the quotas incorporated in the Bantu Trust and Land Act of 1936, fixing a ceiling of 13,7 per cent of South Africa's land space as homeland territory. Early in 1979, however, the government appointed a consolidation commission whose terms of reference enable it to make recommendations for the acquisition of land above this ceiling 'where absolutely necessary'.

The present-day homelands are the shrunken remnants of the areas which earlier African societies regarded as their *lebensraum*. The historian W.M. Macmillan estimated in 1930 that the reserves scheduled in terms of the Natives' Land Act of 1913 constituted approximately one-fifth of the land blacks had formerly occupied.[10] So far as we are aware this estimate has never been authoritatively challenged, although the government adheres to the myth that the present land distribution is a valid reflection of the historical pattern.

The most basic conflict in South Africa is, of course, the exclusion of blacks from any effective share in political power. The whole thrust of official policy has been to frustrate or neutralize black demands by channelling them into homelands political institutions, separated on an ethnic basis, and to deny blacks any representation in a single, interracial political organ. But it should by no means be concluded that there has been a homogeneous black reaction to homelands institutions or to separate development generally.[11] A significant group, especially in the urban areas where people often have no ties with any homeland, completely rejects the homeland concept and will have no truck with homeland leaders. Another group, perhaps larger, is no less emphatic in its rejection of separate development but for instrumental reasons operates the machinery of the system in the hope of increasing black bargaining power within the overall system. Chief M. Gatsha Buthelezi, the chief minister of KwaZulu, is the foremost practitioner of this strategy, for which he has become a target for the younger radicals in the South African Student Organization (SASO). Although Chief Buthelezi's power-base is among the five-million-strong Zulu group his influence among other groups of blacks, as well as among the coloured and Indian people, should not be underestimated. In terms of numbers and potential resources the recently formed alliance between *Inkatha*, of which Buthelezi is president, and the (coloured) Labour party and the (Indian) Reform Party, could become a formidable opponent of the government.

No assumptions can be made about the potential distribution of black voter allegiance in a future open election in which universal suffrage prevails and in which presently banned black organizations are able freely to campaign and mobilize support. Almost certainly sharp policy differences would crystallize among the several political parties that would be bound to arise. Black nationalism in South

Africa has never been a monolithic entity; rather it has been a congeries of groups with different ideological, class and, perhaps, regional interests, held together by a common (and predominantly defensive) rejection of racial discrimination.[12] Moreover, it may not be assumed that purely ethnic black parties (such as Tswana, Xhosa, etc) would be wholly eclipsed in an open election, although it seems likely that support for them would be, relatively speaking, marginal. In this respect the homelands policy has had contradictory effects: on the one hand, its emphasis on ethnic divisions among blacks and on the leadership role of chiefs in the homeland authority structures has appreciably undermined ethnicity and traditionalism (at least as approved by the Nationalist government) as foci of allegiance or adherence; but, on the other hand, these same structures have generated not inconsiderable 'client classes' of politicians, bureaucrats and others, who have operated the system, and who will not lightly be pushed aside by other black political movements who completely reject the homelands concept.

Other ideological conflicts among blacks include those between Marxists and non-Marxists, advocates of various forms of African socialism or 'black communalism' and free enterprise, and between 'multiracialists' and those who accord blacks primacy in their vision of a new society. With the proscription of most major black organizations that operated outside of government-sponsored institutions, it is impossible to say how much weight each ideological segment carries. Nor, we suggest, is it possible to extrapolate from survey findings in the present climate of repression to circumstances in which freedom of association and freedom to mobilize were permitted.

The point has been made that the basic cleavage in South Africa is the exclusion of blacks from power, but the above few paragraphs cast doubt upon any expectation that the black majority would for political purposes form a solidary grouping.

The concomitant inequalities of racial domination have already been alluded to in chapter 2: the distribution of income and wealth is a crucial area upon whose treatment much will depend. Séan Archer has estimated that in 1970–1 the richest decile and quintile in South Africa received, respectively, 58 per cent and 75 per cent of the national income, a pattern that is unique in its inequality among the developed and semi-developed countries of the world. He showed that the overall ratio of white to black (black, Indian and coloured) incomes varied from 8,5 to 1 to 13,6 to 1, while for white/black incomes the range was from 12,1 to 1 and 15,4 to 1.[13]

It is true that a number of studies have indicated that in recent years the wage gap, at least in a number of sectors, has narrowed,[14] but the problem of overcoming relative deprivation remains one of awesome magnitude, especially in circumstances of considerable white resistance to black job mobility and of unemployment, estimates of which vary from 1,5 to 2,3 million.[15] Whatever remedial measures are applied, we fear that there will be a good deal of poverty in South Africa for a long time to come.

Increasing numbers of younger blacks in the urban areas reject capitalism, because they associate it with racial repression, poverty and frustration. Even though the kind of capitalism found in South Africa is unique in the extent to which it is shackled by laws and regulations and differs widely from neo-classical models, it has become a focus of hostility, thereby intensifying the ideological cleavage between white and black. This is not to suggest that all blacks reject capitalism or even that those who espouse black communalism or some variety of African socialism deny a significant role to the private sector. Probably the number of hard-line Marxists is comparatively small, but impressionistic information about the younger militants of Soweto suggests that it will increase quite rapidly.

From this very brief summary of the issues of racial conflict in South Africa certain deductions may be drawn. First, unlike the Swiss or Dutch pattern where cross-cutting lines of cleavage have a moderating effect on the intensity of conflict, the lines of cleavage in South Africa are to a significant extent mutually reinforcing: race, class and nationalism, however much they may be analytically distinct, tend to converge and fuse in the minds of blacks. Secondly, in associational terms, cross-cutting ties are insignificant other than in the economy, where although black and white interact it is almost invariably on an hierarchical or dominative basis. Whatever momentum there may have been for associations to become fully interracial, ranging from universities to recreational clubs, was heavily discountenanced by the Nationalist government; and now, when the government is seeking cautiously to reverse this trend, it seems that there may be an increasing resistance among blacks to accepting such concessions unless accompanied by major structural reforms. The major point is that the capacity of associations to act as nodes of interracial accommodation and generators of a social tissue that could help to reduce conflict is severely limited. Probably they could serve these ends only in an overall context of racial desegregation in the wider society.

Moreover, the rise of black consciousness among the younger generation of blacks is an important manifestation of conflict intensification. While it is as yet too inchoate a bundle of feelings to be described as an ideology, its basis is a refusal to accept white-defined frameworks of reality as applicable to blacks; and it seeks to make blacks, individually and collectively, self-steering actors, who decide and act upon their own initiatives. Black consciousness organizations, before they were proscribed in 1977, were emphatic in rejecting interracial co-operation. This attitude stemmed not so much from a black counter-racism (though this was by no means absent) as from a belief that the easiest basis of mobilization was a common denominator of oppression and, furthermore, that black solidarity was the only instrument capable of mustering sufficient power-resources effectively to challenge white power.

Although the number of adherents to black consciousness is probably comparatively small its influence and capacity for growth should not be underestimated. The banning of its major organizational vehicles will by no means eliminate its influence; in fact it is more likely to heighten it. In the black schools and universities a rising young black élite is being educated in an atmosphere of black consciousness that will not disappear, however many executive measures or prosecutions are directed against its exponents.

Thus far the Nationalist government has shown little sign of willingness to explore effective conflict-regulation machinery. It has become so caught up in its own policy's toils that it can see reality only throug an ideologically refracted prism. In principle it refuses to recognize or deal with black leaders who exist outside of prescribed channels; and it has dealt with them and their organizations with strongly authoritarian measures, thereby increasing the mutual alienation of black and white. A little-explored, but in our judgement, highly significant area of entrenched resistance to change is the bureaucracy. Thirty years of apartheid and separate development have produced an immense juggernaut of administrators, officials and other apparatchiks, dedicated to the enforcement of policy. It is in the nature of civil servants to move in prescribed and predefined grooves only, and to resist deviations and the admission of exceptions. In circumstances where a great deal of rule-making in the form of regulations is delegated to civil servants (which gives them considerable discretionary powers), and where the thrust of official policy has been to treat blacks administratively rather than politically, thereby involving them in a maze of discriminatory regulations and laws, the bureaucracy has become one of the primary interfaces between white and black. The wooden unresponsiveness of the Department of Bantu Education and the Bantu Affairs Administration Boards prior to the Soweto crisis of June 1976 is a case in point. Lawrence Schlemmer has pertinently remarked that 'there is a very real danger that our system of administration and control will become so inured to disturbances that a permanent super-rigidification of practices occurs in our control bureaucracies'.[16]

A number of surveys have shown the large extent to which whites are apparently oblivious of black grievances and needs.[17] Although white industrial and business élites have in recent years become much more conscious of these issues, this awareness has not percolated down to the rank and file of white communities. This gulf in perceptions is attributable to a social mechanism that creates a vicious circle: thoroughgoing racial discrimination cuts groups off from one another on an unequal basis, and subjects dominated groups to regimentation, frustration and social dislocation. In turn these conditions generate anti-social behaviour in a wide variety of forms, while the absence of effective, legal channels for voicing demands forces protest to be illegal; and in white perceptions it is anarchic and anomic behaviour that senselessly destroys amenities which 'we' created for 'them'. Thus it is precisely this kind of anti-social and protest behaviour among blacks that reinforces racial stereotypes among whites, who are substantially incapable of distinguishing cause from effect.

The vicious circle is thus complete, and it is sustained by a cognitive dissonance whereby evidence that reinforces set and internalized ideas and attitudes is accepted, while contradictory evidence is screened out of perception. The whole process is further sustained by a variety of thought-control instruments, ranging from the political use of television to the censorship of literature. Often indoctrination lies not so much in what is said as in what is *not* said.

To most whites the fundamental issues in South Africa are their own retention of political control, the maintenance of their living standards, and the enforcement of order to secure these ends. *Prima facie* these are not negotiable issues, as the Nationalist government has repeatedly emphasized. Its proposals for a new constitutional dispensation are premised upon the assumption of continued white hegemony, however much this fact may be concealed or denied. Fundamentally the proposals seek to create a non-black power-bloc by incorporating the coloured and Indian groups into the white-controlled segment of society, but only in such a way that the incorporation does not jeopardize white hegemony. It is an ingenious step in the dialectic of white-coloured relations: the coloured people were deprived of their franchise rights in 1956 because of their putative threat to a Nationalist majority (see p. 81); now they, together with the Indians, are being reincorporated in a way that strengthens white power but cannot touch its basis.

The constitutional proposals are incorporated in a draft bill (*Government Gazette* no. 6386 of 3 April 1979) which has been presented as evidence to be considered by the joint select committee of Parliament to inquire into the creation of an alternative constitution for South Africa. For our purposes a detailed critique of the bill is unnecessary, and, accordingly, our comments are confined to the broad thrust of the proposals.

The preamble specifically excludes blacks from the new scheme's purview. The black 'nations', it declares, should be given 'separate freedom in the land allotted to them for the exercise of the political aspirations of all the members of those nations'.

The bill provides for white, coloured and Indian parliaments, to be called respectively the Assembly, the House of Representatives, and the Chamber of Deputies. While the seat of the Assembly is specified as Cape Town, the seats of the other two 'parliaments' are left to determination by the State President. The size of each parliament is laid down: 185 members for the Assembly, 92 for the House of Representatives, and 46 for the Chamber of Deputies. Ministerships and deputy-ministerships are also fixed in the same proportion for each body.

Each parliament is required to designate members of the electoral college which is to elect the State President in the proportion 50:25:13 from the white, coloured, and Indian parliaments respectively. Earlier discussions of the scheme indicated that only the majority party in each body would be able to elect members to the electoral college, and, although this is not specified in the bill, the same intention remains and can be implemented in terms of the bill. Under existing conditions, which are meant to be perpetuated, the National party would dominate the electoral college and, conversely, prevent the realization of the party's historic fear of a political alliance between non-Nationalist whites and some black segment(s).

The State President is to be elected for a five-year term, and he can be removed from office by a resolution of a majority of the members of the electoral college. Given the method of election and removal, it is clear that the State President can be little more than a captive of the Nationalist-dominated Assembly. Although there is no specification that he must be white, it is inevitable that he will be. As the former prime minister, Mr B.J. Vorster, informed parliament in 1978,

'It goes without saying that, in practice as well, apart from the theory, my party will propose a White Nationalist as State President . . . as long as this Government is in power, I know who the State President will be. I have no problems in that connection.'[18]

The State President's major function will be to chair the Council of Cabinets, which will be the fulcrum of the new system. It is to consist of the white prime minister and six white ministers, the coloured prime minister and three coloured ministers, and the Indian prime minister and two Indian ministers, the ministers in each case being designated by their respective prime ministers. With the inclusion of the State President's vote a *de facto* majority on the Council is assured to the whites.

The bill provides that the 'legislative power of the Republic' shall be vested in the (white) Assembly, provided that any legislative powers previously vested in the Coloured Persons Representative Council or the South African Indian Council are now to be transferred to the coloured and Indian 'parliaments'. The Council of Cabinets is empowered to vest any legislative power in respect of any matter in the coloured and Indian 'parliaments', but the bill contains nothing to indicate what those powers might be or by what criteria such transfers will be made. In a discussion of the proposals in 1978 (before they had been formulated in the present bill), Mr Vorster said that 'just as a sovereign Parliament may part with powers, so it can take those powers back again'.[19] In the light of the provisions and this comment, doubt must remain whether the proposals as a whole amount to a genuine devolution of power, because the white Assembly is to remain sovereign and by virtue of its *de facto* control of the Council of Cabinets it could resume previously devolved powers. Moreover, in certain circumstances (see below) the Council of Cabinets or the State President can take decisions that bind all three parliaments.

In discussions of the envisaged scheme it has been generally understood that matters which affect all three groups will be dealt with at the Council of Cabinets level, in so far as the Council would initiate legislation. Such 'common' functions would include all the major functions of government, including foreign affairs, finance, defence and justice. On the other hand, matters that are specific to a particular group would be dealt with by its parliament. The bill, however, makes no mention of a division of functions, and it specifically vests the preparation and settlement of legislative programmes in the Council of Cabinets, even where a legislative programme deals with matters peculiar to a group.

The bill provides that the Council of Cabinets may refer any particular proposed legislation on any matter to the coloured or Indian 'parliaments' for disposal; where legislation, in the opinion of the Council, affects more than one group, it may refer the legislation to the parliaments concerned for their consideration. In the event of a disagreement between parliaments the matter is to be reconsidered by the Council, who may either give a decision or refer it to a joint advisory committee composed of members of each parliament in the same numerical proportion as their representation in the electoral college (i.e. a decisive white majority is ensured). If this committee, in the opinion of the Council of Cabinets, is unable to reach a settlement, the matter in question is to be referred back to the chairman of the Council (the State President) for decision.

A further clause in the bill empowers the Council to refer proposed legislation to a parliament for disposal, even after prior reference to another parliament, that is, if one parliament should prove recalcitrant in passing legislation referred to it, the legislation can be passed by another, more compliant, parliament. The same clause provides that even where legislation has been referred to all three parliaments, one may pass the legislation before the views of the other two or the joint advisory committee have been obtained. The purport of this provision is made clear by Mr Vorster's explanation in parliament:

'If the Council of Cabinets lets the legislation go forward, it means that that legislation has been passed by the Council. In that case, we say this expressly, that legislation must be passed by at least one Parliament before it can become law. If the Council of Cabinets decides that the legislation should be submitted to the Parliaments and one Parliament – or even two – were to get it into its head not to discuss that legislation, one cannot undo the consensus emanating from Cabinet government and which is presumed in Cabinet government, simply because one Parliament is recalcitrant. That is why we say that if one Parliament passes it, it becomes law . . . provided that legislation has been approved by the Council of Cabinets.'[20]

It is unclear from the bill how the executive is to be structured in relation to functions involving 'common' or intergroup concerns. Some observers have interpreted the Council of Cabinets as the executive in this respect but little in the bill endows it with the status of an executive. There is no mention of departmental portfolios in the clause dealing with the establishment of the Council, while there is such a reference in the case of ministers who are appointed to the cabinets of the three parliaments.

In view of the reliance placed upon consensus being reached in the Council of Cabinets it may reasonably be asked whether the attaining of consensus will not be made unduly difficult in a body that will consist of three groups of ministers from three different parliaments elected by three different electorates. The Council is to function on the principle of collective solidarity, and each member is required to swear an oath of secrecy which will inhibit his ability to discuss Council matters with colleagues who are ministers at the parliamentary level. Mr Vorster's explanation of the proposed operation drew a misleading parallel with coalition governments in Holland and West Germany, where members of the cabinet are drawn from different parties. Coalitions on the Western European pattern are based upon negotiations and bargains struck between parties of the same parliament, elected by the same electorate, and on the basis of some ideological compatibility.

In the proposed scheme the white group will clearly be dominant, but coloured and Indian ministers may find themselves being expected to acquiesce in legislation which they oppose, or resigning. A situation might easily arise in which no coloured or Indian minister was prepared to serve in the Council because of rooted disagreements with the trend of Council policy. Such a boycott would not paralyze the system because of a provision declaring that a shortfall of numbers will not be able to affect the powers of the Council.

The crucial financial underpinning of the scheme is perhaps the clearest manifestation of the limited intentions of the bill. It is provided that 'No moneys shall be withdrawn from the State Revenue Fund, except in accordance with an Act of the Assembly.' Other financial provisions incorporate the same principle. This gives the white parliament decisive influence in the system, as well as a handy instrument for inducing compliance on the part of the other two 'parliaments'.

As noted, careful attention has been paid in the bill to group numerical ratios, ensuring that whites have a decisive voice in the electoral college and, *de facto,* in the Council of Cabinets. The ratios are said to be derived from existing population figures, but no provision has been made for adjustments in response to changes in the sizes of the respective population groups, as, for example, when the coloured group exceeds the white group, which according to projections will occur some time after the year 2000. The composition of the electoral college may be changed only with the approval of all three parliaments, and other amendments to the constitution generally will require the approval of the white parliament.

We do not dispute the need to maximize consensus in the political process of divided societies, but one of the fundamental flaws of the proposed scheme is that it invokes the principle of consensus in a structural context that seems designed to entrench maximum dissensus. In defending these proposals some Nationalist spokesmen have invoked consociational theorists like Lijphart and the work of

Nordlinger in their support. Thus Denis Worrall makes the astounding claim that 'all the more important conflict-regulating practices or techniques which . . . Nordlinger has isolated and described . . . will be seen on analysis to be built into the proposals'.[21] Lest the work of the consociational theorists and Nordlinger be brought into disrepute by its association with Nationalist policies, it should be unambiguously stated that the consociationalists, in their empirical and normative concerns, have been dealing with democratic political systems, not with a system that excludes 70 per cent of the population from its purview; nor with a system that is based upon tripartite parliaments whose proposed operation appears nevertheless to be based upon a more covert form of white control.

It has been necessary to make these points above with acerbic frankness because if the real consociational model does offer South Africa some hopes of local applicability the concept must not be allowed to become tainted by association with proposals that do not embody its essence. Just as the government's emphasis on ethnicity has led to a counter-reaction to ethnicity that underestimates its real significance and durability, so an unwarranted appropriation of consociational themes will make any application of genuine consociational techniques much less attractive to blacks, whose suspicions will have been aroused that this is another 'white man's trick'.

Obviously the fatal flaw of the proposals is that they exclude the black population, whose political future remains, in terms of policy, tied in with the homelands. No scheme premised upon such an exclusion can hope to cope with the totality of conflict in the society, and it is coping with conflict that is precisely what constitutions are expected to assist in doing. Already significant coloured and Indian groups like the Labour and Reform parties have rejected the new dispensation. A resolution adopted by the Labour Party in 1977 is especially relevant to this discussion:

'The plan seeks to create an alliance of Whites, Coloureds and Indians and . . . even if this "alliance" were to be comprised of fully equal partners which it does not since it fully accommodates white domination and an inferior status for Coloureds and Indians, such an "alliance" is totally unacceptable to the Labour Party because it will completely alienate the overwhelming majority of South Africans from the minority thereby intensifying racial conflict instead of eliminating it.'[22]

A detailed critique of the proposals has been made by a committee appointed by the executive committee of the Coloured Persons Representative Council. The Report's general conclusion is:

'When looked at as a whole, the draft constitution is nothing more than the confirmation of the supreme authority of the existing parliament with the addition of executive bodies. Race classification [i.e. in terms of the Population Registration Act] and group areas – the foundations of the system – remain unchanged and the further the draft law moves away from the central institutions to the provincial and local authorities (and the financial arrangements) the clearer it becomes that one has to do here with the *status quo* in a new dress.'[23]

We concur in this assessment. The new dispensation will not mean the end of racial domination for the coloured and Indian groups. Until laws like those mentioned in the quotation as well as the Mixed Marriages and Immorality Acts, and the Prohibition of Political Interference Act are repealed there can be little serious talk of moving away from racial discrimination and no hope of genuine power-sharing.

A further aspect that has jeopardized the new scheme's acceptability is the way in which it was generated within the National Party, following the recommendation of the Theron Commission in 1976 that the coloured people be granted direct political representation. The plan was drawn up by a Cabinet Committee appointed by the government and prior to its general release to the public it was considered by the Nationalist parliamentary caucus and by closed sessions of National party provincial congresses. Inevitably, given this genesis, the proposals assumed the air of a party political manoeuvre rather than of a serious effort at a legitimate accommodation. This was compounded by making the scheme an issue in the general election of November 1977, even before anything like full details of the proposed system were available to the public.

If constitutions are to provide a durable framework for conflict resolution, they must be acceptable to the population groups that make up the society, and this usually means that representatives of those groups must have had a hand in drawing up the constitution. The National Party's way of presenting its constitutional proposals provided an object lesson in how not to proceed with innovations. The crassness of the following quotation from a National Party magazine should, in the delicate circumstances of attempting intergroup accommodations, be avoided:

Q: What would the position be if the Coloureds or Indians were to withhold their co-operation in the implementation of the plan?

A: Then they will be in exactly the same position as the homelands which are rejecting independence. They then remain where they are. *We lay the table and those refusing to sit down shall do without.* Because the old dispensation is something of the past, we will simply continue with the new dispensation.[24]

Judging by comments offered by Nationalist politicians it is possible to make verligte or verkrampte interpretations of the proposals. Verligte interpretations emphasize the consensual aspect of those common institutions that overarch the three parliaments, and some have hinted (privately) that the scheme has sufficient inherent elasticity to accommodate in the future a fourth parliament representing blacks of the common area. But this does not square with blacks' explicit exclusion from the bill, nor with the steady deprivation of their citizenship rights. Conservative interpretations have emphasized that the proposals do not embody the principle of power-sharing. Dr A.P. Treurnicht has obliquely criticized its allegedly consensual aspects. Perhaps the attractiveness of the plan to some Nationalists lies not least in the very fact that it is amenable to such divergent interpretations, thereby defusing to some extent the ideological differences within the party over the political future of the coloured and Indian people.

Critiques of the plan, however, should go further than pointing out the (by now) rather obvious flaws, and examine whether it offers any scope for what might be called 'creative misuse'. Political history, after all, is full of examples of political leaders making changes to achieve specific goals and subsequently finding the actual results of the changes were far different from what had been intended. The classic instance of this is the Great Reform Act of 1832, which was intended by its sponsors, among other things, to make the British parliament more representative of the rising classes produced by the industrial revolution. Any thought that the Act would be the thin end of the democratic wedge was abhorrent to their thinking: yet this was precisely what the Act achieved, in its inauguration of a long process that ultimately democratized Britain.

A comparable process seems unlikely in South Africa, although, at least, the new constitution seeks in principle to associate coloured and Indian people with the 'white' nation, and this could conceivably increase their political bargaining-power as well. Moreover, after some hesitations expressed by certain ministers, it has now been made clear that within state departments for common affairs there will be no ceiling to coloured and Indian advancement. If these groups were to embrace the scheme enthusiastically and authentic leaders achieved high office in it and the consensual aspects actually succeeded then one might at least concede that its overall impact on the society could be of substantial magnitude, perhaps even tempering white racial fears to the point where a real accommodation with blacks was feasible.

Unfortunately the prospects of this kind of outcome are remote. A more likely scenario is that the only coloured and Indian leaders who will be prepared to operate the new system will be people whose credibility and acceptability in their own communities is limited. In these circumstances the opportunities for creative misuse are limited.

One should not completely exclude the possibility that certain verligte interpretations involving the (partial) incorporation of common-area blacks may ultimately be realized if the Nationalists, as seems likely, find themselves under heavier international pressure and also pressure from an increasingly alienated urban black population. There is no way of foretelling in what way the new constitution might be extended to cater for this contingency or how much real political power would be vested in blacks. This possibility (even if it seems unlikely in the immediate future) ought to be considered, and an attempt be made to examine the parameters of choice in response to it.

At present there are three government-created bodies with terms of reference that have direct constitutional implications. There is of course the Joint Select Committee of Parliament to consider the introduction of an alternative constitution for the Republic. The terms of reference are extremely wide and the Committee can ask for written and oral evidence as well as hear evidence from whoever wishes to give it. This is a far cry from the almost disdainful unilateral action of the government when in 1977 it rushed a draft constitution through the party caucus and congresses of the National party and simply confronted South Africa with a constitutional fait accompli. Secondly, there is the so-called Consolidation Commission which has to investigate the more effective consolidation of the homelands. For the first time the government has agreed that although the 1936 Bantu Trust and Land Act should still serve as the basis of consolidation, the commission could go beyond it where absolutely necessary. Thirdly, there is the Cabinet Committee appointed to investigate the position of the urban blacks. Under this committee there are six multiracial regional committees which have to make recommendations to the cabinet.

These three bodies cover fundamental constitutional problems in South Africa, namely the questions of land, urban blacks and coloureds and Asians. A cynical view would be that the government has simply shelved these problems for the time being by appointing bodies to investigate them. In this way they are taken out of heated political debate. A more charitable interpretation is that the government has at last realized that one-sided or unilateral constitutional action is not going to work and these bodies simply are the first tentative steps towards obtaining co-operation in resolving constitutional deadlocks. Either possibility could become a reality depending on the unfolding of events.

Strong arguments could be adduced for a 'purist' view that rejects any truck with separate development and its institutions, which are premised in reality upon an effective white control and necessarily entail the perpetuation of statutes like the Population Registration and Group Areas acts. As Anatol Rapoport has commented:

'I part company with the "political realists" by rejecting the assumption that proposals for actions should be tailored to the needs and perceptions of *presently* effective actors – the power figures and the powe institutions of our day. For such an accommodation means a tacit acceptance of, in fact a reinforcement of, the currently dominant values, perceptions, and social roles.'[25]

In the context of South Africa's authoritarianly enforced inequality it is likely that *any* proposal emanating from the Nationalist government will meet with rejection by authentic black leaders. The probable fate of the new constitution and the lack of interest in the community councils established in Soweto (whose members were elected in a 6 per cent poll) are indicators of this attitude. Alienation has gone too far to expect blacks to accommodate to white-sponsored initiatives, in which whites have laid down the basic principles and blacks may be permitted to negotiate over the details. As David Curry of the Labour Party informed a recent conference on the constitutional scheme,

'he wished to make it clear that it was really impossible for Black people to come forward now "and shake hands unconditionally. . . . It is like asking the guilty jailor to be reconciled to the innocent prisoner. The guilty jailor must first free the innocent prisoner, then the two can get reconciled." Conversion had to precede forgiveness and until this was a fact "Blacks will reject any new constitutional proposals no matter how good they may seem, because, in their daily lives, they experience oppression. Therefore, the pass law system must go . . . the Group Areas Act must be repealed, the Mixed Marriages Act must go, the Immorality Act – these Acts which are seen to be oppressive – must disappear now before Blacks will be willing to engage in the dialogue on the constitutional proposals." '[26]

On the other hand 'realists' might retort that given the entrenched and massive power of the Nationalist government there is no feasible alternative strategy to trying to make viable those creations of separate development that give blacks a platform and some degree of bargaining power. It can be argued that it is difficult enough to persuade *any* minority to share power with a majority, and impossible so to persuade it if the envisaged change of direction represents a total abandonment of past policies. In other words, if power-holders are to be rendered amenable to change they must not be forced into political corners. It is a rare political leader who, so to speak, can eat his past-political words with good grace.

It may be further argued, from a 'realist' perspective, that orderly and evolutionary political change ought to be based upon existing structures. Marinus Wiechers has persuasively argued this point in an appeal to build on to subordinate governmental structures a firm foundation upon which a consociational central government can eventually rest. He writes:

'Considering the need for change in the Republic and the serious obstacles to evolutionary change which exist, it is also important that we should *move away from the idea of final solutions* to our problems. Rather, we should seek for *a series of progressive settlements.* Nothing could prevent us at this stage, for example, from using the Senate as a centrally representative body in which Coloured and Asian interests could be accommodated by way of direct representations. And we could also institute a Council of State in which the various Homelands could be given representation. Such a Council of State could, in future, prove to be the state institution for a broader South African federation.'[27]

There are attractive aspects to this proposal: it is squarely within the great Burkean tradition of incremental change; it incorporates the wisdom that conflict is easier to resolve if its component dimensions can be disentangled and treated piecemeal; and it offers a face-saving way out of the dilemma for the established political leaders. But one wonders whether the strategy would be acceptable to black leaders, any more than the broadly comparable strategy advocated by the Spro-cas Political Commission in 1973 would be acceptable. As we have emphasized in this chapter, there is no homogeneous black opinion regarding the utility of homelands as instruments for increasing black bargaining-power for their full release from discrimination in the wider society. The vehement repudiation of homelands by urban black leaders, such as Dr N. Motlana, chairman of the Soweto Committee of Ten, is evidence that any such strategy would meet with a great deal of resistance from urban blacks. Yet, if it were demonstrable to these groups that there was a genuine acceptance of the need for real change (change going further than just abolishing 'petty' apartheid) among whites, the position might be altered. The homelands concept is rejected because of the status it imputes to blacks; if that status were to change radically, the status connotations of homelands might also diminish, and urban black leaders could conceivably be persuaded to accept them as the nuclei of potential regions in a federal South Africa in which racial discrimination was being abolished and power was being shared.

It seems to us that this is likely to be the only kind of context in which Spro-cas-type strategies would have a chance of succeeding. Far more problematical is the complex proposal for 'intercommunal power deployment in a South African plural democracy' from Nic Rhoodie, former director of the Institute for Plural Societies, Pretoria University.[28] As this scheme is an example of verligte Nationalist thinking that goes beyond the government's constitutional proposals, its essential points may be briefly reviewed. Rhoodie rejects any dispensation involving simple one-man-one-vote majoritarianism in a unitary state, and proposes a flexible and open-ended model involving federal and confederal elements. The federal bloc will comprise a partnership or alignment of the white, coloured and Indian groups, and possibly smaller black homeland communities and 'denationalized or de-ethnicized' blacks in the white areas, who may apply to enter the federal bloc on the understanding that it will remain a white-dominated entity. For the most part blacks will make up a black bloc comprised of either a single state or separate units based upon the homelands. The two blocs, the white-dominated and black, will come together in a confederal arrangement whose consultative, decision-making powers and functions will be vested in a confederal council. The council's competence will include only matters of common interest such as infrastructural services, regional monetary and fiscal matters, economic and technological co-operation, customs agreements and regional defence. Rhoodie does not spell out how confederal decision-making will take place, but he indicates that this will be a matter for negotiation by the interested parties through an ongoing process of conciliation and compromise.

Rhoodie emphasizes that this is no sterile or fixed formula, and he expresses the hope that the emergence of 'an inclusive South Africanism' could enable the confederal units to cohere more closely into a federal type of accommodation. He further emphasizes that his proposals will have no chance whatever of succeeding unless they are accompanied by a thoroughgoing abolition of colour discrimination.

Inevitably so brief a summary of a detailed set of proposals does violence to their complexity, but the main principles have been indicated. Clearly, their adoption would mark a signal advance from the present log-jam, and the insistence upon 'multiple majorities' in decision-making at the federal and confederal levels need not be inconsistent with democratic government. Nevertheless the scheme would be incapable of succeeding because when it is laid bare it is still whites that will control the major resources and their allocation for the whole society, and such a dispensation would not be acceptable to majority black opinion. Moreover, the plan suffers from the entrenchment of race as an organizing principle of the dispensation as a whole, which makes it doubtful if an 'inclusive South Africanism' could conceivably emerge.

Consideration of the government's constitutional scheme and of proposals such as Rhoodie's point to a difficult issue with which any would-be architect of a new dispensation for South Africa would have to grapple: if group identities, solidarities or attachments (whatever material or power aspirations they may embody) are going to remain a feature of South African society, even if racial discrimination were abolished, how does one deal with the argument that groups in a multi-group society are, normatively speaking, entitled to self-determination? This, we may note, is a major prop in Nationalist ideology and therefore deserves careful consideration. For all that it is a principle that is more honoured in the breach than in the observance, national self-determination as a concept enjoys a respectable pedigree in liberal and even Marxist–Leninist thought, and it retains a powerful persuasive force; and even a cursory review of the wretched treatment of minorities by dominant majorities inclines one to be favourably disposed to claims for self-determination.

While a detailed examination of the issues surrounding claims to national self-determination is beyond the scope of this chapter, the issue may be located in a South African context by raising the question: what rights, if any, should groups have in a democratic (or democratizing) framework? and should these rights be given some form of legal or constitutional expression? Clearly 'group rights' or rights of national self-determination are in no sense absolute. As Walker Connor points out, a 'principle' of self-determination can be countered by other 'principles', such as the right of states to protect themselves against disruptive claims.[29]

A critical problem arises where a group invokes the principle of self-determination in circumstances where it is highly interdependent with other groups, and any decision it might take to act unilaterally, using its superior power-resources, would have negative consequences for those other groups. In other words the obverse of self-determination for group A might be oppression for groups B, C, and D. In South Africa the government, in terms of its constitutional proposals, acknowledges, by providing for a substantial area of common interests or functions, that no group's self-determination is unfettered; it accords to a group, theoretically, the power to control 'their own affairs'. Now, a further problem arises if one poses the question: what are a group's 'own affairs' where its activities, levels of prosperity and so forth are inextricably bound up with those of the other groups?

The Report of the Theron Commission in 1976 illustrated just how difficult it is to separate coloured and white interests. In a discussion of the effectiveness of the Coloured Persons Representative Council as an instrument of self-determination one paragraph opens with the words, 'Insofar as coloured, white and joint spheres of interest can be separated . . . , ' and it avers that 'the supposed "coloured sphere of interest" has not yet been clearly delineated'. The Commission acknowledges that educational and welfare spheres have not posed particular jurisdictional problems as both have reference to specialized and delineated functional services specifically provided for the coloured people. Although it concludes that the provision of services on a community basis does not necessarily have to be problematic, it qualifies this with the acknowledgement that 'fragmentation can give rise to unnecessary duplication and divergent standards'.[30]

These considerations point to the central problem of separate development: that separate political institutions are incapable of succeeding because they seek to separate groups that are effectively interdependent and whose interdependence is the product of a long historical process *initiated by the dominant white group.*[31] The Theron Commission's analysis was concerned with the coloured people, but in principle the same kind of conclusion can be made in respect of the Indians and blacks in the common, white-controlled areas. It is only marginally less true for the homelands (independent or not) as these have developed, or rather, have remained undeveloped, within the historic context of an integrated political economy. A vote in an election to an institution that controls a group's 'own affairs' has little significance: hence the widespread lack of interest in, and hostility towards, all those separate political institutions that are not 'plugged in' to effective power sources.

A further consideration is the need to scrutinize claims for group autonomy or self-determination to ascertain whether they are façades for claims to the retention of group privileges. Lawrence Schlemmer's survey findings show that, 'among Afrikaners generally, concern with identity and concern with privilege were completely interwoven' and that 'it does not seem that there is a strong majority conviction underlying those ideological justifications which relate purely to Afrikaner identity'.[32] There is a strong case to be made for the right to cultural self-determination but this must in no way be confused with the entrenchment of group privilege.

In the analysis of consociational democracy in the preceding chapter it was shown how groups are the salient political units, and how 'segmental autonomy' vests control in the group itself over its area of exclusive concern. It is perhaps a paradox of South Africa that for all the intensity of its racial antagonisms and the thoroughgoing statutory delineation of group boundaries we cannot be certain, in advance, of what groups might present themselves as candidates for being vested with 'group rights'. At various points in this work we indicate how at least one population category has formed an ethnic group, with a corresponding bureaucratic network, while others, like the English-speaking whites and the coloured people, have lacked the political inducements to do so; and in yet another configuration, the 'black' (African, coloured, and Indian) categories have, through the Black Consciousness movement, sought to mobilize on a group basis.

No purpose will be served by attempting to anticipate the configuration of politically salient group identities in a democratic South Africa, and any constitutional provision for the protection of 'group rights' should be a permissive one, enabling such a group, when it crystallizes, to avail itself of the protection offered. The danger of calling groups into existence must be guarded against, as should the danger that any entrenchment of 'group rights' might perpetuate and exacerbate inter-group antagonisms. Moreover, membership of a group for the individual must be voluntary, in respect of both leaving and joining it.

It is surely a matter of justice that groups who wish to protect their cultural identity should be entitled to do so. We would take cultural identity to include spheres like language, religion, art and literature. Group or community councils, on the Belgian model, might even be considered. An issue would be how far such protection would require statutory enforcement. In the case of language, enforcement (at least in particular areas) would be necessary. Another problem might be that a group which demands the erection of legal barricades around its culture might attract more hostile attacks and pressure against itself, thereby weakening it more than might have been the case had it seen protection as best secured by its members' determination and efforts to ensure the viability and vitality of their culture. In general we are sceptical of the idea of legally enforced 'group rights', although we accept completely the right to cultural self-determination. If individual rights are adequately enforced, 'group rights' will look after themselves.

An explosive area intimately concerned with the socialization of the young and, hence, with the passing on of cultural traditions lies in the field of education. A detailed examination of this issue and the likely consequences of different policies in South Africa would require another book. One is faced here by an antinomy: on the one hand, if groups are entitled to protect their cultures then they should be entitled to control their own schools, including admissions, if schooling is a vital part of cultural protection. Rhoodie, for example, rejects equal decision-making capabilities in all matters for white and black because 'this notion conjures up visions of Zulus deciding jointly and equally with Afrikaners how the latter should educate and socialize their children'.[33] On the other hand there is the powerful principle that all public amenities and publicly funded services, including educational institutions, should be open to all; and in racially divided societies there is compelling evidence to suggest that in the field of education 'separate' cannot be 'equal'.

A possible way out of the dilemma, which involves strategies as much as principles, might be to permit schools and universities, while insisting upon their openness in principle, to maintain particular cultural environments – a formula similar to that recently adopted by Stellenbosch University when it agreed to admit blacks, subject to certain conditions, provided that the admission of such students does not harm the character and identity of Stellenbosch University as an Afrikaans university for whites.[34] Minus the racial overtones and the restrictive conditions imposed in conformity with government policy, the formula might prove to be a valuable means of creating nodes of interracial accommodation in education, thereby defusing a potentially explosive issue and simultaneously permitting groups that so wish to enable their children to attend culturally congenial schools. (It goes without saying that the gross disparities in expenditure on white and black education respectively would have to be overcome.)

It may seem that the discussion has veered far from the main focus of the chapter, which is to explore the possible bases of a democratic South Africa; but the issues of group rights, group autonomy, or group self-determination are of critical importance to such a discussion, because upon their satisfactory resolution depends, to a large extent, the likelihood that South Africa could develop the social tissue upon which a multiracial democracy could be established.

The question of group rights leads directly to an examination of whether consociational techniques have relevance for South Africa. It may be recalled here that consociationalism is a variable which may be adopted to greater or lesser extents, and therefore need not be construed as a matter of 'all-or-nothing' application. Given the very wide differences between South Africa and the four classic consociations or the other societies where consociational techniques have been attempted, it is prima facie unlikely that the full model would fit South Africa's circumstances.

Certain preconditions (see pp. 63–4) are clearly absent in the South African setting: there is hardly a predisposing amenability to conciliation embedded in the South African tradition, which, Daalder argued, facilitated the implementation of consociational techniques in Switzerland and Holland. South Africa's history is marked by a great deal of raw conflict, including conquest and the imposition of gross forms of exploitation and authoritarian regimentation. The traditional way of dealing with conflicts has lain not so much in seeking to regulate and resolve them as in taking forcible action against those members of the subordinate groups who have sought to break out of their subordination. Moreover, whatever difficulties there may be in placing the intensity of different conflicts on a scale, there can be little doubt that the intensity of South Africa's racial conflict is substantially greater than that experienced in any of the classic consociations, and it is not mitigated to any comparable extent by cross-cutting axes of division. Rather, as has been argued, in South Africa the lines of cleavage have a strong tendency to be mutually reinforcing or cumulative in their effect. The extreme gaps in the pattern of income distribution are a major component of South Africa's conflict, which has no parallel in any of the European consociations. Indeed, it is highly unlikely that the magnitude of the wage gap in South Africa has been exceeded in any other society that has undergone an industrial revolution; and, moreover, the size of the relatively better-paid (white) category in South Africa has been substantially larger than its counterparts, at least in Europe.

In the discussion of 'group rights', it was noted that the configuration of groups in South Africa differed in some crucial respects from that posited in the consociational model. It would also appear that another highly significant factor conducive to the success of consociationalism, a multiple balance of power among the groups, is also absent. In his analysis of the applicability of consociationalism to Northern Ireland, Lijphart says that it exemplifies the least favourable situation, being characterized by 'a dual division into political subcultures without equilibrium and with one subculture capable of exercising hegemonic power'.[35] Prima facie, the disequilibrium of South African society seems comparable, but, as has been stressed, the future profile of group solidarities is hard to discern in advance. Schlemmer has noted:

'At some future stage it is possible that whites, Coloureds, urban

Africans and those non-urban Africans in Homelands which have not taken independence could potentially provide a rough demographic equilibrium. Under the circumstances leaders may be willing to enter into the kind of association required. Further speculation is, however, impossible.'[36]

It may further be doubted whether distinct lines of cleavage exist in South Africa in such a way as to be conducive to consociationalism. Interracial contact is ubiquitous in South Africa, and it is highly prone to generating conflict, because nearly universally the contact occurs upon a basis of unequal status, such as between employer and employee. Lijphart's principle that 'good fences make good neighbours' is not validated by the historical and contemporary South African experience in which the fences have been established by the dominant group in the interests of protecting its privileges.

If external threats have generated a degree of internal unity in the European consociations, their function in South Africa has not been the same. There are blacks who welcome and applaud external threats, ranging from foreign criticism to economic sanctions, that will undermine white domination.

To estimate the likely acceptability of the grand-coalition or élite-cartel form of government as a normative model is difficult. Given the strongly competitive and zero-sum conceptions of politics in South Africa, and its corollary that South Africa's political system must embody either white minority rule (under the guise of separate development) or black majority rule, the adoption of a more coalescent style of politics would require a substantial modification of attitudes. Such a modification may be facilitated, at least at the ideological level, by the government's recently espoused emphasis on the importance of consensus, as in the new constitutional proposals, and the repudiation of Westminster-style, zero-sum politics by some of its spokesmen. Of course these changes of emphasis have not occurred in the context of their contemplation of a possible full consociational scheme for South Africa. A further factor that may facilitate the emergence of consensus/coalescent political attitudes is their broad congruence with the style of political decision-making in traditional African societies. It is this consensual tradition and the absence of structural adversary groups in the political process that has enabled leaders such as Julius Nyerere to rationalize the modern one-party state in Africa. We may note here the conclusion of a recent study of party systems in Africa that the consociational model is eminently applicable to contemporary Africa:

'The emphasis on élite accommodation to stabilize situations of cultural fragmentation is the main insight. But only slightly less striking is the observation that élite accommodation works best if "mass" cultural groups are not only kept out of national political accommodation processes but are discouraged from intercultural contacts.'[37]

It is a matter of hope rather than of hard analytical insight that the consensual attitudes of African traditional politics will somehow rub off on modern African political leaders and converge with possible incipient predispositions towards consensual practices among white leaders.

In general African nationalism has not viewed the constitutional provision of guarantees for minority ethnic or racial groups with much favour. This attitude is understandable in the light of the nationalist movements' aim to maximize the solidarity of the 'masses' in the anti-colonial struggle. To acknowledge minority claims through federal or other constitutional means detracted from this solidarity, and, more importantly, was seen as giving these minorities a political base from which to mount secessionist and other disintegrative moves. Ali A. Mazrui has argued that since the idea of self-determination seemed to imply the freedom of cohesive subgroups, leaders like Tom Mboya of Kenya preferred to emphasize the rights of individuals, regardless of their ethnic ties. He writes:

' . . . what Africa voiced was not the demand that every culturally distinct group should determine its own future but simply that there should be "majority rule" in each territorial unit. Independence for a country as a whole could thus be secured without any implicit commitment to give every culturally distinctive group internally an additional right to determine its own independent future.'[38]

Almost certainly the ideological predispositions of black nationalists in South Africa will be against the constitutional protection of minority rights. These predispositions stem partly from the 'majoritarian' assumptions of the limited democracy that has prevailed in parliamentary politics in South Africa (see p. 85), and partly from their complete repudiation of the political manipulation of 'ethnicity' practised by the South African government to thwart black unity.

The traditions of the African National Congress were essentially those of constitutional liberalism and, as a recent analysis records, were not opposed to the principle of constitutional rights for minorities. The same analysis notes, however, that the breakaway Pan Africanist Congress rejected this idea and spoke of the forging of an ultimate, single, national identity. R.M. Sobukwe, the P.A.C. leader, is quoted as saying

'To us the term "multiracialism" implies that there are such basic insuperable differences between the various national groups here that the best course is to keep them permanently distinctive in a kind of democratic apartheid. That to us is racialism multiplied, which probably is what the term truly connotes. We aim, politically, at government of the Africans by the Africans for Africans, with everybody who owes his only loyalty to Africa and who is prepared to accept the democratic rule of an African majority being regarded as an African. We guarantee no minority rights, because we think in terms of individuals, not groups.'[39]

More recent black consciousness thought is likely to follow Sobukwe's approach and to reject in principle anything less than full 'non-racialism'.

These attitudes have to be reckoned with because, as we repeatedly emphasize, no new political and constitutional dispensation can be forced unilaterally upon blacks by whites. But, at the same time, views like Sobukwe's need not be read as the final, non-negotiable statement of the black political bargaining position. Not all blacks would insist on them, and many, we believe, would be prepared to relax ideological rigidity in the interests of reaching an accommodation based upon a mutual compromise.

Black nationalists have tended to invest the idea of 'freedom' with qualities that are different from its connotations in much of Western liberal democratic thought. In the latter 'freedom' is usually identified negatively with the absence of restraints and positively with the protection of civil rights under the rule of law. In much African nationalist thinking, however, 'freedom' is much more closely tied in with the ideas of 'equality' and 'progress'. These differing emphases partly account for the scant regard which a regrettably large number of African governments have paid to classic notions of civil liberties.

In consolidating their power, often with limited political resources, and launching ambitious development programmes, many African leaders have all too easily curbed freedoms for the ostensible cause of promoting progress, equality and national integration. Given the underdeveloped and dependent nature of most economies in black Africa this outcome was hardly surprising. It does not, however, automatically follow that a similar process will ensue in a democratizing South Africa. South Africa is a far more developed country and possesses a sophisticated infrastructure and a rich resource-base that may enable it to surmount many of the developmental problems encountered by other African states. But any optimism in this respect should be tempered by consideration of the problems that will have to be faced in reducing income inequalities and eliminating unemployment.

The establishment and legitimation of a suitable political structure for South Africa will be complicated by these differing predispositions and expectations, but the task is not impossible.

The prospects are not auspicious that some degree of national solidarity, and a common will transcending the cleavages to make a democratic accommodation succeed, will emerge; and certainly they are less auspicious than they were in the broadly comparable phases of development in the European consociations. As Schlemmer notes, ideological polarization is increasing, and the black critique of society correspondingly involves a fundamental rejection of any form of racial or ethnic separation as well as a trend towards the rejection of capitalism.[40] The only hope that some narrow basis for consensus could be established and consolidated is if the antagonists have a glimpse into the abyss of violence, economic disaster and all the miseries that go with unrestrained conflict. There would be a mutual appreciation that a 'no-win' state of deadlock had been reached and that it would be better to look for an accommodation than inflict enormous damage upon one another. To repeat a point that has been emphasized: a durable political settlement in South Africa requires a recognition among all groups that they have more to gain by co-operation and reconciliation than by the perpetuation of a conflict that could prove to be mutually devastating.

South Africa has reached the precipice; the abyss is an ominously close reality. It is only the quality of the *authentic* leaders of the rival groups that will determine whether violence can be averted, and whether rival claims can be sufficiently abated in the interests of a compromise. One may only speculate about this critical variable: much of the authentic black leadership is either unrecognized by the government or has been placed under restraints of one kind or another; and one has seen mostly the 'hard-line', intransigent aspects of the white leadership. It is, moreover, true that the circumstances of bitter racial conflict are not such as to produce capacities for tolerance, mutual understanding and flexibility in political leaders; but it would be wrong to infer from this that such qualities are incapable of being generated in changed contexts. The very business of negotiation can be a learning process, and bitter rivals can acquire a grudging respect for one another that could be extended into an acceptance of one another's good faith, which is a necessary condition of successful negotiation.

7 *Negotiating for a democratic dispensation*

We have identified the present nature of the conflict in South Africa as institutionalized inequalities of power, wealth, opportunity and status between black and white people. This conflict manifests itself politically in patterns which are typical of politics in deeply divided societies where, in addition to other factors, racial, ethnic and cultural mobilization are particularly salient in the competition for power and the distribution of opportunities. Is democratic government possible in such societies? If by this question is understood a system of government where: (a) there is universal adult suffrage with regular elections to determine the composition of government; (b) all the major political interest groups can compete for and influence the exercise of political power; and (c) freedom of association, freedom of the press, and the independence of the judiciary are constitutionally guaranteed, and upheld – then divided societies pose severe difficulties for democratic government. Nevertheless we have seen that there are societies where more or less democratic governments prevail. The style of government tends to avoid simple majoritarianism in elections and decision-making and heavy emphasis is placed on proportionality, intergroup bargaining and compromise. South Africa, by definition, fails to be a democracy. The vast majority of people subjected to political decision-making cannot call to account or electorally remove those who take decisions that fundamentally affect their daily lives, and structure the opportunities for the pursuit of income and livelihood. In a previous chapter we gave a brief historical overview of how this has come about.

The question to be considered now is: How can a democratic dispensation come about in South Africa? There are those who believe that the only way it is going to happen is through some violent overthrow of the present regime. Obviously no one is in a position to judge the validity of this strategy at this stage. What appears to us reasonable to anticipate, however, is that such an approach is likely to entail untold misery, struggle, sacrifice and bloodshed, with the desired outcome of a more just and democratic South Africa in no way certain. What is also clear to us is that for as long as the present system prevails there will also be untold misery, struggle, sacrifice and bloodshed.

Can a more democratic dispensation be negotiated as a possible alternative? In a sense this is a rhetorical question, because our normative preference for such an alternative is evident throughout what has been said so far. But moral preferences aside, what are the conditions under which such an alternative could become a real option and what would such a process of negotiation entail?

When will the white government be prepared to negotiate for a more democratic dispensation? No doubt the answer is to be found somewhere in the many 'when-the-chips-are-down-no-win' scenarios one has read on South Africa. All of them make it clear that the white government will not easily relinquish its position of entrenched privilege and power. It is likely to happen when the costs of domination are outweighed by the possible advantages of negotiation. That the costs are going to increase is almost a unanimous theme in analysis of South Africa, whether the internal, international or African situation of South Africa is the object of investigation. It is of course not possible to predict when exactly the combined pressures of, for example, increasing isolation, shortage of capital, sanctions, economic recession, urban unrest, etc. will fall into a jig-saw puzzle where the last piece is a cost-benefit decision on the part of the white government to relinquish domination in favour of a negotiated democratic alternative. What will no doubt be of crucial importance is the quality and style of political leadership in the white government. The more intelligently the leadership can anticipate the costs of domination and avoid them through effective negotiations, the less likely that a 'no-win' situation has to be experienced in order to move away from it. It is not necessarily inevitable that the representatives of the conflicting parties have to crawl in exhaustion over the corpses of their followers to conclude a truce and begin negotiations.

A major complicating factor, however, is that many of the same pressures that increase the costs of domination also stimulate enthusiasm for violent change. The extent and intensity of this enthusiasm in itself can increase the costs of domination, but a critical threshold can be reached where those dominated reject negotiation as a viable option, irrespective of the decision of those who dominate. Then the 'no-win' situation proper is likely to begin. In other words, once those dominated perceive the conflict as winnable on their own terms by means of violence, even if this does not turn out to be the case, then untold misery, struggle, sacrifice and bloodshed will be the order of the day, before and if negotiations begin. Then you may very well find the situation that Lewis Coser describes when he says:

'The parties to the conflict may be willing to cease the battle when they recognize that their aims cannot be attained or that they can be attained at a price they are not willing to pay, or, more generally, when they conclude that continuation of the conflict is less attractive than the making of peace. In neither of these cases will they be willing to accept defeat although they are willing to stop short of victory. In such situations they may be impelled to explore the chances for a compromise.'[1]

We emphasize that, although the initiative for avoiding an actual 'no-win' situation is the sole prerogative of those who govern in South Africa, there is no significant indication at present that they find the costs of domination unbearable. There are a few government-supporting institutions and individuals who make 'five-minutes-to-midnight' noises, but the relevance of such thinking is nowhere evident in political decision-making. Yet the objective conditions are still such that negotiating for a democratic dispensation is a viable option for the white government. The major missing ingredient is a hard assessment on the part of those who govern of the escalating costs of domination, and an implementation of appropriate measures to bring about an effective process of negotiation.

What would such measures entail? Obviously there is no exhaustive checklist that could be presented but within the South African context certain fundamental steps on the part of the white government seem to us to be essential. These steps must all be designed to demonstrate the government's credibility and clear desire to enter into effective negotiations.

The first move on the part of the government would be to announce a statement of principle which, by implication, rejects fundamental aspects of government policy that have been a source of frustration and aggression to blacks. Thus the government would have to commit itself to the principle of full and equal citizenship for all South Africans and effective participation in the same government irrespective of race. We cannot conceive of a viable constitutional structure evolving through a process of negotiation where these principles are not enshrined.

By committing itself to these principles the government would definitely take a great deal of heat out of the internal situation and create a new climate for pursuing negotiations. It would also indicate quite clearly that it was not simply consulting blacks on how to make its own policy work more smoothly but that as the government it was actually interested in negotiation.

There has been a persistent confusion on the part of government over the difference between consultation and negotiation. Negotiation, if it is 'genuine' and is to have a chance of being 'effective' refers to situations in which bargaining occurs among parties all of whom have a measure of mutually acknowledged power-resources. Clearly it is greatly to the advantage of the major power-holders to begin negotiations sooner rather than later, when their resources may have been eroded or drained in a protracted struggle. Notwithstanding the recent internal settlement, the case of Mr Ian Smith and the Rhodesian Front may be cited as an instance of a group that might have secured a more favourable dispensation for themselves had they not commenced negotiation only when their position had been substantially weakened. Negotiation for total capitulation, which is surrender rather than a matter of bargaining, is the logical consequence of excessive delay, resulting from an unwillingness or an inability to gauge correctly changes in the balance of power-resources.

A statement of principle, as mentioned above, must obviously be followed by an unambiguous invitation to those excluded from effective political participation to come and negotiate at a constitutional conference or convention on an acceptable alternative constitutional structure for the country. We want to state quite categorically that such an invitation would not signify an abdication of sovereignty on the part of the government nor that the convention would take over any of the functions of government. *De facto* the government would control security, defence and police forces, and would go on doing so even after the invitation had been extended. The convention would stand in an advisory capacity towards government but not in a simple take-it-or-leave-it relationship. The alternative to what could be agreed upon at the convention is confrontation and violence and it is the extent of the awareness of this alternative among all parties which will bring them to negotiations. Therefore one can safely accept that the 'advice' given by a convention will carry a great deal of weight.

One must assume, given the existing circumstances, that a statement of principle and an invitation such as has been mentioned, will happen at a time when goodwill and mutual trust will be at a low ebb between black and white in South Africa. Again, it is only the government that will have the power and the ability to initiate moves that could improve goodwill and establish acceptance of bona fides. Therefore we believe it to be absolutely fundamental for effective negotiations that any invitation to deliberate as a convention must allow the potential political groups or movements to be represented there, to elect those whom they regard as their true representatives. Clearly those who come to such deliberations, by their very presence, indicate that they prefer to talk rather than fight, and if any significant leader indicates this and is deliberately excluded by government, the credibility of such deliberations could be damaged immeasurably. No one would wish to underestimate the extreme difficulties that would have to be faced in reversing the sequence of events and allowing political movements to indicate freely whom they would prefer to represent their respective interests at a convention. In South Africa political movements and individuals have been banned, persons have been detained indefinitely without trial, some sentenced to jail in terms of security laws, others placed under house arrest, and yet others have fled the country or accepted 'one-way tickets' out. In short it is impossible for the government to maintain the status quo without the use of a whole array of coercive measures. It is these very measures which have contributed significantly to erosion of goodwill and trust between black and white: a first step would be to review these measures and make it possible for political movements to appoint their own representatives to attend a convention. The implications of this have to be stated frankly: persons and organizations that have been banned must have their restrictions lifted and be allowed to mobilize their support and engage in political campaigning for the purpose of participating in peaceful negotiations; persons convicted under the various security laws must be amnestied. These are tough demands for any ruling group to accept, especially where the persons or organizations concerned have been guilty of violence. In claiming such amnesty one is not necessarily condoning past illegal acts: one is saying that a new dispensation is being created and that in doing so it is necessary for the past to be transcended. Neither side will benefit from acrimonious and inconclusive wrangles over how blame for past actions is to be apportioned. A settlement will not be durable unless authentic leaders have been party to it. The price of enabling them to do so must be lower than the cost of failure.

In a paper on the legislative pre-conditions for peaceful change John Dugard has spelled out in some detail what the need to allow authentic black leaders to operate entails. His conclusion may be quoted:

'Discrimination and repression stand in the way of peaceful change in South Africa. Both these obstacles are incorporated into the South African legal system – indeed they could be said to be the foundations of the existing legal order. Until they are removed, it will be difficult, probably impossible, for any power-sharing to take place as they obstruct an equal and free exchange of ideas between members of the different communities that comprise South African society. . . . But until the discriminatory and repressive laws that compromise the South African legal order have been repealed there will be no possibility of trust and confidence between the races of South Africa.'[2]

The refusal of white South African leaders to acknowledge the authenticity of black leaders who have emerged through unofficial, anti-system channels amounts to an attempt to impose leaders on the black communities. The former prime minister has dismissed claims that Nelson Mandela is a leader of consequence:

'My immediate reply was that he was not. I took up the attitude that he was neither an elected nor a natural leader of Black peoples in South Africa, but just the leader of an organization, the African National Congress, an organization with a limited membership.'[3]

The attitudes which these comments reveal are not only misconceived but dangerous as well because of the ostrich-like thinking that is manifest. A government that restricts political organization and association within the limits of its own ideology, bans opposing black political movements and individuals and then sanctimoniously declares that there are no 'natural or elected' black leaders from such movements simply ignores the reality of conflict underlying the situation. As it happens a recent survey has shown that among urban blacks, who overwhelmingly reject the homeland or Bantustan dispensation, Nelson Mandela (the leader of the banned African National Congress) enjoys the support of 18 per cent, which is a remarkable indication of his stature when it is recalled that he has been in prison since 1964.[4] (The survey in fact excluded from its purview urban centres where the African National Congress has the highest degree of support such as Port Elizabeth and East London. No doubt Mandela's support would be even stronger if these were included.) It also follows that the A.N.C. has a limited membership, if Mr Vorster was referring to it in the present, when it is illegal and convictions for membership are visited with heavy penal retribution. Moreover, one is entitled to ask, if the government's view of the A.N.C. is that it is of such limited significance, what then does it have to fear from it? In any case, the point is clearly made: negotiations can take place between effective and representative leadership only.

Assuming that such representative leadership is locked into negotiations it is fairly self-evident that the first priority will be the formulation of a common declaration of intent in terms of which negotiations can proceed. No one bargains in a vacuum of commitment and principle and it is therefore quite clear that the establishment of a common declaration of intent between black and white negotiators would involve determining what either side regards as negotiable and non-negotiable in the bargaining process. We suspect that this would be the point of intersection between white fears and black aspirations, and problems of political domination and racial repression and exploitation will no doubt figure prominently in such a declaration of intent. Inevitably in this initial negotiating phase the rival groups will present inflated demands and make exaggerated claims regarding their power-resources; but the early posturing need not be taken as statements of non-negotiable positions. The very process of bargaining involves give-and-take, and compromise.

We believe that many obstacles will have to be overcome before a common declaration of intent will have been established. This process would however be greatly facilitated if the government embarked on a programme, in the interim, of systematically removing statutory and *de facto* forms of discrimination and points of friction. The manner in which the government did so would greatly improve the climate in which negotiations could take place. We may consider in this context the crucial question of how far, in fact, the issues in racial conflict are likely to prove bargainable, that is, where on a rigidity/flexibility continuum are the parties to racial conflict likely to stand? Partly, of course, a party's rigidity in a bargaining situation will depend on its power-resources:if it is powerful and its adversaries are incapable of inflicting any real damage on it, there will be few inducements for it to compromise its stance; but bargainability is determined also by the nature of the issue itself. Richard Rose, in a study of Northern Ireland, makes the following observations:

'In so far as political discord arises from substantive issues, then the crucial question is the extent to which the chief issues are bargainable. Peaceful bargaining is possible, if the matter in dispute permits negotiations that can lead to an outcome acceptable to all. An issue is not bargainable if there is no way in which all concerned can be sufficiently satisfied to accept the outcome – or at least not be so dissatisfied that they will wish to repudiate the regime that fixes the terms. Whether or not an issue is bargainable is reflected by three characteristics: whether it involves a zero-sum conflict; whether it involves private or collective goods, and whether competing claims are stated as absolute values or advanced as demands for more or less of something.'[5]

In terms of this framework class issues are likely to be the most easily bargainable, being pre-eminently concerned with allocative, 'slice-of-the-cake' considerations in societies without sharp social discontinuities. Religious issues, on the other hand, being concerned with rival world-views and transcendental values, are notably non-bargainable, especially where, as in Northern Ireland, they are fused with ethnicity. Prima facie ethnic issues are likely to be located at the non-bargainable end of the continuum, especially where they involve questions such as which group's language is to prevail as the official one; whose symbols are to enjoy the status of national ones; and the critical question, which group is to be dominant? It is clearly the latter issue which is at the heart of the South African problem.

The thrust of the argument in chapter 2 was that race derives much of its salience from the institutionalized inequalities with which it is associated. It follows, therefore, that if these inequalities could be reduced and eliminated and no negative consequences were to flow from membership of a particular racial category, a good deal of the steam could be taken out of race conflict. This is of course much easier said than done. It seems to us highly doubtful that, short of applying the most authoritarian methods, inequalities in income distribution could be reduced to reasonable dimensions in much less than a generation – and time is a critical factor in making settlements durable. The point is that the issue of race conflict needs to be 'de-mythologized' and broken into its component aspects: if a significant part of the South African conflict is class-like in character, it may be that its resolution or regulation will be easier than if the conflict involved an all-or-nothing contest between rival world views. But it should not be forgotten that race imparts to class-like issues an additional crust of intractability. Nevertheless, the National Party government accepts in principle the desirability of reducing the wage gap, and in the near future one is likely to see further far-reaching moves to dismantle the colour bar in industry and to vest more bargaining power in the hands of black workers.

Separate development does not conform to the model of a rigid, unbending and immutable set of ideas, incorporating an inviolable world view. To appreciate this one need only compare the formulation of apartheid in the earlier days of Nationalist rule, when the appeal was made in outright white-supremacist terms, with later versions of the same policy, which incorporate at least an indirect affirmation of the principle of non-discrimination. There is an instrumental dimension to the policy, acknowledged by some verligte Nationalists who describe it as a 'method' rather than an ideology, dogma or principle.[6] It may, therefore, when subjected to pressures, become more amenable to pragmatic adjustments, whose cumulative impact may create an irresistible momentum. One must not overlook the likely fact that in the present climate concessions to blacks do not damp down their demands; rather the effect is the opposite, a probability with profound implications for both separate development *and* some future government based upon power-sharing.

The negotiating forum convened to produce a new political dispensation for South Africa will face the prodigious task of attaining a substantial degree of consensus among deeply conflicted parties. We have presumed a prior 'no-win' situation in which the parties, instead of continuing to inflict enormous damage on one another, opt instead for a negotiated settlement. The possibility of such a settlement will depend on the extent to which the parties recognize and acknowledge a common predicament that will be magnified unless the conflicts are restrained and regulated. In his work on conflict resolution Muzafer Sherif employs the concept of 'superordinate goals' to describe the necessary condition of securing co-operation among previously antagonistic rivals. He writes:

'Superordinate goals cannot be fabricated or unilaterally proposed. They arise in the functional relations between groups, and their possibilities increase with the diversity and volume of concerns affecting both groups. With increased contact and a growing diversity of concerns affecting both sides, each group in an intergroup system becomes more dependent upon the other, so that what happens *within* its bounds is increasingly conditioned by its relations with the other groups in the system. Such mutual dependence, even though it may be decried within each group, furnishes fertile soil for common predicaments. The predicament of one group becomes a predicament to the other groups in the system. Thus, the attainment of compelling goals to which all aspire becomes contingent upon all parties pulling together in the same direction. Superordinate goals are not "devices" to be manipulated in dealing with intergroup tensions. They must arise from the relations between groups in a fashion so compelling that they can be recognized within each group.'[7]

In the South African situation the building materials for the mutual acknowledgement of superordinate goals lie in the economic interdependence of all groups, although, in view of the racially stratified nature of the society, the nature of the co-operation involves at the same time a significant measure of antagonism. It remains true, however, that white and black, whatever the inequalities between them, share a common economic base whose potential can be realized only by joint endeavours. Vigorous efforts to break the association of race and class would surely heighten the awareness of superordinate goals by bringing increasing numbers of blacks into executive, managerial, professional and supervisory capacities, from which vantage points the delicate web of economic interdependence may be more readily appreciated.

The absence of cross-cutting ties of any significance in the social structure of South Africa has been emphasized previously; an emphasis on cross-cutting *needs* could be stimulated by intelligent leadership at all levels in the society: whatever the differences among the groups, all people share a number of needs and wants in common, which have nothing intrinsically to do with their colour. Governments that are committed to interracial harmony can do a great deal to propagandize the benefits that flow from co-operation. Sherif's experiments with group encounters have relevance for divided societies: when two groups of young schoolboys were pitted against each other in a number of contrived competitions, strong antagonisms and prejudices were generated; it was only when the experimenters contrived tasks that required co-operative efforts by the boys for their common well-being that the antagonisms and prejudices abated, and new solidarities that cut across previous lines of division were developed.[8] Practically every task of any consequence in South Africa requires interracial co-operation, and when the statutory and social barriers to full and equal status co-operation are removed, a powerful generator of intergroup harmony could come into being. In dealing with these possiblities, we are not alluding to a potential role for the state or other governmental structures only. Local-level initiatives in towns and villages, churches, industrial and commercial enterprises, and associations of all kinds could help greatly in creating nodes of interracial co-operation and accommodation that could form the social tissue of a democratic society. It may be that the roles and capacities of the national political élites will be decisive in reaching an overall accommodation, but its chances for durability will be strengthened if its terms and quality are congruent with patterns in the wider society.

The stress that has been laid upon the need for an awareness of superordinate goals relates to the need to break out of zero-sum conceptions of political conflict. The expectation or hope is that if a resolution of conflict can be negotiated all parties will be better off, at least in some dimension. Morton Deutsch offers as a proposition that 'any attempt to introduce a change in the existing relationship between two parties is more likely to be accepted if each expects some net gain from the change than if either side expects that the other side will gain at its expense'.[9] Prima facie it would appear that in the South African situation negotiation between white and black can lead only to substantial gains by blacks at the expense of whites.

Clearly any chance of a settlement would require the complete abolition of racial discrimination, from which the dominant white group benefits substantially. Moreover, something like a charter of distributive justice would have to be adopted to enable a fairer sharing of wealth and incomes to be effected.

The supreme advantage for whites in negotiating a settlement would be the improvement in their chances of surviving as a vigorous community enjoying full political equality, and a real share of power in a racially tolerant society. The alternatives, to quote the previous prime minister, might be 'too ghastly to contemplate'. Whatever happens in South Africa, a substantial number of whites are likely to remain: if power had to be wrested from them by force, economic sanctions and the like in a protracted struggle, they might survive only as a persecuted minority, subjected to the vengeful repression of a revolutionary and authoritarian black regime.

For blacks the advantages of a negotiated settlement would be more direct: the release from racial discrimination would have both a material and a psychic dimension, and it could avert the massive bloodshed that must necessarily occur if a racial war were to engulf South Africa. By comparison the wars in Moçambique, Angola and Zimbabwe-Rhodesia would seem trivial, and there would be no guarantee of a decisive black victory.[10] The major inducement for both white and black to negotiate ought surely to be that neither can win a civil war, but in a real sense both can lose.

The possibility of a negotiated settlement in South Africa depends critically upon the quality of the leaders who are involved in the negotiations – a point that has been made several times in this work. Vision, the capacity for compromise and empathy, and flexibility, apart from sheer negotiating skill, will be required if they are to transcend the past and escape out of the racially determined grooves on which South Africa's social structure has been run. South Africa has produced impressive leaders in the past: Smuts, Hertzog, Abdurahman, Malan and Lutuli, whatever one may think about their policies and deeds, were men of stature who, had they been faced with South Africa's supreme crisis, might well have shown the qualities required to overcome it.

There can be no guarantee that the present and future political leaders will be capable of summoning up the requisite qualities; no less can there be any certainty that the respective leaders will be able to carry their followers with them in accepting and abiding by the terms of a settlement. Anthony Oberschall has written:

'Any conciliatory enterprise is complicated: on top of the substantive issues causing the conflict in the first place there arises the question of allocating responsibility for the injuries that both sides have inflicted upon each other during the confrontation period, of punishment for those held responsible, and of compensation for damages and injuries incurred. Not only do negotiations take place against a background of past humiliations, broken promises, recriminations, injuries, and disappointments, but the atmosphere of hostility and mistrust is re-enforced by new incidents that lead to doubts about the good faith of one's opponents, that call for retaliatory action and thus might be the occasion for resuming full-scale overt conflict. Such incidents strengthen the complementary negative images of the adversaries and the position of the hard liners in both camps who were opposed to conciliation to begin with. . . . Consequently the chances of fruitful negotiations are enhanced to the extent that both sides are highly organized, united, and strongly led, with leaders able to enforce discipline down to the rank-and-file who man the front lines, since then the likelihood of injurious incidents poisoning the conduct of negotiations is low.'[11]

Negotiations in South Africa might involve at least three and possibly as many as ten politically significant groups. While it may be that alliances or linkages across the group divisions could achieve a rough balance of power or mutually deterrent effect that could mitigate the conflict, there is a stronger possibility that the negotiating situation and an ensuing democratic political system would be characterized by the politics of racial outbidding, that is, attempts made by more radical parties or factions within parties to undermine support for more moderate leaders who have struck bargains. A comparable situation has arisen in Northern Ireland.[12] There is no way of evading this issue and no effective institutional safeguard that could prevent its occurrence. It may be possible to outlaw racist appeals and proscribe parties that seek to undermine democratic institutions or the possibility of creating them but, if these appeals and anti-democratic intentions catch on among sizeable segments of the population, it would not augur well for the successful creation of a democratic political system and its viability thereafter. Only strong leaders with a commitment to racial peace could obviate this contingency.

It may seem that the consideration of possible institutional frameworks has been unduly deferred, but the underlying thesis has been that without some prior commitment among the groups to explore collectively possible models of the political system, constitution-making is likely to be a fruitless exercise. The crucial aspect of the settlement will be whether a formula could be agreed upon whereby power is shared, and a situation of group domination is avoided. It is a chimerical hope to expect that the strong feelings of racial antagonism that have been generated will evaporate easily or quickly; but strong and sensible leadership could contain them and inaugurate a dispensation that will erode their basis. Conflict, of course, is basic to society, and the racially determined contours of South African society will continue to be the major source of conflict for a long while to come. Political settlements and constitutions are not intended to eliminate conflict, but to provide the means of containing and regulating it, and blunting its cutting edge so that diverse and divided groups can accommodate to one another.

8 *An alternative political framework*

It was argued in the preceding chapter that the *sine qua non* of a durable political settlement and a viable political system was that all significant political groups must be party to it. Under no circumstances should what follows in this chapter be construed as a blueprint: it is presented rather as a set of suggestions or guidelines for those who wish to see South Africa transformed into a democratic society.

Certain related principles stand out in the light of the analyses in preceding chapters and, as they underlie the suggestions that follow, they are presented here in summary form:

(1) As simple majoritarianism has in no deeply divided society had a democratic outcome, the principle of power-sharing among all groups must be institutionalized.

(2) The operation of the political system must, as far as possible, provide incentives for coalescent rather than adversary politics: that is to say, the zero-sum style of politics must be avoided.

(3) The operation of the political system must, as far as possible, deny or minimize the pay-off to racial or ethnic appeals; and conversely, it must provide rewards to coalescent, linkage, or simply interracial, movements.

(4) Without rejecting or diminishing the importance of formal safeguards, such as a justiciable bill of rights, the fundamental safeguards for groups and individuals must as far as possible be woven into the operation of the political system itself.

(5) As far as possible, potentially disruptive issues must be settled by inter-party negotiations that avoid submitting them to open competitive politics. In Nordlinger's terms, there must be purposive depoliticization.

Institutions that create the possibilities for these principles will be suggested below but, it must be repeated, institutions themselves, unless they are very firmly entrenched and hallowed by a longstanding legitimacy, cannot also create the political culture that will enable the principles to be realized. South Africa's present political institutions are discredited among a large section of the black population. While the Burkean tradition may prescribe piecemeal adjustments and reforms to a continuing set of institutions, there is little chance now that a strategy based upon this approach would succeed. Accordingly, and mindful of the risks and imponderables that are involved, our suggestions amount to a systematic and sustained departure from the past. Existing institutions will have to be manipulated, changed – or jettisoned.

THE STRUCTURE OF GOVERNMENT

Should a new South African constitution be unitary or federal in character? Should a Westminster-type parliamentary system be retained, or should there be a presidential system in which the executive and legislature are formally and actually separated? While these questions will form the main substance of this section, it should be noted they are not necessarily amenable to 'either/or' answers: combinations are possible, as will be indicated.

As was shown in chapter 5, some attention was given to the possibility of federation rather than union for South Africa at the National Convention in 1908, and a number of writers have argued that a federal South Africa might have prevented or inhibited the development of the racial problem into its present impasse. Several organizations, black and white, have in recent years advocated federalism in one form or another.

A federal alternative for South Africa needs careful examination lest the enthusiasms of its proponents and detractors blind us to some of its merits or demerits. In a much-quoted remark W. Ivor Jennings said that 'nobody would have a federal constititution if he could avoid it'. Federations are notoriously cumbersome and unwieldy political instruments, whose operation requires patience, negotiating skill and a large amount of resources to cope with the duplication of civil services, police forces and so on. Moreover, federalism is not a concept that excites people: as G.F. Sawer remarks: 'It is not a swinging system. People are not likely to go to the stake, or the barricades, to defend federalism as such.'[1] This is a serious disadvantage, because the prospects for federalism, or for any kind of constitution, depend upon its acceptability. In his analysis of the requisites for successful federation Thomas M. Franck argues that the absence of positive political or ideological commitment to the primary goal of federalism as an end in itself among the leaders and people of the federating units makes the success of federation improbable if not impossible. He writes:

'For a federation to be able to resist failure, the leaders, and their followers, must "feel federal" – they must be moved to think of themselves as one people, with one, common self-interest – capable, where necessary, of over-riding most other considerations of small-group interests.'[2]

The aspirant federalist in contemporary South Africa may be daunted by the wreckage of failed federations in the modern world, not least in Africa. Federalism's track record in developing countries has not been an encouraging one. Of the modern democratic federations (excluding West Germany) only India has survived, while Malaysia, shorn of Singapore, barely qualifies as a survivor. The failure of the Federation of Rhodesia and Nyasaland particularly affected Nationalist thoughts about federalism for South Africa, giving them additional reasons for rejecting it beyond the fact that it involved power-sharing.[3] The collapse of the original Nigerian federation has also been adduced by Nationalists as evidence of the unworkability of federalism, at least in African conditions.

Both these examples deserve brief mention for neither proves anything about federalism *per se.* The Central African Federation failed not so much because of federalism, but because its federalism lacked a democratic content and because its slogan of 'partnership' was not expanded into a meaningful reality of intergroup co-operation. The federation was conceived out of the joint efforts of the British Colonial Office and white politicians in the Rhodesias, who saw in the federation a means of reducing British colonial control and enhancing their own political and economic power. In none of the three federating territories were Africans properly consulted, and it was this omission and the failure to create pro-federal sentiment among them that led to the federation's termination.

The prospects for federal success in Nigeria were jeopardized from the very start by an unworkable configuration of regions. Like consociationalism, federalism is more likely to succeed in circumstances where a multiple balance of power obtains among the units. As B.O. Nwabueze says:

'Federalism thrives upon a multiplicity of interest-groups reacting upon one another to produce an equilibrium. A multiplicity of units creates a feeling of interdependence, which, in turn encourages co-operation and mutual tolerance.'[4]

Federal Nigeria began with three regions, one of which, the Northern Region, comprising 75 per cent of the land area and 60 per cent of the total population of Nigeria, was larger than both of the other regions combined.[5] Prior to independence, demands had been voiced by minorities in each of the regions, which were dominated by a single ethnic group, for the creation of additional regions; but the demands were rejected by the (British) Minorities Commission in 1957. Post-independence politics saw a heightening of ethnicity, with political parties in the Ibo-dominated Eastern Region and the Yoruba-dominated Western Region realizing that the road to national political power lay in securing a foothold in the North, which had been allocated nearly one-half of the national parliamentary constituencies.[6] Such a situation, as Nwabueze indicates, pointed to a strategy whereby two regions could gang up and make life uncomfortable for the third. This is precisely what happened between 1959 and 1964 when a Northern–Eastern coalition ganged up against the Western Region.[7]

A further structural problem in the Nigerian federation was that insufficient powers were vested in the centre, with the result that national politics did not attract the real regionally based leaders, who sought to control the actions of their lieutenants at the centre.[8] As Olorunsola points out, while the federal prime minister was theoretically the most powerful individual in Nigeria, in reality the (Northern) Sardauna of Sokoto was more powerful by virtue of being the pivot of Northern cultural sub-nationalism.[9]

It is no part of the argument that had Nigeria started with ten or twelve regions federation would have succeeded. There were additional reasons for the federal failure, such as the disparities in regional levels of development; but a more flexible basic structure might have enabled Nigeria to surmount its problems, without military coups and a bloody secessionist war. It should also be pointed out that whatever the failings of federalism in Nigeria were, it is most unlikely that a unitary system would have overcome them. As we have noted in an earlier chapter, Nigeria's current efforts to restore democracy still rest upon a federal base.

It has often been argued that federalism is an appropriate form of government for ethnically divided societies where ethnicity is territorially based. Thus F.G. Carnell, in one of the classic expositions of federalism, writes:

'Federalism is an attempted solution to territorial rather than racial conflicts of interest. It endeavours to square unity with diversity, but it can only do so on the supposition that the major diversities are territorially expressed. If the major diversities have no inclusive territorial base but traverse the whole society in the form of racial or communal conflict between intermingled communities, it is extremely doubtful if federalism can serve any useful purpose.'[10]

On the other hand, it can equally be argued that where federalism grants partial autonomy to a territorially based ethnic or racial group, that group may use its autonomy as a lever for making increased demands or even as a base for possible secession. The case of Quebec comes to mind, as well as the attempted Ibo-led Biafran breakaway from Nigeria. But it does not follow from this argument that a unitary system would have overcome the problem, unless the minority groups were forcibly assimilated or dispersed.

In a critique of the federal idea William H. Riker has raised some fundamental questions, including ones that relate to the problem of coping with diversity. He writes:

'Federal governments are not the only ones that permit regional diversity nor do they support diversity particularly well. It is well known that some federalisms, e.g., the Soviet Union, hardly support diversity at all and it is equally well known that some unitary governments do support diversity very much. For example, after five hundred years as centralized unitary governments England, France and Spain all have provinces where minority languages are still spoken and the culture of these languages is so alive in the hearts of the people that movements for provincial autonomy are almost as strong as in some federalisms. Indeed it is legitimate to ask: Does federalism make any difference in the way people are governed? If one controls for political culture, is there not about the same amount of diversity and local autonomy in both federal and unitary governments? . . . Whether or not local autonomy and diversity exist is a matter of whether or not such local officials are permitted to respond to local pressures for regional variation. Federalism is one way to provide for such a response; but so is any system – federal or unitary – that provides for the responsiveness of local officials . . . the essence of local autonomy has little to do with whether or not the central constitution grants particular rights to local officials but has very much to do with whether or not local officials are elected by or are in some other way responsive to local citizens.'[11]

These comments were written in 1969; since that time pressures for decentralization in Britain have increased; Breton subnationalism in France has not abated; and in Spain, which has been democratized in the intervening period, Basque and Catalan subnationalisms will surely have to be accommodated by a substantial degree of decentralization, if not by federalism. Moreover, it is very doubtful whether Swiss, Canadian or Yugoslavian citizens would accept any proposition that the existence of federalism makes little or no difference to their ability to exert pressures at local levels.

But Riker's remarks do point to the fact that federal and unitary forms of government are located on a continuum, containing a penumbral zone where the more centralized federations and the more decentralized unitary systems are located in close proximity to one another. In one of the many definitions of the federal principle, K.C. Wheare wrote that it is 'the method of dividing powers so that the general and regional governments are each, within a sphere, co-ordinate and independent'; and in the same book he says:

'What is necessary for the federal principle is not merely that the general government, like the regional governments, should operate directly upon the people, but, further, that each government should be limited to its own sphere and, within that sphere, should be independent of the other.'[12]

More recent scholarship on federalism, however, has shown that Wheare's emphasis on the mutual independence of central and regional governments is obsolete. Terms such as 'interdependent federalism' and 'co-operative federalism' indicate that central and regional governmental functions interact and interpenetrate in many ways that reflect both co-operation and rivalry. There may be concurrent powers for which both the centre and the regions have responsibility, and the regions may be responsible for executing central policy. All modern governments have become more centralized under the impact of war, the adoption of Keynesian economic practices, the provision of welfare services and so on. Federations have not been exempt from this process although, in the case of Canada, the renaissance of French-Canadian ethnicity has involved a strong resistance to it, which has succeeded in restoring to Quebec significant powers of initiative previously assumed to be vested in the central government.[13]

In a review of federalism in Canada, Australia and the United States a leading student, William S. Livingston, writes:

'The changed interpretation of powers, together with the growth of fiscal resources, has lodged an authority in the national government that is unlike anything contained in the traditional conception. The power of the purse has given to the national government a control over activities at both state and national level that was unknown in earlier years. In effect the court has abandoned its role as arbiter of the system – almost wholly in the United States, nearly as much in Australia and to a very considerable extent in Canada. The consequence of these two developments, judicial and fiscal, is that federalism in all three federations has come to be more and more a political matter and less and less a legal matter.'[14]

In the analysis of federalism by recent scholars a great deal of emphasis has been laid upon the consideration that the federal principle is as much a process, or a particular way of conducting politics, as it is a formal, written constitutional document.

In particular the party system has been singled out as a key variable, both shaping and being shaped by the federal structure and, in particular, by whether its executive is parliamentary or presidential.[15] Daniel J. Elazar has argued that a non-centralized party system is perhaps the most important single element in maintaining a non-centralized federal system;[16] other authors have argued that the type of executive influences the party system. Thus Ronald L. Watts and William S. Livingston show that in the parliamentary federations the thrust of the executive system has been to encourage nodes of concentrated power in the central and regional sites of decision-making, while in the United States and Switzerland (whose collegial-type executive is sui generis) the tendency has been to diffuse power within each level of government. In the parliamentary federations parties are more centralized (though not to the same extent as in the United Kingdom), contrasted with the United States or Switzerland whose parties are decentralized and relatively undisciplined, executive stability not being dependent upon party support in the legislature.[17] A further consequence of the parliamentary-type executive is to weaken the second chambers in parliaments. Livingston remarks that 'the introduction of parliamentary government in a federal system inevitably leads to the decline of the second chamber and to the weakening of whatever representation of state interests that chamber is intended to provide'.[18] These points will be picked up subsequently when we examine the question of what kind of executive is best suited to South Africa.

Federalism, we have noted, is not a simple type of government to operate. It requires among the citizenry 'a high degree of rule-consciousness',[19] a strong and universally respected judiciary, whose role in interpreting the constitution and conciliating conflict will be crucial, and a capacity among politicians and administrators for flexibility and negotiation. Elazar writes:

'The successful operation of federal systems requires a particular kind of political environment, one which is conducive to popular government and has the strong traditions of political co-operation and self-restraint that are needed to maintain a system which minimizes the use of coercion. Beyond the level of tradition, federal systems operate best in societies with sufficient homogeneity of fundamental interests – or consensus – to allow a great deal of latitude in political operations and to place primary reliance upon voluntary collaboration.'[20]

In a survey of the findings of various scholars on federal requisites Carnell writes:

'A "federal situation" is . . . a highly delicate balance of coalescing and conflicting forces. There must be a feeling of insecurity, but not too much of an outside threat, such as war. There must be economic divergence of interests between the units, but no one unit should have an overwhelming preponderance in population or resources. Differences of race, religion or language may help to maintain the federal balance, but fundamental cleavages may shatter it.'[21]

In assessing the possibilities of federation for South Africa it must be remembered that federation will entail the partial, at least, dismantling of what has become a highly centralized system of government. This need not be an insuperable problem: Latin American federations, and federal West Germany were created in this way.[22] It will require also that the map be redrawn to carve out perhaps ten regions that constitute reasonably coherent entities, none of which has an overwhelming influence or leverage within the system.

Prima facie South Africa does not seem promising as a federal situation, the major reason being that its diversity has no territorial nexus. Whichever way regional boundaries were drawn each region would be likely to have a heterogeneous population and the problem of creating a more coalescent style of politics would exist in each.[23]

It would be difficult to create even a rough balance, in terms of population and resources, among ten regions, given that South Africa has only four major areas of extensive industrial concentration, namely the Pretoria-Witwatersrand-Vereeniging triangle, Durban-Pinetown-Pietermaritzburg, the Cape Town Metropolitan region, and Port Elizabeth-Uitenhage area.

It would make little economic sense to divide any of these areas by regional boundaries. Other growth points, fostered by industrial decentralization, may develop, but their wealth-generating capacity and ability to sustain a heavy fiscal load will be limited for some time to come.

In other words, a South African federation would have to face one of the classic difficulties of federation – serious disparities in wealth and resources among the regions. Of course, the federal government could equip itself with machinery to redistribute wealth and thereby ensure that no region was markedly worse off than others in terms of functions like education and social services.[24] A number of federations have evolved such equalizing agencies, but the possibility is that wealthier regions will resent being required to subsidize the poorer ones –

a phenomenon found even in the socialist federation of Yugoslavia.

So far the discussion of a federal system for South Africa has inclined to a pessimistic view of the possibilities, but a major consideration in its favour lies in the possibility that it can fragment power and thereby avoid its concentration in a single, decisive site. A federal system may be so structured that no one site is decisive. Robert A. Dahl isolates a group of countries, including the United States, Switzerland and West Germany, where 'the absence of a decisive site has been produced by a deliberate dispersion of legal authority through constitutional devices such as federalism, separation of powers, and checks and balances'.[25]

A political party in such a system, if defeated in one site, may win in another and because this possibility exists it does not become alienated or 'anti-system' in character. Nwabueze makes the related important point that

' . . . the mere fact of decentralising functions makes the question of the control of the centre less embittering than it would be under a unitary system; with the diminished powers exercisable centrally, the central government cannot become an instrument of total domination'.[26]

As we have indicated, there is no way of foretelling what configuration of political parties would emerge in a democratic election in South Africa. It may, however, be reasonably conjectured that no single black-dominated party would win an overall majority in the federal parliament and in all of the regional assemblies. The electoral leverage of non-black minorities would vary among the constituencies for the national parliament, and regionally their overall political influence would vary in strength from region to region depending upon their population concentrations. It is quite possible that predominantly black parties might vie for minority support and build coalitions with minority parties. It is in this kind of coalition-building or linkage politics that the best political safeguards for minorities are likely to be found.

Massive concentrations of power are always potentially inimical to liberty, and to the extent that federalism fragments power by diffusing it to other sites it may facilitate the protection of liberty. As Montesquieu said, power can be checked only by power: if the federal society can create and entrench countervailing centres of power the dangers of an omnipotent centre can be checked.

Nothing in these arguments should be construed as support for the proposition that federalism 'guarantees' democratic freedom – which is particularly untrue, as the abuse of freedom in a number of federations shows (for example, the historic status of blacks in the American South). The argument is rather that federalism may be supportive of democratic values and practices after they have been mutually agreed upon and given expression to in a federal constitution. Moreover, whatever powers were vested in the regions, the entire society would fall under a common bill of rights.

A further advantage that might accrue from a federal decentralization in South Africa is that conflict may be regionally localized. In Switzerland a good deal of conflict occurs and is regulated at the cantonal level, thereby obviating the development of nation-wide polarization. A recent study of this aspect of Swiss politics concludes that '. . . to the extent that political power is dispersed in an ethnically divided nation, the probability of cleavages finding political expression nation-wide across the many arenas of party competition is reduced'.[27]

Of course, as has been stressed, the cleavage pattern of Switzerland is very different from South Africa, and no facile extrapolation from Swiss experience can be made. South Africa's cleavages have already polarized society and one may doubt whether even under conditions of democratic federalism, it will be possible to confine particular issues to regional significance only. Nevertheless it may occur, and even if it does so only to a limited extent initially, regional fractionalization of conflict may increase as federal institutions and practices take root. It may even happen that a particular region's malpractices (of whatever nature they may be) could be curbed by that region's becoming an object of national derision, much as Pretoria's recalcitrant city council was forced, in June 1978, to back down from its previous stand and acquiesce in the opening of one theatre to all races.

If power can be checked only by power, it follows that the regions of a federal South Africa must be vested with sufficient authority to enable them, individually and collectively, to stand up to the centre, and to evoke the interest of their citizens. This raises the crucial question of what division of powers and functions between the centre and regions would be appropriate in South Africa, bearing in mind the possibility that some powers may be concurrently exercised by both the centre and the regions.[28] Certain subjects are, in their very nature, federal-wide, and therefore fall within the federal sphere: foreign affairs, defence matters, currency and foreign exchange, foreign and internal trade, shipping and transport. The regional sphere might include agriculture and land, forestry, education, public health and social welfare, local or municipal government, and town and country planning. A third or concurrent category of powers would include economic affairs, labour issues and industrial relations generally.

These categories are not necessarily hard and fast. Historically federations have had to adapt to new demands made upon government or to readjust to cope with new circumstances.[29] Elazar writes:

'In any federal system, it is likely that there will be continued tension between the federal government and the constituent polities over the years and that different "balances" between them will develop at different times. The existence of this tension is an integral part of the federal relationship, and its character does much to determine the future of federalism in each system. The question of federal–state relations which it produces is perennially a matter of public concern because virtually all other political issues arising in a federal system are phrased in terms of their implications for federalism. In this way federalism imposes a way of looking at problems that stands apart from the substantive issues raised by the problems themselves. This is particularly true of those issues which affect the very fabric of society. In the United States, for example, the race question is a problem of federal–state as well as Negro–white relations, and the same is true of the cultural question in Canada and the linguistic question in India.'[30]

This discussion of the implications of federalism has necessarily been cursory, but our emphasis has been that federalism is no panacea. As Jennings's remark (see p. 134) implied, federalism is something of a 'second-best' option, chosen because none of the other options seems to have a better chance of viability. Consensus on a democratic constitutional framework for South Africa will be difficult to attain: our reason for suggesting federalism is that it is more likely than other models of the political system to enable that consensus to be reached. There should, however, be no naive utopianism in espousing the federal idea. As André du Toit has pointed out, white and black advocates of federalism may have very different expectations of what goods federalism could deliver.[31] If predominant white opinion views federalism as a technique of fragmenting black power and thereby enabling them to maintain their privileges, federalism has no chance of succeeding; conversely if predominant black opinion regards the federal structure as an intolerable brake on their aspirations to unbridled majoritarianism, federalism will similarly fail.

There are no inherent reasons why federalism should be incompatible with redistributive policies and steps towards social democracy or an extended welfare apparatus, which will be necessary. It may be that the political process is slower and more complex than in a more homogeneous unitary system, where majoritarianism is accepted, but this is a cost worth bearing if it supports constitutionalism and the respect for democratic freedoms.

As we have noted, federalism has, for many radicals, a tinge of 'neo-colonialism' about it, and a conservative bias is imputed to it. It should be pointed out (for what it is worth) that the U.S.S.R. is ostensibly a federation, and Yugoslavia is one in theory as well as in practice. But this is a debating point: the nettle to be grasped is Tocqueville's paradox of equality and freedom: 'in proportion as equality . . . was established by the aid of freedom, freedom itself was thereby rendered more difficult of attainment'. In other words freedom and equality stand in a certain antithetical relationship to each other: unrestrained freedom (as under a laissez-faire system) is likely to result in gross inequalities; pulverizing equalitarianism (such as under Stalin) will obliterate freedom. A balance between the two goals must be struck, whereby the grosser inequalities of society are overcome and a real equality of opportunity is established, while civil liberties are protected.

A critical component of any structure of government is the executive. The effect of the type of executive on federal government has already been referred to, and it was noted that democratic federalism is compatible with both parliamentary and presidential executives. In asking what kind of an executive would be best suited to South Africa, the issue turns on which type would be more encouraging of, and congruent with, a more coalescent, consensus-maximizing style of politics. These questions cannot be considered in isolation from the party system, which, in turn, is shaped to a significant extent by the type of electoral system. For reasons that will be examined below, the adoption of proportional representation is being advocated here, with the likely result that a multiparty system will emerge, at both federal and regional levels.

The pros and cons of presidential and parliamentary executives must be considered point by point. It has been argued that the United States's executive (which may be taken as a prototype of presidential systems) induces political parties, seeking to capture this crucial single office, to maximize their support by building coalitions, offering compromises and so forth. The presidency, in other words, is an office whose filling is an integrative or bridge-building process, that has to be sustained even after the incumbent has been elected. In South Africa, however, it is doubtful whether a comparable integrative effect would be achieved by a national election for a single office-holder. The American presidency is supported by a political environment that accords considerable legitimacy to America's political institutions; in South Africa that supportive environment will still have to be created, and a presidential election would be more likely to have a divisive effect on the society.

It is arguable that in a system of the American type, where the separation of the executive from the legislature is both formal and real, the executive is far more amenable to control by the legislature than in parliamentary systems, where the common tendency has been for the role of parliament to degenerate into a rubber-stamping agency for the actions and initiatives of the cabinet. One may question whether the structured antagonism of the American system, and the fluidity of party alignments in Congress, did not have a great deal to do with the uncovering of the Watergate scandal, which, in a parliamentary system, may more easily have been covered up.

There can be little doubt that the relative lack of cohesion of the American parties permits a greater degree of flexibility in the building of coalitions and alignments (even if for ad hoc legislative purposes) across party lines than in a parliamentary system of the Westminster type, where parties are disciplined and marshalled to a far greater extent by the party leaderships. In the American system the elected representatives are not responsible to the president (even if his popularity helped the election of many of his party's candidates); and the president's term of office is not dependent upon legislative support, although that support would facilitate the passage of his legislative programme.

A further consideration is that in presidential federations upper houses have been far more influential bodies than in parliamentary federations – a point that has already been noted in another context. The same is true of the Swiss system. R.L. Watts has shown how in the United States and in Switzerland second federal chambers, in which the states or cantons are equally represented, have curbed the considerable power that representation by population alone gives to majority groups in the lower houses. By separating the powers and creating a framework of checks and balances, these systems have encouraged searches for compromise because minority groups and parties have been able to block action at a number of points in the system. By contrast, in parliamentary federations, substantial, if not complete, sovereignty has been vested in a parliamentary majority with no institutional checks on it.[32] As Watts notes, while parliamentary systems offer scope for rapid and effective action, and in this respect are more efficient than presidential systems, the relative lack of restraints upon majorities puts the onus for reconciling conflict and aggregating support across the lines of cleavage upon the parties themselves; and if the parties fail to do so, the consequences for the federation's stability as a democracy may be serious.[33]

It must be noted, however, that these remarks about parliamentary federations all relate to those that retained Westminster-oriented institutions in a federal setting – Canada, Australia, India, Nigeria, Malaysia and the West Indies. Whatever virtues it may have, it is hard to detach the Westminster system from an adversary, zero-sum form of political conflict. In principle it may be possible to establish a parliamentary executive in a more coalescent context, thereby retaining its advantages of greater efficiency and flexibility, while avoiding its anti-consensual bias. Before exploring this possibility we may examine the structure and operation of the Swiss executive, which is an interesting mutation of the American system standing somewhere between the presidential and parliamentary types.[34]

The Federal Council of Switzerland, as the executive is called, consists of seven individuals, elected by the Federal Assembly (i.e. the National Council and the Council of States sitting together) for four-year terms of office. Since 1959 the Federal Council has been elected on the basis of the 2:2:2:1 formula, whereby each of the major parties has two representatives, while a smaller party, the Democratic Centre Union, has one. The formula, which is a political convention and not a constitutional provision, also requires that no more than five members may be German-speaking, and that the three biggest cantons, Zurich, Bern and Vaud, should each have a permanent seat. Under the constitution, however, no canton may be represented by more than one member.

The members of the Federal Council, although they have been party men (though not necessarily members of the Federal Assembly), cease to be party representatives on election to the Council. Although there may be quite wide divergencies of political views among the members, they are expected, in the Swiss tradition of 'amicable agreement', to co-operate in the national interest as a collegiate body. It is said that decisions are taken on a majority basis, but that all decisions must be supported by at least three members.[35] The president and vice-president of the Federal Council are elected annually by the Federal Assembly and neither incumbent may serve for more than one year at a time – a constitutional provision that reflects a characteristic Swiss rejection of 'any exclusive personal pre-eminence'.

The president has no greater powers than any of his colleagues; he is chairman of the Council, and titular head of state, but his status among his colleagues is that of *primus inter pares.* Each member of the Council is responsible for an administrative department of state, and may be called upon, by 'interpellation', to defend the Federal

Council's policies in regard to the department concerned before the Federal Assembly. Most legislation originates in the Federal Council, and a particular councillor will be assigned to see the bill through the legislative process in the Federal Assembly.

Despite the different points of view within the Federal Council, it develops its own programme, which is reported to Parliament, and extensively debated in both houses of the Federal Assembly. Nevertheless, the Federal Councillors, as C.F. Strong notes,

'are not the leaders of the Houses, but their servants. The Ministry has no partisan character; it stands outside party; it does not do party work; and it does not determine the policy of the various parties in the Houses.'[36]

The Federal Council, as noted, is elected for a fixed four-year term of office, and it may not be removed by parliamentary votes of no-confidence. The Federal Assembly, however, is required to enact legislation (other than emergency measures during crisis times such as during the world wars); it can exert pressure over the Federal Council through standing committees, debates and through the right of interpellation, which requires the government to defend its actions in parliament.[37] A further principle of the Swiss system is the right of popular recourse to referenda to repudiate federal laws and to approve or reject proposed constitutional changes.

Although there is no suggestion that this peculiarly Swiss institution could be transplanted into a South African context, it has certain important aspects which may have relevance for us.[38] First, the stability of the executive is ensured by the fixed term of office; secondly, there are adequate checks on the executive; and thirdly, the executive embodies the principle of coalescent politics in that it seeks to be maximally representative while operating on a broadly consensual basis. It may be difficult to imagine how consensus could succeed in situations of deep cleavage, which is not the case in Switzerland, but it is not impossible for politically disparate individuals, when freed from *immediate* party restraints and obligations, to achieve some kind of accommodation among themselves.

While it is not practicable to replicate the Swiss model in South Africa, the principle that all or most of the politically salient groups should be represented in the executive is one that could well be adopted here. In their study of the politics of pluralism Smock and Smock concluded:

'Only when a system that gives the constituent groups a belief that they are equitably represented in the central decision-making organs can be devised, has the most fundamental issue been resolved.'[39]

They recommend, accordingly, that a broadly accepted formula for cabinet composition applicable to all governments be worked out in advance, and more specifically, in the interests of embodying the coalescent style in politics, they suggest the adoption of a constitutional provision requiring that all parties winning more than a certain minimum percentage of seats should be invited to join the government.[40]

In South Africa the adoption of proportional representation (PR) in the electoral system might be matched by a similar principle in membership of the cabinet. The minimum percentage might be fixed at 10 or 15 per cent of the seats, which, under PR, would be an accurate reflection of the number of votes cast for individual parties. Moreover, this relatively low ceiling would ensure a cabinet that was broadly representative of all groups in society. The further advantage would be that the necessity for legislatively expressed group representation in the cabinet would be obviated, and advantages would accrue to those parties that sought to build as wide (and, hence interracial) an electoral base as possible.

This suggested scheme might also secure the best possible safeguard for minority groups, namely one that is woven into the operation of the political system itself by making the votes of minority members important. Power-sharing in a coalescent system of politics that avoided domination of one group by another would also defuse the explosive issue of group control at the centre. If the play on words will be forgiven, to defuse it will be necessary to diffuse.

On balance it would seem that it would be best, in the circumstances of South Africa, to retain a parliamentary executive. It may be, as Claire Palley has suggested, that executives that are outside the legislature are more independent and enable the élites to co-operate more easily;[41] but the further requirement that élites exert a measure of control over their parliamentary followers would be better served by a parliamentary executive. The attractiveness of an American-style presidential executive is unquestioned, but it is difficult to see how the structured conflict between the executive and the legislature would yoke easily with a more coalescent type of politics. Carl J. Friedrich's observation that 'the more divided the power of government, the greater the opportunities for an opposition' is apposite.[42] The political systems of deeply divided societies require a plurality of sites to afford minority groups maximal access to influence and power, but this access should be in a co-operative, coalescent context, and not merely oppositional.

The executive system suggested here presupposes coalition government. PR alone would almost certainly suffice to achieve a multiparty system and the strong likelihood of coalition government as the norm. Coalitions go against the grain of Anglo-Saxon political habits, an attitude expressed in Disraeli's remark that 'England does not love coalitions'. Coalitions have been regarded as inherently unstable, incapable of providing strong government and so on. The empirical evidence, however, does not support these views. S.E. Finer has shown that 'if by stability we mean "steering the same course over periods that are longer than the lifetime of single parliaments", then all the evidence shows that the PR coalition governments of Europe have outperformed Britain in this respect'.[43]

A detailed study of coalition government in a Western democratic political system reaches the following conclusion:

'Political choice among several minority parties need not undermine political stability; quite the contrary, a party system reflecting a moderately diverse range of views conceivably could integrate the citizenry through open recognition of a competition between competing minority perspectives, activating the instinct for community by the development of widespread appreciation of and commitment to democratic processes. A wider range of party system structures may be appropriate to the democratic polity than analysts have recognised. As party coalitions are not necessarily antagonistic to cabinet durability, multiparty politics may not be necessarily antithetical to responsive, authoritative government.'[44]

To be sure, the cleavages between parties in a South African multiparty system may well be wider than in the average Western multiparty system; but those cleavages would surely be more effectively and expeditiously narrowed if all parties had a realistic possibility of a share in power where it counted, namely in the executive.

We are under no delusions about the difficulty of operating a power-sharing cabinet system. The major experiment of this kind in recent times was in Northern Ireland in 1974, where an intersectarian cabinet's capacity to govern was destroyed after a few months by a massive general strike by Protestant workers. The experiment has not been repeated, and power-sharing is not regarded as a viable option, at least for the time being. In a critique of the possibility of a power-sharing cabinet for Northern Ireland John Oliver writes:

'It is difficult for any Prime Minister to manage a Cabinet; to manage a coalition Cabinet is still more difficult; to manage an enforced coalition of disparate partners borders on the impossible; when those partners are so disparate as to hold opposing views on the very existence of the state (or, what is just as serious, are widely believed to hold such views underneath their apparent readiness to co-operate), Cabinet management becomes a most dangerous occupation. The Prime Minister . . . would, for a start, have no disciplinary powers outside his own party. He could not sack a minister who was misbehaving or proving obstructive. In the absence of any agreed programme put to the electorate and converted into a mandate, every important issue would be the subject of inevitable controversy at the Cabinet table. . . . What happens when one member of such a Cabinet retires in a huff and upsets the delicately constructed balance? What happens when the government is defeated on a minor matter emanating from one party within the Cabinet? What happens when the government is defeated on a major matter?What happens when one party starts losing support in the country, say at successive by-elections? What happens when backbenchers revolt out of dissatisfaction with the unrewarding role they have been given? The answers to those unpleasant questions are probably the same in all cases: the government collapses and the country loses not just a government but a constitution as well, because it proves impossible to put Humpty Dumpty together again and because the country by that time has lost confidence in the system.'[45]

The religious dimension and the fundamentally opposed views of Catholics and Protestants on the unity of Ireland give a peculiar intractability to the Northern Ireland conflict; but Oliver's questions raise pertinent issues for power-sharing proposals for South Africa. He assumes that adversary-style politics will continue, while power-sharing is premised upon coalescent or co-operative politics; he assumes further that the self-interest of parties and politicians will lead them to disruptive behaviour, while power-sharing assumes, or rather, hopes, that self-interest might be a basis of co-operation in the interests of avoiding mutual destruction. The conflicts from which Oliver's questions emanate will arise *whatever* form of government is devised, and the real question is whether a potentially more effective system of conflict regulation than power-sharing, in spite of all the difficulties, has yet been thought of. Oliver's book does not offer any more hopeful alternative for Northern Ireland. Other than power-sharing there is no middle ground between the options of forcibly reunifying Ireland, which would surely lead to a Protestant rebellion, and restoring the Protestant ascendancy, which would leave the Catholic minority powerless.

There is perhaps an over-deterministic streak in Oliver's pessimistic views about the capacity of politicians to transcend their differences in the interests of negotiation and co-operation. Loss of office is usually a powerful deterrent to rocking the boat; and, as far as the legislature is concerned, their ability to bring down governments might be restricted by a constitutional device, similar to that in West Germany, which requires the legislature itself to vote a successor into office, where it has voted the chancellor out of office. This device is said to strengthen executive stability and independence.

THE FRANCHISE AND THE ELECTORAL SYSTEM

In much of the discussion about political change in South Africa the franchise is accorded a central role. This is rightly so, for the franchise, as the indicator of the individual's rights to participate in electing a government, reflects the broad constellations of power in society. Unenfranchised groups have little direct, effective say in government, and accordingly, as politics is largely about the allocation of resources, they tend to be neglected or even discriminated against.

What is less appreciated in discussions of the franchise is the context in which it exists. In particular the electoral system – whether it is a plurality, first-past-the-post, single-member constituency system, or some form of PR – is of critical importance, as is the whole structure and style of government – whether it involves power-sharing and coalescent politics, or zero-sum, adversary politics.

The view adopted here is that the level of the franchise qualifications is not where safeguards for minorities in South Africa are to be sought or found. Indeed, attempts to manipulate the level of franchise qualification in the interests of protecting minorities are more than likely to be counterproductive. The implication of these considerations is that South Africa needs to have universal suffrage on common electoral rolls. The time when a qualified franchise would be acceptable to a majority of Africans has passed. Perhaps right down into the 1960s a qualified franchise might have had some chance of acceptability among Africans. For many years the African National Congress requested (as a traditionally moderate body it seldom 'demanded') the extension of the Cape's qualified non-racial franchise to the rest of the country; and it was only in 1945 that the demand for universal suffrage became its official policy. Today, even among moderate Africans, the acid test of white bona fides has become acceptance of universal franchise. S.A. de Smith writes:

'A limited, qualitative franchise, designed to give special weight to the votes of particular interest groups, can be dismissed from consideration. Universal adult suffrage is an article of faith in almost every new state.'[46]

South African blacks are unlikely to differ very much in their attitudes, and nowadays, moreover, no political party, including the National party, advocates a qualified franchise.

Constitutions and political systems ought to be designed to institutionalize peaceful conflict arbitration and regulation: the sooner *all* adult citizens are brought within the ambit of politics on an equal basis, the greater the chances of successful conflict regulation will be. It was this thought that prompted William Porter, the attorney-general of the Cape Colony, to remark in 1853 that he would 'rather meet the Hottentot at the hustings, voting for his representative, than meet the Hottentot in the wilds with his gun upon his shoulder'.[47]

Universal franchise must be distinguished from 'majority rule': in advocating the former one is not necessarily advocating the latter. A major theme of this book has been to emphasize the inappropriateness of majoritarianism in deeply divided societies; but majoritarianism will not be averted by seeking to block access to an equal franchise by certain disadvantaged categories. The avoidance of simple majoritarianism lies, in the final analysis, in the attitudes of the political leaders who operate the system, and in the institutional mechanisms of the kind of political system advocated here.

The question of who has the vote is obviously only part of the issue. What kind of electoral system is an equally significant question. As indicated above, our suggestions include the adoption of PR as the electoral system. PR is more easily harnessed to the cause of coalescent politics; it is more equitable in translating votes-won into seats-won; it obviates the need for specifically communal or racial representation and could encourage the development of cross-group linkage politics, while at the same time ensuring minorities of fair representation, and tending to inhibit the formation of large voting blocs.

The mechanics of the various forms of PR are a complex issue which we cannot explore fully here.[48] The two main systems of PR are the single transferable vote (STV) and the party list system. Under STV the individual voter ranks his preferred candidates on a first, second, third, etc. choice basis, whereas under the list system generally the voter must vote for one or another party's list of candidates either *in toto* or with some limited range of choice within the list. (Exceptions to this rule are Switzerland and Luxembourg where, although the list system is employed, voters are not confined in their choice to candidates of one list.)

The pros and cons of these two systems are finely balanced. STV, which has been favoured in the small number of English-speaking countries that have adopted PR, gives the voter a free choice to vote for candidates on party as well as personal grounds; while under the list system his choice is much more constrained by party considerations. STV, then, is more democratic in allowing a greater range of choice, but as Lijphart points out, this could be a disadvantage in systems that depend on inter-party negotiations because the greater freedom of the voter weakens the control of party leaders.[49]

THE MINORITY VETO

We have repeatedly emphasized that simple majoritarianism is incapable of bringing democracy to divided societies. The logic of this conclusion is that a democratic political system in South Africa must involve a minority veto in the legislative process, whereby laws can be passed in parliament only if a substantial majority of the members agree to them or, put differently, a minority of between 10 and 15 per cent can prevent the legislation from being passed. Democracy in South Africa will require maximal consensus as an on-going feature of the legislative process. The main purpose of the minority veto is to force negotiation and consensus between parties. We do not envisage it as a permanent blocking device or as a means of creating deadlocks in government. What has to be visualized is not the present adversarial, 'winner-takes-all' system where the majority in government can simply impose their will on the minority, but a situation where the parties negotiate and compromise beforehand on any issue that is likely to affect their interests.

Horse-trading, give-and-take, bargaining and trade-offs are common features of all democratic governments, and it is often the threat of deadlocks or vetos that induces a consensus. The parties to this process may not necessarily agree on everything, but a kind of lowest common denominator of agreement could be reached whereby, in the case of a particular decision, each will be somewhat advantaged, though not as much as if it had got its own way completely. Compromise, in other words, is a fundamental requirement.

Our suggestion of a minority veto is liable to be construed as a device to entrench the racial privileges of whites. We have no such thoughts in mind, and they would be inconsistent with the thrust of our analysis. We have shown that the genesis of the conflict in South Africa is in the inequalities of the status quo, and our proposals for resolving or regulating the conflict could hardly be based upon maintaining that status quo.

The minority veto that we envisage would operate only in the context of a constitutional dispensation that outlaws racial discrimination: it could not, therefore, be used to entrench something which is, by definition, illegal.

A further consideration is that the degree of unity which exists among blacks derives largely from their rejection of the present system. This solidarity cannot be seen as reflecting a complete unity of purpose among them as to what kind of alternative dispensation is appropriate for South Africa. There is no reason to suppose that under conditions of voluntary association and for the purpose of effectively participating in government, the spread and diversity of political-interest groupings among blacks will not be as great as or greater than among whites. Surely it is not only whites who differ on political issues. Among blacks there are regional, urban/rural, class and ethnolinguistic differences and it would be shortsighted to underestimate the potential political significance of such differences. The minority veto simply implies that those differences must be resolved through consensus and compromise rather than confrontation and domination.

In his survey of consociational systems Lijphart acknowledges the danger that minority vetos can lead to minority tyranny and paralysis of government, but he points out that the danger is not as serious as it might seem. First, a minority segment (however constituted) would be chary of using the veto too often because it will recognize that the veto could be used against its interests by other minorities; secondly, the mere existence of the veto as an instrument of protection will give minorities a sense of security which could make the actual use of the veto less probable; and thirdly, minorities will appreciate the dangers of deadlock and paralysis in the system.[50] If they abuse their veto rights a frustrated majority may be tempted to try and sweep away the restraints upon its freedom of action and govern by domination.

Radical critics may not be persuaded by our arguments, but we challenge them to suggest a more feasible mechanism, or to explain how simple majoritarianism is compatible with effective democracy in a society like South Africa.

Constitutions are not immutable, and their provisions may change to meet new circumstances. It may be that the minority veto could help to build up mutual trust in the South African political process, and once that trust had established itself, the veto provision could be abolished. Drawing upon his experience as a participant in British colonial constitutional conferences, Richard Luyt has said:

'The main lessons that seem to me to be available to us from the experiences of Kenya and Zambia are that elaborate constitutional curiosities, designed to protect minority race interests, are unlikely to last in circumstances where the numerical strength of a majority race hugely transcends that of the other races. This does not mean, however, that these devices did not play an important part at a most difficult stage in the experience of both of those countries. They gave an important degree of confidence, however temporary, at periods when confidence was needed, when fears about black majority government were great, and when any kind of trust in their future rulers still had to be developed.'[51]

South Africa's configuration of majorities and minorities is different from Kenya's or Zambia's, and simple majority rule is not a democratic option here, as the argument has shown, but the point about the value of minority safeguards is well taken.

FORMAL SAFEGUARDS AND RELATED MATTERS

The trend of the argument so far has been to suggest that the workability of formal safeguards depends to a large extent upon the attainment of a prior consensus about the political dispensation in its totality; and moreover, it has been indicated that the more effective safeguards for individual and group rights are likely to be those that exist as a function of the actual operation of the political system.

Nevertheless, there is a strong case for adopting a bill of rights in the South African constitution and rendering it amenable to judicial review. The bill of rights, in addition to spelling out the liberties of individuals, might also incorporate sections that seek to protect those groups who wish to avail themselves of rights of cultural self-determination.

It has been easy to dismiss the idea of a bill of rights as 'not worth the paper on which it is written', as Nationalists are wont to do. (No doubt their contemptuous disregard of the spirit of the South African constitution, manifested in the 1950s, has enabled them to realize how fragile constitutions are.) But the spirit of these proposals envisages a different structural position and role for the South African Supreme Court, by vesting it with judicial powers of review, which traditionally it has substantially lacked.

The courts have usually performed a critical role in federal systems, as arbiters of the constitution. As Livingston observes: 'A federal constitution tends to be what the judges, rather than the founding fathers, say it is.'[52] In the new South African dispensation the courts will be required to play a creative, constructive and conciliatory part, transcending the positivist, 'slot-machine' role which they have played in recent times, and helping in the arduous process of social and economic reform that must necessarily underpin basic human rights if they are to be meaningful.

Another critically important role for the courts relates to their significance as instruments of conflict regulation. Although, as A.S. Mathews has argued, it is not realistic to expect the judiciary to settle or compromise on the major conflict issues of a divided society[53] – a task which can be achieved only by political leaders – its ancillary role in conflict regulation is by no means negligible. A universally respected judicial system can be a valuable agent of depoliticization, dealing with issues in the quiet sobriety of the courtroom, far removed from the passions of politics. By their training, and by the ambience of their profession, judges tend to be independent, dispassionate and objective, and these are qualities which, along with skills in conflict resolution, can play a valuable part in knitting together a divided society. W.H.B. Dean has made the important point that the *de facto* involvement of the judiciary in the formulation of state policy is

'. . . a mechanism of further diffusion of political power which does not reflect the ethnic divisions within a particular society . . . this kind of division cuts across the other divisions which exist in the particular society. It can therefore operate as a means of defusing conflict and competition between those groups'.[54]

The discussion of the possible role of the courts has necessarily been brief, and a more precise statement of the mechanics of judicial review will require the skills of a constitutional lawyer. Our concern has been to indicate a possible role for the judiciary and its quasi-political use as a cross-cutting agency. Whatever formal role is accorded to the judiciary, however, an equally critical variable determining its effectiveness is the calibre of the people who become judges and, to a lesser extent, magistrates. Their formal independence can be safeguarded and this has been satisfactorily achieved in the South African legal tradition. But equally important is the inculcation in them of attitudes that are resistant to 'executive-mindedness'. Real judicial independence of the executive may be aided by altering the present method of judicial appointment by the Minister of Justice, and vesting the power of appointment in a Judicial Service Commission, presided over by the Chief Justice and composed mainly of judicial members. In other words, the role of the (political) executive would be eliminated, or at least radically diluted. A comparable appointment procedure ought to be devised for appointments to lower-echelon courts, corresponding to present-day magistrate's courts. In contemporary South Africa the magistrate is part judicial officer and part civil servant, a combination that has not enhanced his reputation for independence.

A major problem facing the judiciary, if it is to be respected as a dispenser of justice, is its racial composition. To fulfil the role imputed to it in our suggestions, the judiciary, at all levels, will have to become multiracial in composition. As with the civil service and the armed forces, this is going to be an exceedingly difficult and problem-prone area. The goals of merit and proportionality or representativeness will be to some extent in conflict, as a result of the historic inequalities of black education and their right of access to occupations in these spheres. As far as the courts are concerned, no pat formula is available for the transitional period, before suitably qualified blacks in reasonable numbers become eligible for elevation to the bench. One may hope that common sense will prevail and that the situation of a *de facto* white-preponderant bench can be mitigated in the interim by the judicious and sensitive use of black assessors, especially in cases involving black and white.

It may reasonably be expected that in the transition towards an open society, threats to security will be manifold.[55] Much of the volatility, potential aggression and explosiveness has been contained by the use of harsh and repressive methods of coercion. It would be unrealistic to assume that the lifting of these restrictions and the abolition of discrimination could not be accompanied by serious outbreaks of disorder. However firm one's commitment to civil liberties and the rule of law may be, the possibility that emergency measures will have to be resorted to cannot be ruled out. Present-day South Africa resembles, in its security legislation, a society in a permanent state of emergency. One may hope that radical and determined attacks on the causes of disaffection will in time eliminate the need of the disaffected to have recourse to unlawful and violent ways of voicing their demands. Order, as Ortega y Gasset has said, 'is not a pressure which is imposed on society from without, but an equilibrium which is set up from within'. It is order in this sense of a voluntary restraint that South Africa must aspire to. If emergency measures have to be employed, it must be emphasized that they do not necessarily entail the elimination of the rule of law.

Further attention will have to be paid to other uses of the law in social reform. South Africans may learn a great deal from American experience in combating racial discrimination. Thomas F. Pettigrew has written:

'Contrary to the old adage . . . law *can* change the hearts and minds of men. It does so through a vital intermediate step. Enforced law first acts to modify behaviour, and this modified behaviour in turn changes men's hearts and minds. . . . The legally established *fait accompli,* unlike exhortations for intergroup tolerance, generates its own acceptance. The situational face lifting it achieves is a year-round process, a constant, institutionalized reminder that intergroup harmony is the sanctioned norm. Finally, the new behaviour required by the law commits the individual psychologically; for he who has publicly behaved in a new manner and been rewarded for doing so is likely to become personally committed to the intergroup change.'[56]

Another issue that will soon loom up on the agenda for the nation's business is that of 'affirmative action', that is, programmes designed to enable groups to overcome the effects of discrimination and catch up with others. Again, this issue has focused primarily on American blacks and other minority groups, and has generated a controversy from which we can learn.[57] Whatever government is in power South Africa is going to face problems of poverty, un- and under-employment for a long time to come. It will serve little purpose to insert into a bill of rights, as many radicals propose, lists of economic and welfare rights that are incapable of immediate realization. Instead, we suggest that realistic goals for overcoming these problems be established, and their attainment be regarded as the nation's number-one priority.

Agreement upon a possible charter of distributive justice among black and white might serve to depoliticize the issue of income inequality; even if it were only partly successful in this respect some of the potentially disruptive effects for democratic government might be avoided. Primarily, distributive justice is an ethical concept; and therefore it implies choice or political options; but partly it is a technical question of how chosen goals may be attained with the minimum of human cost. The skills of experts, black and white, need to be invoked here, as in the case of other problems which have an important technical dimension to them, aside from the question of choice. A good deal more work needs to be done on the political possibilities of income redistribution, bearing in mind the antithesis of liberty and equality, mentioned above. Utopian schemes or vast blueprints for the future should be avoided. Peter L. Berger has written:

'Social reality is hard, obstreperous, resistant to our wishes. Any situation of policy making should embrace as clear an awareness as possible of the likely limits this reality will set to the intended projects. In view of the postulated state of ignorance, it will be advisable to define these limits narrowly rather than broadly, thus possibly reducing the probability of failure. In other words, since we know so little it is wiser to act towards goals that are relatively proximate and therefore relatively calculable, than towards goals that are so broad and remote that all calculations break down.'[58]

A further issue to be explored is the possibility of power-sharing in industry and commerce. We raise this in the context of our personal conviction that the 'socialism versus capitalism' debate is a sterile one and that the dichotomy implied is false. No society describing itself as 'socialist' is at the same time a democracy, as we have employed the concept in this book; and no 'capitalist' society operates purely on market forces. There is surely a convergence emerging that transcends the simple dichotomy. Perhaps these are the simplistic views of non-economists, but the intention behind them is to urge that the ideological blinkers of dogmatic devotees of either system be set aside in the quest for a possible *via media.* Power-sharing in industry, it seems to us, may be part of such a *via media.* It would be congruent with the political principle proposed here, and it could further help to create nodes of interracial accommodation.

The invoking of experts is not a reflection of any undue reverence for technology; rather, it stems from a belief that experts can establish more readily than laymen the parameters of choice in policy options. In their fields they are inclined to be passionless and emotionless, and whatever other differences may divide them, they speak a common language. Although South Africa is sorely short of highly skilled technical blacks in practically every field, their numbers must increase, even under the present restraints; and when those restraints are abolished the increase will be more rapid. Interracial task forces of experts could address themselves to all the problems that confront South Africa, and their passionless, emotionless qualities could perhaps defuse hot issues into technical problems.

The discussion of safeguards has strayed far into a consideration of issues that are associated with any attempt to provide constitutional protection of civil liberties. Certain fundamental issues remain: should the constitution be rigid or flexible? and should formal safeguards for groups be further incorporated into the political process and the amendment procedure?

To the first question the answer should be a qualified 'rigid', and the qualification serves to remind us of Salmond's warning that a constitution that will not bend will sooner or later break. Amendments of the constitution should require maximal consensus among regional assemblies and the federal parliament; but by the same token it should not be impossibly difficult, so that provisions of the constitution that are shown to be anomalous or unworkable can be changed. Attention should be paid to the provision of the Belgian constitution (Article 3b) which provides, in effect, that legislation affecting relations between the linguistic groups requires the support of a majority of the members of both groups in parliament and an overall two-thirds of the total parliamentary vote. No less relevant are the provisions of the new Nigerian constitution (see pp. 47–8).

PROPORTIONALITY

Desegregating the civil service, police force, and the armed services will prove to be a major issue. As far as possible, these institutions must be insulated from political interference and they must not be allowed to become assimilated into the political resources of any group or party, or used as avenues for the sponsored advancement of its members. At the same time it must be recognized that they represent massive focal points of racial privilege in South Africa (to say nothing of their change-resistant qualities). The most equitable principle, as part of the proposed redistributive measures, is that of proportionality – as far as possible members of each politically salient group should be employed at each level proportionately to the size of the group in relation to the others. Smock and Smock write:

'The introduction of some kind of an ethnic quota system in recruitment to government could serve both as a conflict-settling device and as an integrative mechanism. By enabling each ethnic group to have more equitable opportunity to benefit from government employment, such an ethnic quota system would remove a serious source of intergroup envy and hostility. Moreover, by bringing into regular relationship within the civil service, large numbers of persons from diverse ethnic backgrounds, an important integrative end can be served.'[59]

Recommendations such as these will be anathema to those raised in strictly meritocratic traditions. But merit alone, however desirable a principle it is, has to be balanced against other desirable principles, even if the price is a temporary decline in efficiency. The quota would not necessarily have to be a rigid one requiring something like the Population Registration Act for its application. Observance ought ideally to be carried out carefully and discreetly by bodies of unimpeachable integrity, insulated from manipulation by politicians seeking to distribute patronage. Again, if prior agreement could be reached on the proportionality principle, it could be taken out of the political arena and relegated to be more or less routinely monitored.

The police and the armed services pose an additional set of problems, because they are the state's coercive agencies and can intervene directly in political matters. Ideally, the coercive agencies ought to be insulated from society's conflicts, but this is difficult to achieve. In a federation it is possible to decentralize police forces so that one has local-authority-controlled, regionally controlled, and federally controlled forces, something after the American pattern. The question of the armed services is more difficult. Fundamentally they can be kept out of direct political involvement only to the extent that they are imbued with respect for the principle of their subordination to the civilian government. Unfortunately these principles are easily forsaken, as the number of military coups in Africa by Sandhurst-trained men suggests.

It may be possible so to structure the armed services that in time of peace they are decentralized, even fragmented, and therefore not easily capable of mobilization for domestic political purposes, such as a coup. Hopefully, South Africa's standing army might need to be only small, spending a good deal of its energies on peaceful activities of development. It may also be that an effectively integrated army, as the Israeli army is said to be, could establish bonds of common interest among its diverse members.

To a considerable extent the armed services' behaviour will depend on the kind of threats posed to a democratic South Africa: will the threats serve to unify or intensify the divisions of the society? The answers can only be speculative.

THE POLITICS OF TRANSITION

Our analysis has focused on the roots of South Africa's conflict and on an alternative structure that could reduce the conflict and enable it to be peacefully and creatively regulated. We are conscious of our vulnerability to the criticism that we have paid insufficient attention to the question of transition, of how one gets away from the status quo and moves into an era of racial equality and democracy. If we believed that such a transition were impossible, then obviously we would not have written this book. We have assumed that when the costs – material, physical, and moral – of maintaining white domination increase to an unacceptably high point, most whites will want to, or could be persuaded to, move away from it, provided they could be reassured that such a move would not inevitably lead to their own domination or would not entail massive disruption and instability for South Africa.

It is not possible for us to specify in advance what particular forces or events might be the catalyst of change; nor can we rule out the possibility that the obduracy of the white leadership will blind them to the need for negotiating real change. As the costs of maintaining white domination mount, the more white resources will be eroded, and the less their bargaining power will become. Conversely, the more black political resources are mobilized, the greater black bargaining power will become. Imponderables such as these would have a vital effect on the course which transition politics might follow, on what kind of institutional vehicles might be used, and on what kind of a dispensation we would end up with.

For many advocates of change a national convention of representatives of all identifiable, salient political groupings in South Africa is the optimal forum for deliberating on a new political framework. There is a precedent for this (albeit racially restricted) in our history, and a number of significant black and opposition white groups favour it strongly. We agree with this proposal, which flows logically from our recommendation for a jointly negotiated settlement. We believe that if a constitution is to bring about co-operation between groups then groups should co-operate in bringing about the constitution.

Three issues will be raised immediately by critics of the idea. Who is to be invited to the convention and on what criteria? Would there be any hope of reaching agreement, in view of the wide ideological differences? In what relation would the government stand to the convention? These issues have formed the substance of Nationalist opposition to the idea.

Representatives of *all* significant political groupings must be enabled to attend the convention if it is to have any chance of reaching a durable accommodation. This implies that leaders of banned organizations may be included, subject to their commitment to negotiating, rather than fighting, for an accommodation. It would make little sense for organizations to have representatives negotiating peacefully while the same organizations are simultaneously engaged in guerrilla warfare. We are fully aware of the danger that racial polarization may go so far that a liberation movement may spurn the idea of negotiation and seek to achieve its aims by violence, as the Patriotic Front in Zimbabwe-Rhodesia is doing. This possibility underlines the urgency of starting real negotiation sooner rather than later.

We doubt that there would be much of a problem in identifying who the significant political groupings are. It may be that an election could be held and its results would show with reasonable accuracy what configuration of political groupings exists among blacks and what their respective influences are. The disadvantage of this method would be that an election might aggravate an already tense situation and spill over into widespread unrest. It would be preferable to avoid this possibility and adopt an entirely different method by creating a judicial commission charged with the task of identifying the salient organizations that deserved representation. In principle such a commission would be not unlike the Pearce Commission, which investigated African attitudes to a possible settlement in Rhodesia in 1972 and produced what was widely considered to be a pretty accurate profile of African opinion. In terms of our proposals such a commission would have to consist of people whose integrity was acknowledged across a wide spectrum of opinion.

In answer to the second question, whether a convention could reach agreement, a short response might be that the only possible way to find out would be to hold the convention and see what happens. Obviously there will be wide differences: if there weren't there would be no need to have a convention in the first place. The object of negotiation is precisely to try and bridge differences by bargaining, compromise and trade-offs. Moreover, attempting to reach an accommodation in the sequestered environment of a convention, whose proceedings are confidential (at least for its duration), would be very different from trying to do so in the glare of publicity, with the pressure for maintaining postures that this creates. It is a well-known fact that the private qualities and capacities of individual politicians are often very different from the apparent qualities that their public postures convey. We emphasize a point made already: the very process of negotiating together can be a learning experience. 'Personal chemistry', as it has been called, can significantly reduce the distance between even bitter adversaries. (This phenomenon, incidentally, seems to have been an important factor in the negotiations between Begin and Sadat that resulted in the Israeli–Egyptian peace treaty in 1978.)

We are assuming, moreover, that self-interest will lead the parties or groups to negotiate with, rather than confront, one another. The advantages to be derived from a negotiated accommodation, compared with the costs of heightened polarization and uncontrollable conflict, are self-evident. We do not say that they will be a solvent of differences; but at the very least they can serve as a vitally important lubricant and inducement.

A final consideration in relation to this question: let us assume the worst: negotiations break down, the convention grinds to a halt and is disbanded. Undoubtedly this would be a serious and tragic development, but would the participants in the abortive exercise be any worse off than they were before their agreeing to try negotiation? We cannot see any way in which they would. In fact in some circumstances they might find themselves marginally advantaged by having shown some preparedness to reach an accommodation by peaceful means. Let us, for purposes of the argument, assume a hypothetical situation in which black intransigence causes whites to break off negotiations. The whites' position will be parlous because it will have been demonstrated that black alienation is so great as to make negotiation impossible, but at least they will have shown to a hostile and sceptical world that they were prepared to try and negotiate.

It is most unlikely that any group of people, let alone a convention of the kind we envisage, would be able to reach absolute and total identity of opinion on issues that they are tackling. The consensus which we hope would be reached by a convention does not presuppose this illusory goal. All that consensus implies in this context is a general agreement to co-operate within a framework that establishes procedures and norms for the peaceful arbitration of conflict.

In response to the third question, concerning the relationship of a convention to the government, we repeat that the convention is not a sovereign or law-making body. It stands in an advisory relationship to the government, and it is only the government that can accept the convention's recommendations and enact them into a new constitution. The kind of convention we envisage would be a lengthy, wide-ranging process, and it could take eighteen months or two years to complete its task. As we have emphasized, it will be the duty of the government to do all in its power to create favourable conditions for the convention. It need not wait for the conclusion of the convention's proceedings to abolish or relax discriminatory measures or to tackle problems like housing shortages and poverty. Tangible gestures such as these can do a great deal to create an auspicious climate for negotiation. Moreover if the government could, in this transition period, break the back of organized resistance to the abolition of racial discrimination, it would greatly ease the load and strain which the government under the new dispensation would have to bear.

Our argument throughout this analysis derives from our conviction that the advantages of negotiation greatly exceed the costs of confrontation. We have appealed to the self-interest motives of the antagonists, although we do not dismiss considerations of ethics and justice. What precisely do 'costs' and 'advantages' mean in this context? Prima facie it would seem in the South African context that a negotiated settlement between whites and blacks could lead only to substantial gains by blacks at the expense of whites. If the *sine qua non* of a settlement is the abolition of race discrimination not only in a statutory sense but also effectively in everyday life, then one of two processes can be initiated: either a deliberate planned programme of reducing white standards of living and increasing black standards of living, or stimulating the economy to such an extent that black living standards rise rapidly without undue decrease in white standards of living. Obviously the latter process is the preferable one but whichever one is followed whites cannot possibly hope to enjoy the structured privilege of the past. A leading Nationalist academic and member of the Broederbond, Professor Sampie Terreblanche, has recently made the following remarks:

'Our standard of living is too high. The unavoidable structural changes that we will have to bring about will carry the consequence that in real terms the whites' standard of living will have to be scaled down.'[60]

This prospect must be faced squarely. We would point out, however, that the perpetuation of domination is likely to have an even more catastrophic effect on white (to say nothing of black) living standards. Already the costs of defence and fuel have perceptibly lowered living standards, and the downward spiral is likely to continue, with the serious prospect of far tougher economic sanctions being applied to South Africa.

Any argument, then, that whites would suffer economically through the dismantling of racial discrimination has to be placed in this wider perspective, and our conclusion is that in material terms their losses would be relatively small in comparison with the losses that isolation and the garrison-state situation would bring.

The abolition of racial privilege would bring *moral* advantages to the whites of great proportions: their pariah-status in the modern world would be overcome; the guilt that some, perhaps many, feel about being the beneficiaries of discrimination could be eliminated; but above all the tensions and neuroses of life in a siege-culture, with its increasingly hostile and aggressive subject population, could be ameliorated. The effects of racial discrimination on its victims have been widely examined; but less frequently explored are its corrosive and debilitating effects on those who practise it. To view life through a racially refracted prism is to be blinkered.

These considerations may be nebulous and difficult to convey in the clinical language of the social sciences, but they are real nevertheless. The abolition of racial discrimination throughout the American South in the 1960s produced a great surge of release and relief among both white and black. If it could be achieved in an orderly and controlled way there are good grounds for hoping that its effects in South Africa would be comparable. There is, moreover, the exciting prospect of unleashing the full creative potential of the society in all its spheres.

9 *In conclusion*

It is inevitable that when one reaches this stage in an analysis one begins to think of issues and factors that may have been underemphasized or ignored, of possible misunderstandings that may arise or possible criticisms that may be levelled at the work from various ideological or analytical perspectives. Every analysis of South Africa, whether it be social, economic, political or all three, ends up with its agenda of unfinished business. So it is with this book as well. However, we would like to conclude by referring briefly to some of the issues on our agenda of unfinished business in the hope that this might anticipate and obviate unnecessary criticism and stimulate more constructive debate.

(1) *The problem of evolutionary change*

Anyone who claims that 'white politics is irrelevant in South Africa' neither cares for, nor understands the problem of evolutionary change towards a more democratic alternative. By evolutionary change we do not necessarily mean a smooth, peaceful transition to a new dispensation. We do not exclude conflict, tension and even sporadic violence. What we do most emphatically mean, however, is that whatever constitutional change occurs, or whatever a new democratic South Africa is going to look like, it will come about through the active participation and volition of those who govern in the existing undemocratic dispensation. If this is seen as not possible, then evolutionary change in South Africa is not possible. For us this is a fundamental analytical point of departure in looking at the South African situation and failure to be clear on it has obscured many analyses of South Africa. Once one accepts or rejects evolutionary change as a possibility for South Africa a value-added or periscopal logic is introduced into one's analysis.

For example if one accepts, as we do, the possibility of evolutionary change, then one has to try and identify the factors in the present South African situation which could under certain circumstances contribute to such change; whereas someone committed to, or interested in, revolutionary change of some sort would obviously have to identify factors in the situation with that in mind. But not only is there a selective emphasis in one's analyses, certain options are excluded as well and certain phrases have different meanings, depending on which point of departure one adopts.

For example, a simplistic one-man-one-vote majority-rule political programme appears to us not to be capable of implementation in an evolutionary way in South Africa. We do not say this approvingly but as a result of our understanding of the present political situation. For it to be possible, those who govern must voluntarily hand over sovereignty to a new constitution in which the likelihood is great that they will not participate in government. This seems to us extremely unlikely in the South African situation. A further example concerns the phrase 'redistribution of wealth'. Revolutionary and evolutionary agendas give entirely different meanings to this phrase. In the one case, the existing structure of economic life has to be destroyed; in the other, existing institutions and organizations have to be used and changed and new ones created to bring about redistribution.

We make this point about the problem of evolutionary change to prevent the debate from proceeding at cross-purposes. It is quite likely that those committed to revolutionary change will dismiss our analysis with a few standard ideological epithets. It is possible, however, to enter into the debate 'for the purpose of argument', as it were, and criticize our analysis in terms of its own assumptions, and this we would welcome.

(2) *Ethnicity, culture and race once again*

One of the persistent criticisms against the approach to conflict resolution that we have adopted here is that it overemphasizes the cultural or ethnic dimension; that in doing so it tends to ignore or underplay the importance of the 'structural' or 'real' factors of conflict in South African society. In fact there are those who argue with a great deal of conviction that to use concepts such as race, ethnicity or culture in analyzing the situation is to indulge in 'mystification'.

We want to make it quite clear that we do not deny or ignore the structural or underlying factors of conflict in society. Thus we have defined the nature of the conflict as structural inequality of wealth, status, and power. But we must insist that in a racially divided or plural society there is a very strong tendency to articulate the structural inequalities in racial or ethnic terms and South Africa is no exception in this respect.

Because this is so, an additional factor enters into conflict resolution which simply cannot be ignored and that is the question of 'deracializing' or detribalizing the conflict potential in our society. It does not help to argue that those who believe in a nationalist, ethnic or racial ideology simply labour under a 'false consciousness'. If that consciousness is the prevailing ideology of a significant section of the population then it vitally shapes and influences the conflict itself. That is why the problem of racial domination in South Africa, whether by white or black, has such an all-or-nothing character to it. We deplore and abhor racial mobilization for the purposes of achieving political ends, but sadly we have come to the conclusion that its occurrence cannot be ignored when considering ways and means of promoting evolutionary change in South Africa.

(3) *The problem of economics*

There are those who argue that the problem in South Africa is fundamentally an economic one, a struggle between the haves and the have-nots, and that this is brought about by the particular mode of production operative in South Africa. Consequently an approach such as ours completely misses the point and is essentially irrelevant.

Again we must respond by saying that we do not deny the fundamental importance of the economic problem, but in the political arena the problem is seldom articulated purely in economic terms or in terms of the interests of a particular economic class.

As Chaliand (a Marxist analyst) observes, in the third world there is a great deal of socialist rhetoric but very little socialism![1] One reason for this, he claims, is that for many countries the major preoccupation with liberation during 'decolonization' is with political rather than economic liberalization.[2] Where in Africa has the liberation struggle been only a class struggle? Again, we would like to suggest that one of the important reasons is that with the process of decolonization factors such as race and ethnicity become involved in the problem.

South Africa is no exception in this respect, although, as we have pointed out, colonial withdrawal is not an available option for conflict resolution. Precisely because this is so it would seem that the problem of political liberation will remain the paramount one. To say this is not to force a false dichotomy between economics and politics. On the contrary there has been a common assumption in many African states that the acquisition of political power for its own sake will 'automatically' resolve economic problems. Nor do we deny that the economic problem will have to be faced. Our main preoccupation throughout has been to explore the possibilities of an alternative democratic dispensation in which the political problems can be resolved – problems of access, distribution and use of power – so that economic problems can be identified and rendered bargainable. If this cannot be done we are very much afraid that South Africa is doomed to attain its own version of political liberation without solving or coming to grips with the economic problem. It will not be the first time that a liberation movement, with every good intention, uses socialistic rhetoric to justify its action, and yet the society ends up with a new ruling class just as reactionary as the one it has eliminated. After all, a petit bourgeois is a petit bourgeois whether he is white or black.

(4) *Why not partition?*

Lately, and of course from a vastly different ideological perspective from the one alluded to above, there has been a renewal of interest in partition as a solution to the conflict in South Africa.[3] The most radical and equitable suggestion in this respect comes from Blenck and Van der Ropp. It is almost of the 'we-cut-the-cake-and-you-choose' variety, which is morally quite defensible provided all concerned want it. Most other forms of partition are suggested unilaterally and less equitably,[4] that is, they are a variation on the present policy, which is essentially a policy of inequitable partition.

Rather than go into the merits or demerits of various partition schemes we offer a few general comments on the principle:

(a) It is conceivable that partition may be a last-resort option in a no-win situation, but quite likely the line will be drawn where the battle has ended and not where it has been thought out in morally and intellectually defensible terms in some scholar's study.

(b) Radical partition on an equitable basis as a party-political programme in white politics has a very poor chance indeed. To put it graphically it all depends which geographic half of the white electorate you wish to alienate completely. The present government has had great difficulty in consolidating land in terms of the Bantu Trust and Land Act of 1936 and has now caused a great deal of uncertainty by appointing a commission of inquiry into consolidating the homelands beyond the limits of the 1936 Act if this is absolutely necessary. Land is a major political hot potato in South Africa and it seems highly unlikely that the problem will be solved by simply partitioning it even if it is suggested that it be done equitably.

(c) No inequitable form of partition done unilaterally by whites has any chance of resolving conflict. Further comment is superfluous if one keeps the history and record of white domination in South Africa in mind. In any case partition as such has very low support among blacks in South Africa.

(5) *Social control and change*

During any period of major planned social change in a society the issue of control is of crucial significance. It would be naive in the extreme to assume that in South Africa an entrenched bill of rights will suffice to maintain control and stability during a period of transition. In a perceptive and disturbing paper A.S. Mathews formulates the problem as follows:[5] 'What kind of security programme will be needed to ensure that change follows a peaceful course without too much social dislocation?' This question is posed against the background of a prevailing security situation where

'The idea that the law may be used to secure justice *between* racial groups as well as *for* them, that the function of the legal system is in part to strike an equitable balance between competing interests, has been undermined by the vast programme of repressive legislation during the past thirty years. One of the truly stupid features of South African internal security policy is its tendency to destroy belief in, and support for, some of the better features of our inherited political and social tradition.'

In a nutshell then the problem of social control and change in South Africa is the following: for evolutionary change to take place in an orderly fashion, strict but fair security measures must obtain, respect for the law and its impartiality must be fairly pervasive and the legal system must not be seen as one of the instruments of domination and subjection. One thing is patently obvious and that is that there will have to be an extensive and intensive review of existing security measures as a first step towards such a goal. Essentially we agree fully with Mathews when he says:

'Security can only be enhanced by the inclusion in the bodies responsible for it of responsible and independent men of the presently excluded groups. If security is not made the common concern of all it will never be lasting and effective.'

A democratic South Africa: is it possible? Yes, we believe it is, even though nowhere in the modern world can it be conclusively shown that the problem of race has been 'solved'. Perhaps for the next few hundred years race will be one of the world's great problems. Our problems are common to a large number of the world's states, and our attempts to find a modus vivendi for diverse peoples will attract continuing attention. If we could establish a durable and democratic accommodation, it would not only be one of the major feats of political engineering in the modern world, it would also stand as a beacon to numerous other societies that are wracked by racial and ethnic conflict.

Max Weber once wrote: 'All human experience confirms the truth – that man would not have attained the possible unless time and again he had reached out for the impossible.' It may be that politics in South Africa will be the art of the impossible. Is this not a challenge worth accepting?

Notes

1. INTRODUCTION: SOME OPTIONS FOR POLITICAL DEVELOPMENT IN SOUTHERN AFRICA (pages 1–9)

1. Heribert Adam, 'When the Chips are Down: Confrontation and Accommodation in South Africa', *Contemporary Crises* 1, 1977, pp. 417–35.
2. André du Toit, 'Different Models of Strategy and Procedure for Change in South Africa', unpublished paper delivered at a workshop on *Socio-economic and Constitutional Alternatives for South Africa*, 24–5 August 1978, Rhodes University, p. 2.
3. Du Toit, p. 4.
4. Du Toit, p. 2.
5. This is very clearly shown in research done by the Arnold Bergstraesser Institute and published under the authorship of Theo Hanf, Gerda Vierdag and Heribert Weiland in *Süd-Afrika: Friedlicher Wandel?* (Kaiser Grünewald, Munich 1978).

2. THE NATURE OF THE CONFLICT (pages 10–30)

1. Donald L. Noel (ed.), *The Origins of American Slavery and Racism*, pp. 106–27.
2. Winthrop D. Jordan, *White over Black: American Attitudes toward the Negro 1550–1812*, p. 20.
3. Roger Bastide, 'Color, Racism, and Christianity' in John Hope Franklin (ed.), *Color and Race*, p. 42.
4. Hiroshi Wagatsuma, 'The Social Perception of Skin Color in Japan', in Franklin, p. 129.
5. Bernard Lewis, *Race and Color in Islam*, pp. 14–28.
6. Philip Mason, *Patterns of Dominance*, p. 31.
7. Donald L. Horowitz, 'Three Dimensions of Ethnic Politics', *World Politics* 23, 1971, pp. 232–42.
8. Hubert M. Blalock, *Toward a Theory of Minority-Group Relations*, pp. 199–203.
9. John C. Leggett, *Class, Race and Labor – Working Class Consciousness in Detroit*, pp. 14, 18–19.
10. J.F.C. Harrison, *The Early Victorians 1832–51*, p. 45.
11. Asa Briggs, 'The Language of "Class" in Early Nineteenth Century England', in M.W. Flinn & T.C. Smout (eds.), *Essays in Social History*, p. 157.
12. Léon Poliakov, *The Aryan Myth – A History of Racist and Nationalist Ideas in Europe*, p. 32.
13. John Rex, *Race Relations in Sociological Theory*, p. 36.

14. Percy Cohen, 'Race Relations as a Sociological Issue', in Gordon Bowker & John Carrier (eds.), *Race and Ethnic Relations: Sociological Readings,* pp. 13–14.
15. Leo Kuper, *Race, Class and Power,* p. 224.
16. Frederick A. Johnstone, *Class, Race and Gold – A Study of Class Relations and Racial Discrimination in South Africa,* p. 2.
17. Johnstone, p. 50.
18. Johnstone, pp. 74–5.
19. H.J. & R.E. Simons, *Class and Colour in South Africa 1850–1950,* p. 37.
20. Katharine West, 'Stratification and Ethnicity in "Plural" New States', *Race* XIII, 1972, p. 495.
21. Johnstone, p. 208.
22. Johnstone, p. 64.
23. Franz Neumann, *The Democratic and the Authoritarian State – Essays in Political and Legal Theory,* p. 268.
24. Simons & Simons, p. 618.
25. Simons & Simons, p. 618.
26. John Stone, 'Race Relations and the Sociological Tradition', in John Stone (ed.), *Race, Ethnicity and Social Change,* p. 64.
27. Frederick C. Barghoorn, 'Soviet Dissenters on Soviet Nationality Policy', in Wendell Bell & Walter E. Freeman (eds.), *Ethnicity and Nation-Building: Comparative, International and Historical Perspectives,* pp. 117–33; Gary K. Bertsch, 'Ethnicity and Politics in Socialist Yugoslavia', *Annals of the American Academy of Political and Social Science,* Sept. 1977, pp. 88–99; June Teufel Dreyer, *China's Forty Millions – Minority Nationalities and National Integration in the People's Republic of China,* pp. 261–2.
28. Frank Parkin, *Class Inequality and Political Order,* pp. 36–7.
29. Walker Connor, 'Eco- or Ethno-Nationalism?', paper delivered at the International Political Science Association Round Table, Oxford, March 1979, p. 15.
30. Ronald Hyam, *Britain's Imperial Century 1815–1914: A Study of Empire and Expansion,* p. 299.
31. David Welsh, 'The Politics of White Supremacy', in Leonard Thompson & Jeffrey Butler (eds.), *Change in Contemporary South Africa,* pp. 51–78.
32. R.A. Schermerhorn, *Comparative Ethnic Relations: A Framework for Theory and Research,* p. 68.
33. Blalock, chap. 4.
34. Robert H. Mast, 'Some Theoretical Considerations in International Race Relations', in Bell & Freeman, p. 64.
35. Herbert Blumer, 'Race Prejudice as a Sense of Group Position', in *Pacific Sociological Review* 1, 1958, p. 4.
36. Blalock, p. 114.
37. Donald G. Baker, 'Politics, Power and Race Relations', in Donald G. Baker (ed.), *Politics of Race,* p. 7.
38. Milton J. Esman, 'Communal Conflict in Southeast Asia', in Nathan Glazer & Daniel P. Moynihan (eds.), *Ethnicity: Theory and Experience,* p. 393.
39. Anatol Rapoport, *Conflict in Man-Made Environment,* p. 236.
40. Rapoport, p. 201.
41. Max Gluckman, 'The Bonds in the Colour Bar: South Africa', in Paul Baxter & Basil Sanson (eds.), *Race and Social Difference,* pp. 284–5.
42. Heribert Adam, *Modernizing Racial Domination: The Dynamics of South African Politics,* p. 175.

3. THE POLITICS OF DIVIDED SOCIETIES (pages 31–49)

1. Cited in Christopher Hewitt, 'Majorities and Minorities: A Comparative Survey of Ethnic Violence', *The Annals of the American Academy of Political and Social Science,* Sept. 1977, p. 151.

2. Walker Connor, 'The Politics of Ethnonationalism', *Journal of International Affairs* 27, 1973, p. 1.

3. Walker Connor, 'Nation-Building or Nation-Destroying?', *World Politics* 24, 1971–2, p. 32.

4. See, e.g., Dept. of Information, *Multi-National Development: The Reality* (Pretoria, 1974), ch. IX.

5. E.K. Francis, *Interethnic Relations,* pp. 73–4.

6. Walker Connor, 'National-Building or Nation-Destroying?', *passim.*

7. Alvin Rabushka & Kenneth A. Shepsle, *Politics in Plural Societies: A Theory of Democratic Instability,* pp. 91–2.

8. Harold Jackson, *The Two Irelands – A Dual Study of Intergroup Tensions,* p. 6.

9. Crawford Young, *The Politics of Cultural Pluralism,* p. 125.

10. James E. Blackwell, 'The Power Basis of Ethnic Conflict in American Society', in Lewis A. Coser & Otto N. Larsen (eds.), *The Uses of Controversy in Sociology,* pp. 179–80.

11. David Welsh, 'English-speaking Whites and the Racial Problem', in André de Villiers (ed.), *English-speaking South Africa Today,* pp. 217–39.

12. For a broadly comparable case study see Orlando Patterson, 'Context and Choice in Ethnic Allegiance: A Theoretical Framework and Caribbean Case Study' in Glazer & Moynihan (eds.), pp. 305–49.

13. Milton M. Gordon, *Assimilation in American Life.*

14. Robert Melson & Howard Wolpe, 'Modernization and the Politics of Communalism: A Theoretical Perspective', *American Political Science Review* LXIV, 1970, pp. 1113–14.

15. E.E. Mahant, 'The Strange Fate of a Liberal Democracy', *Round Table* 265, 1977, p. 78.

16. Mahant, p. 85.

17. Embert Hendrickson, 'New Directions for Republican Guyana', *World Today* 27, 1971, pp. 35–6.

18. Robert N. Kearney, *Communalism and Language in the Politics of Ceylon*; A.B. Mendis, 'Sri Lanka', *World Survey,* 89–90, 1976.

19. Paschalis M. Kitromilides & Theodore A. Couloumbis, 'Ethnic Conflict in a Strategic Area: The Case of Cyprus', in Abdul A. Said & Luis R. Simmons (eds.), *Ethnicity in an International Context,* p. 177.

20. Bruce Hutchinson, 'Canada's Time of Troubles', *Foreign Affairs* 56, 1977, pp. 175, 179.

21. Milton M. Gordon, 'Toward a General Theory of Racial and Ethnic Group Relations', in Glazer & Moynihan (eds.), p. 109.

22. Quoted in R.M. Burns (ed.), *One Country or Two?,* p. 1.

23. Arend Lijphart, 'Cultural Diversity and Theories of Political Integration', *Canadian Journal of Political Science* IV, 1971, p. 12.

24. Robert A. Dahl, *Polyarchy: Participation and Opposition,* pp. 117–18.

25. Gary K. Bertsch, 'Ethnicity and Politics in Socialist Yugoslavia', *The Annals of the American Academy of Political and Social Science,* Sept. 1977.

26. Nikolaos A. Stavrou, 'Ethnicity in Yugoslavia: Roots and Impact', in Said & Simmons (eds.), p. 143.

27. Bertsch, p. 94.

28. William S. Livingston, 'A Note on the Nature of Federalism', in Aaron Wildavsky (ed.), *American Federalism in Perspective,* p. 37.

29. Carl J. Friedrich, *Limited Government: A Comparison,* p. 11.

30. Harry Eckstein, 'Constitutional Engineering and the Problem of Viable Representative Government', in Harry Eckstein & David E. Apter (eds.), *Comparative Politics: A Reader,* p. 102.

31. S.A. de Smith, *The New Commonwealth and its Constitutions,* p. 129.

32. De Smith, pp. 107-9.

33. Quoted in De Smith, p. 110.

34. Jack Lively, *Democracy,* p. 87.

35. J.A. Laponce, *The Protection of Minorities,* pp. 63-4.

36. David M. Rayside, 'The Impact of the Linguistic Cleavage on the "Governing Parties" of Belgium and Canada', *Canadian Journal of Political Science* XI, 1978.

37. Alfred Latham-Koenig, 'Shadow of Marxism over Mauritius', *Round Table,* 266, 1977.

38. Donald L. Horowitz, 'Multiracial Politics in the New States: Toward a Theory of Conflict', in Robert C. Jackson & Michael B. Stein (eds.), *Issues in Comparative Politics,* pp. 172-76.

39. Cynthia H. Enloe, 'Police and Military in the Resolution of Ethnic Conflict', *The Annals of the American Academy of Political and Social Science,* Sept. 1977, p. 147.

40. Dov Ronen, 'Alternative Patterns of Integration in African States', *Journal of Modern African Studies* 14, 1976, p. 580.

41. For more detailed information on Sudan see John Howell, 'Politics in the Southern Sudan', *African Affairs* 72, 1973; Timothy C. Niblock, 'A New Political System in Sudan', *African Affairs* 73, 1974.

42. Mohamed Omer Beshir, *The Southern Sudan – From Conflict to Peace,* pp. 110-63.

43. *Financial Times,* London, 21 March 1978.

44. M.J. Dent, *Improving Nigeria's Draft Constitution.*

45. *West Africa,* 9 October 1978, p. 1983.

46. *West Africa,* 30 January 1978, p. 174.

4. THE POSSIBILITY OF DEMOCRATIC GOVERNMENT IN DIVIDED SOCIETIES (pages 50-76)

1. Robert N. Kearney, *The Politics of Ceylon (Sri Lanka),* p. 103.

2. Robert N. Kearney, *Communalism and Language in the Politics of Ceylon,* p. 140.

3. Alfred Latham-Koenig, 'Shadow of Marxism over Mauritius', *Round Table* 266, 1977, p. 178.

4. Christopher Bagley, *The Dutch Plural Society,* pp. 115-27, 233-4.

5. E.E. Mahant, 'The Strange Fate of a Liberal Democracy', *Round Table* 265, 1977, pp. 86-8.

6. Mahant, p. 85.

7. Young, pp. 516–17.
8. William T. Bluhm, *Building an Austrian Nation: The Political Integration of a Western State,* pp. 24, 26.
9. Bluhm, pp. 1–5.
10. Alfred Diamant, 'Austria: The Three Lager and the First Republic', in Kenneth McRae (ed.), *Consociational Democracy: Political Accommodation in Segmented Societies,* p. 155.
11. Peter Pulzer, 'Austria: The Legitimizing Role of Political Parties', in McRae, p. 168.
12. G. Bingham Powell, Jun., *Social Fragmentation and Political Hostility – An Austrian Case Study,* p. 10.
13. Val R. Lorwin, 'Belgium: Religion, Class and Language in National Politics', in Robert A. Dahl (ed.), *Political Oppositions in Western Democracies.*
14. Kenneth D. McRae, 'Introduction', in McRae, pp. 20–1.
15. Arend Lijphart, *The Politics of Accommodation: Pluralism and Democracy in the Netherlands,* p. 17.
16. Lijphart, *Politics of Accommodation,* p. 23.
17. Lijphart, *Politics of Accommodation,* pp. 18, 33, 78, 58.
18. Lijphart, *Politics of Accommodation,* p. 109.
19. Jürg Steiner, *Amicable Agreement Versus Majority Rule: Conflict Resolution in Switzerland,* p. 58.
20. G.A. Codding, Jun., *The Federal Government of Switzerland,* pp. 8–12.
21. R.L. Watts, 'The Survival or Disintegration of Federations', in R.M. Burns (ed.), p. 43; T. Rennie Warburton, 'Nationalism and Language in Switzerland and Canada:, in Anthony D. Smith (ed.), *Nationalist Movements,* p. 96.
22. Francis, p. 107.
23. Kenneth D. McRae, *Switzerland – Example of Cultural Coexistence,* pp. 33–4.
24. Warburton, pp. 99–100.
25. Donald Eugene Smith, *Religion and Political Development,* p. 136.
26. Kurt Mayer, 'Cultural Pluralism and Linguistic Equilibrium in Switzerland', in Pierre van den Berghe (ed.), *Intergroup Relations – Sociological Perspectives,* p. 80.
27. Bluhm, p. 65.
28. Bluhm, pp. 54, 62.
29. Lorwin, 'Belgium . . .', p. 150.
30. Martin O. Heisler, 'Managing Ethnic Conflict in Belgium', *The Annals of the American Academy of Political and Social Science,* Sept. 1977, p. 36.
31. Heisler, p. 37.
32. Lijphart, *Politics of Accommodation,* p. 204.
33. Lijphart, *Politics of Accommodation,* p. 111.
34. Heisler, p. 34.
35. Eric A. Nordlinger, *Conflict Regulation in Divided Societies,* p. 45.
36. Arthur A. Stein, 'Conflict and Cohesion – A Review of the Literature', *Journal of Conflict Resolution* XX, 1976, p. 165.
37. Nordlinger, pp. 42–53.
38. Bluhm, p. 70.
39. Bluhm, pp. 69, 73; McRae, 'Introduction', in McRae (ed.), *Consociational Democracy,* p. 18.
40. Lijphart, *Politics of Accommodation,* pp. 131–2.

41. Lijphart, *Politics of Accommodation,* p. 125.
42. Steiner, pp. 35–6.
43. Steiner, p. 6.
44. K. Rimanque, 'Devolution in Cultural Affairs in Belgium', in Harry Calvert (ed.), *Devolution,* pp. 149–54.
45. Ilhan Arsel, 'Belgium', in Albert P. Blaustein & Gisbert H. Flanz (eds.), *Constitutions of the Countries of the World.*
46. Nordlinger, pp. 26–7.
47. Lijphart, *Politics of Accommodation,* pp. 129, 113–15.
48. Lijphart, *Politics of Accommodation,* pp. 143, 116.
49. Nordlinger, p. 40.
50. For an analysis of variations in strength on this dimension see Val R. Lorwin, 'Segmented Pluralism: Ideological Cleavages and Political Cohesion in the Smaller European Democracies', in McRae (ed.), *Consociational Democracy.*
51. Lijphart, 'Cultural Diversity and Theories of Political Integration', *Canadian Journal of Political Science* IV, 1971, p. 11.
52. Brian Barry, 'Review Article: Political Accommodation and Consociational Democracy', *British Journal of Political Science* 3, 1977, pp. 481–7.
53. Lijphart, 'Review Article: The Northern Ireland Problem; Cases, Theories and Solutions', *British Journal of Political Science* 5, 1976, pp. 99–101.
54. S.E. Finer (ed.), *Adversary Politics and Electoral Reform.*
55. Lijphart, 'Review Article', p. 101.
56. Lijphart, 'Consociational Democracy', in McRae (ed.), *Consociational Democracy,* p. 84.
57. Barry, 'Review Article'.
58. Bluhm, p. 80.
59. Young, p. 326.
60. Steiner, p. 67.
61. Lijphart, *Politics of Accommodation,* p. 205.
62. Nordlinger, pp. 93–102.
63. Hans Daalder, 'On Building Consociational Nations: The Cases of the Netherlands and Switzerland', *International Social Science Journal* 23, 1971, pp. 367–8.
64. Daalder, 'The Consociational Democracy Theme', *World Politics* 26, 1974, p. 618.
65. Lijphart, *Politics of Accommodation,* p. 202.
66. Karl von Vorys, *Democracy without Consensus – Communalism and Political Stability in Malaysia,* pp. 28–9.
67. Milton J. Esman, 'Malaysia: Communal Coexistence and Mutual Deterrence', in Ernest Q. Campbell (ed.), *Racial Tensions and National Identity,* p. 229.
68. Esman, 'Communal Conflict in Southeast Asia', in Glazer & Moynihan (eds.), pp. 404–5.
69. Von Vorys, p. 133.
70. 'Malaysia's Linguistic Maze', *Race Today,* Jan. 1972, p. 21.
71. *Guardian,* London, 29 March 1979.
72. Michael Leifer, 'Malaysia after Tun Razak', *Round Table* 276, 1976, pp. 154–5.
73. Von Vorys, pp. 394, 416–17; Stuart Drummond, 'Towards a New Order in Malaysia?', *World Politics* 29, 1973, p. 440.
74. Esman, 'Malaysia', in Campbell (ed.), pp. 238–9.

75. *Times,* London, 30 Sept. 1965.
76. *Guardian,* London, 14 Aug. 1965.
77. Quoted in R.S. Milne, ' "The Pacific Way" – Consociational Politics in Fiji', *Pacific Affairs* 48, 1975, p. 420.
78. *Times,* London, 21 April 1970; *Financial Times,* London, 6 May 1970 and 7 Oct. 1970.
79. *Financial Times,* London, 14 Sept. 1977; *Guardian,* London, 26 Sept. 1977; *Daily Telegraph,* London, 27 Sept. 1977.
80. Michael C. Hudson, *The Precarious Republic – Political Modernization in Lebanon,* pp. 23, 42–4.
81. David R. Smock & Audrey C. Smock, *The Politics of Pluralism – A Comparative Study of Lebanon and Ghana,* pp. 114–15.
82. Richard Hrair Dekmejian, 'Consociational Democracy in Crisis: The Case of Lebanon', *Comparative Politics* 10, 1978, pp. 254–5.
83. Smock & Smock, pp. 153–4.
84. Dekmejian, p. 259.
85. Frank Stoakes, 'The Civil War in Lebanon', *World Today* 32, 1976, p. 8.
86. De Smith, *Constitutional and Administrative Law,* pp. 26–7.
87. Stanley Kyriakides, *Cyprus: Constitutionalism and Crisis Government,* pp. 57–63, 66–7, 69, 71.
88. De Smith, *Constitutional and Administrative Law,* p. 26.
89. Paschalis M. Kitromilides & Theodore A. Coloumbis, 'Ethnic Conflict in a Strategic Area: The Case of Cyprus', in Said & Simmons (eds.), p. 173.
90. Kyriakides, p. 76.
91. Smock & Smock, p. 166.
92. Bagley, p. 121.
93. Bagley, p. 234.
94. Nordlinger, p. 35.
95. Smock & Smock, p. 318.
96. Smock & Smock, p. 18.
97. Smock & Smock, p. 270.

5. THE EVOLUTION OF SOUTH AFRICA'S CONSTITUTIONAL AND POLITICAL STRUCTURE (pages 77–89)

1. James Bryce, *Impressions of South Africa* (third ed.), p. 469.
2. Edgar Walton, *The Inner History of the National Convention of South Africa,* p. 55.
3. Walton, p. 59.
4. R.H. Brand, *The Union of South Africa,* p. 130.
5. Brand, p. 74.
6. Brand, p. 72.
7. David Welsh, 'The Politics of White Supremacy', in Leonard Thompson & Jeffrey Butler (eds.), *Change in Contemporary South Africa.*
8. P.J. Cillié, *Konstitusionele Verandering in Suid-Afrika (2),* p. 5.
9. L.M. Thompson, *The Cape Coloured Franchise,* p. 55.
10. B. Beinart, 'The South African Appeal Court and Judicial Review', *Modern Law Review* 21, 1958, p. 600.
11. W.H.B. Dean, 'The Judiciary', in Anthony de Crespigny & Robert Schrire (eds.), *The Government and Politics of South Africa,* p. 40.

12. Alexander Brady, *Democracy in the Dominions* (third ed.), p. 374.
13. A.J. Milnor, *Elections and Political Stability,* pp. 25–6.
14. W.H.B. Dean, *The Riots and the Constitution in 1976,* p. 15.
15. Kenneth A. Heard, *General Elections in South Africa 1943–1970,* p. 236.
16. W.B. Vosloo & R.A. Schrire, 'Subordinate Political Institutions', in De Crespigny & Schrire (eds.), pp. 77–80.
17. Vosloo & Schrire, p. 84.
18. A.N. Pelzer (ed.), *Verwoerd Speaks,* p. 127.
19. C.J.R. Dugard, *The Judicial Process, Positivism and Civil Liberty,* p. 7.
20. A.S. Mathews, 'Judicial Activism and Internal Security', in J. Midgley, J.H. Steyn & R. Graser (eds.), *Crime and Punishment in South Africa,* p. 180.
21. Dean, 'The Judiciary', p. 36.

6. POSSIBILITIES FOR A DEMOCRATIC SOUTH AFRICA
(pages 90–119)

1. Cf. *Report of the Spro-cas Political Commission: South Africa's Political Alternatives* (Johannesburg, 1973), pp. 48–50.
2. Leo Kuper, 'Political Change in White Settler Societies: The Possibility of Peaceful Democratization', in Leo Kuper & M.G. Smith (eds.), *Pluralism in Africa,* p. 169.
3. Cited in S.A. Institute of Race Relations, *A Survey of Race Relations in South Africa 1977,* p. 51.
4. For a possible scenario see R.W. Johnson, *How Long will South Africa Survive?* esp. pp. 320–7; on the possibility of sanctions see Clyde Ferguson & William R. Cotter, 'South Africa: What is to be done', in *Foreign Affairs* 56, 1978.
5. Lewis Coser, *The Functions of Social Conflict,* p. 135.
6. Anthony Oberschall, *Social Conflict and Social Movements,* p. 262.
7. *Survey of Race Relations 1977,* p. 51.
8. *House of Assembly Debates* (cited afterwards as *H.A.D.*), 7 Feb. 1978, col. 579.
9. *Survey of Race Relations 1977,* p. 337.
10. W.M. Macmillan, *Complex South Africa,* p. 120.
11. For an incisive overview of political differences among Africans see Lawrence Schlemmer, 'Conflict and Conflict Regulation in South Africa' in De Crespigny & Schrire (eds.), *Government and Politics in South Africa.*
12. Peter Walshe, *The Rise of African Nationalism in South Africa: The African National Congress 1912–1952.*
13. Séan Archer, address to Jewish Leadership Seminar, Cape Town, 4 June 1978 (unpublished).
14. *Survey of Race Relations 1977,* pp. 206–8.
15. *Survey of Race Relations 1977,* p. 215.
16. Lawrence Schlemmer, 'The Urgent Need for Fundamental Change in South Africa', pp. 22–3, in S.A. Institute of Race Relations, Papers Given at the Forty-Seventh Annual Council Meeting, Durban, 1977.
17. Schlemmer, 'White Voters and Change in South Africa', *Optima* 27, 1978, p. 68.
18. *H.A.D.,* 12 April 1978, col. 4546.
19. *H.A.D.,* 12 April 1978, cols. 4547–8 (italics added).

20. *H.A.D.*, 12 April 1978, col. 4555.

21. D. Worrall, 'The South African Government's 1977 Constitutional Proposals', in John A. Benyon (ed.), *Constitutional Change in South Africa*, p. 129.

22. Labour Party of South Africa: *Resolutions Adopted at a meeting of the National Executive Committee held at Stellenbosch on 10 September 1977.*

23. *Report of the Committee on Alternative Constitutional Proposals* (Cape Town, 1979), p. 17.

24. 'Questions and Replies on Constitutional Plan' in *Pro-Nat*, September 1977 (italics added).

25. Rapoport, p. 241.

26. Quoted in Benyon (ed.), p. 90.

27. Marinus Wiechers, 'Possible structural divisions of power in South Africa', in Benyon (ed.), p. 116.

28. Nic Rhoodie, 'Key Socio-Political Determinants of Intercommunal Power Deployment in a South African Plural Democracy', in S.A. Institute of Race Relations, *Papers given at the Forty-Eighth Annual Council Meeting*, Cape Town, 1978.

29. For a trenchant overview of the literature and discussion of the issues see Walker Connor, 'Self-Determination: The New Phase', *World Politics* 20, 1967–8.

30. *Verslag van die Kommissie van Ondersoek na Aangeleenthede Rakende die Kleurlingbevolkingsgroep* (RP 38/1976, Government Printer, Pretoria), pp. 372–3 (translation).

31. For an account of white efforts to incorporate Africans into a white-controlled economy see David Welsh, *The Roots of Segregation: Native Policy in Colonial Natal, 1845–1910.*

32. Lawrence Schlemmer, 'Social implications of constitutional alternatives in South Africa', in Benyon (ed.), p. 267.

33. Rhoodie, p. 1.

34. *Survey of Race Relations 1977*, p. 525.

35. Lijphart, 'Review Article: The Northern Ireland Problem', p. 100.

36. Schlemmer, 'Social Implications', p. 263. This essay contains a useful discussion of the possibilities for a South African consociational democracy and we acknowledge Professor Schlemmer's influence on our assessment.

37. Roberta E. McKown & Robert E. Kauffman, 'Party System as a Comparative Analytic Concept in African Politics', *Comparative Politics* 6, 1973, p. 72.

38. Ali A. Mazrui, 'Borrowed Theory and Original Practice in African Politics', in Herbert J. Spiro (ed.), *Patterns of African Development*, p. 97.

39. Gail Gerhart, *Black Power in South Africa: The Evolution of an Ideology*, p. 195.

7. NEGOTIATING FOR A DEMOCRATIC DISPENSATION
(pages 120–132)

1. Lewis Coser, *Continuities in the Study of Social Conflict*, p. 50.

2. John Dugard, 'Legislative Preconditions for Peaceful Change', in S.A. Institute of Race Relations, *Papers given at the Forty-Eighth Annual Council Meeting*, Cape Town, 1978, pp. 19–20.

3. *H.A.D.*, 12 April 1978, col. 4502.

4. Hanf, Vierdag & Weiland.

5. Richard Rose, *Governing without Consensus: An Irish Perspective*, p. 397.

6. Gerrit Viljoen, *Ideaal en Werklikheid: Rekenskap deur 'n Afrikaner,* p. 35.
7. Muzafer Sherif, *Group Conflict and Co-operation,* p. 147.
8. Sherif.
9. Morton Deutsch, *The Resolution of Conflict: Constructive and Destructive Processes,* p. 98.
10. Heribert Adam, 'When the Chips are Down: Confrontation and Accommodation in South Africa', *Contemporary Crises* 1, 1977, p. 420.
11. Oberschall, p. 264.
12. Rose, *Northern Ireland: A Time of Choice,* pp. 30–1, 122, 133.

8. AN ALTERNATIVE POLITICAL FRAMEWORK (pages 133–165)

1. G.F. Sawer, *Modern Federalism,* p. 186.
2. Thomas M. Franck (ed.), *Why Federations Fail: An Inquiry into the Requisites for Successful Federalism,* p. 173.
3. Cf. Wiechers in Benyon (ed.), p. 113.
4. B.O. Nwabueze, *Constitutionalism in the Emergent States,* p. 112.
5. Nwabueze, p. 117.
6. Victor A. Olorunsola, 'Nigeria', in Olorunsola (ed.), *The Politics of Cultural Sub-Nationalism in Africa,* p. 23.
7. Nwabueze, p. 112.
8. Nwabueze, p. 111.
9. Olorunsola, pp. 32–4.
10. F.G. Carnell, 'Political Implications of Federalism in New States', in U.K. Hicks et al, *Federalism and Economic Growth in Under-developed Countries,* pp. 22–3.
11. William H. Riker, 'Review Article: Six Books in Search of a Subject on Does Federalism Exist and Does it Matter?' in *Comparative Politics,* Oct. 1969, pp. 138–9.
12. K.C. Wheare, *Federal Government* (fourth edition), pp. 10, 14.
13. For an account see Donald V. Smiley, *The Canadian Political Nationality.*
14. William S. Livingston, 'Canada, Australia and the United States: Variations on a Theme', in Valerie Earle (ed.), *Federalism: Infinite Variety in Theory and Practice,* p. 129.
15. Livingston, pp. 109–12.
16. Daniel J. Elazar, 'Federalism', in *International Encyclopedia of the Social Sciences* (Crowell Collier and Macmillan, New York, 1968), vol. 5, p. 359.
17. Livingston, pp. 108–9; Ronald L. Watts, *Administration in Federal Systems,* pp. 17–20.
18. Livingston, p. 111.
19. Sawer, p. 137.
20. Elazar, p. 365.
21. Carnell, p. 24.
22. R.D. Dikshit, *The Political Geography of Federalism: An Inquiry into Origins and Stability,* p. 239.
23. Leo Marquard, *A Federation of Southern Africa,* p. 125.
24. Rufus Davis, 'The "Federal Principle" Reconsidered', in Aaron Wildavsky (ed.), *American Federalism in Perspective,* pp. 19–23.
25. Robert A. Dahl, 'Patterns of Opposition', in Dahl (ed.), *Political Oppositions in Western Democracies,* p. 340.

26. Nwabueze, p. 97.
27. Henry H. Kerr, *Switzerland: Social Cleavages and Partisan Conflict*, p. 31.
28. Watts, *Administration in Federal Systems*, pp. 62–71. This book contains a useful comparative survey of federal administrative practices.
29. For an interesting discussion of some of the issues facing Canadian federalism see A.W. Johnson, 'The Dynamics of Federalism in Canada', in *Canadian Journal of Political Sciences*, March 1968.
30. Elazar, pp. 360–1.
31. André du Toit, *Federalism and Political Change in South Africa* (1974 Maurice Webb Memorial Lectures), pp. 13–15.
32. Watts, 'The Survival or Disintegration of Federations', in Burns (ed.), p. 64.
33. Watts.
34. See Codding, ch. 6; P.F. Barchi, 'Political Institutions', in *Focus on Switzerland* (Lausanne, 1975), pp. 93–103.
35. Codding, p. 91.
36. C.F. Strong, *Modern Political Constitutions*, p. 268.
37. Barchi, p. 100.
38. Cf. Wiechers, p. 110.
39. Smock & Smock, p. 265.
40. Smock & Smock, pp. 269–70.
41. Claire Palley, *Constitutional Law and Minorities*, p. 20.
42. Carl J. Friedrich, *Trends of Federalism in Theory and Practice*, p. 59.
43. Finer, p. 27.
44. Lawrence C. Dodd, *Coalitions in Parliamentary Government*, pp. 243–4.
45. John Oliver, *Ulster Today and Tomorrow*, p. 30.
46. De Smith, *The New Commonwealth*, pp. 119–20.
47. Quoted in Simons & Simons, p. 23.
48. See Enid Lakeman, *How Democracies Vote: A Study of Electoral Systems* (fourth edition).
49. Lijphart, *Democracy in Plural Societies: A Comparative Exploration*, pp. 136–7.
50. Lijphart, *Democracy in Plural Societies*, p. 37.
51. Richard Luyt, 'African Constitutionalism: Constitutions in the Context of Decolonization', in Benyon (ed.), p. 22.
52. Livingston, p. 100.
53. A.S. Mathews, 'Discussion', in Benyon (ed.), p. 86.
54. Dean, 'Discussion', in Benyon (ed.), p. 87.
55. For a useful discussion of this contingency see A.S. Mathews, *Freedom and State Security in the South African Plural Society*.
56. Thomas F. Pettigrew, 'Race Relations: Social-psychological Aspects', in *International Encyclopedia of the Social Sciences*, vol. 13, p. 281.
57. See, e.g., Nathan Glazer, *Affirmative Discrimination: Ethnic Inequality and Public Policy*.
58. Peter L. Berger, *Pyramids of Sacrifice: Political Ethics and Social Change*, p. 156.
59. Smock & Smock, pp. 272–3.
60. Quoted in *Rapport*, 20 May 1979.

9. *IN CONCLUSION* (pages 166–171)

1. G. Chaliand, *Revolution in the Third World,* p. xv and ch. 4.
2. Chaliand, p. 189.
3. Jurgen Blenck & Klaus van der Ropp, 'Republic of South Africa: Is Partition a Solution?', *South African Journal of African Affairs* 1, 1976.
4. See Roelf Botha, *South Africa: Plan for the Future – A Basis for Dialogue;* Wolfgang Thomas, *Plural Democracy – Political Change and Strategies for Evolution in South Africa,* pp. 19–21.
5. A.S. Mathews, 'Security Legislation and Peaceful Change in South Africa', unpublished paper delivered at a Workshop of the Institute of Social and Economic Research, Rhodes University, Grahamstown, August 1978.

Bibliography

A. BOOKS AND PAMPHLETS

Adam, Heribert, *Modernizing Racial Domination: The Dynamics of South African Politics* (University of California Press, Los Angeles, 1971).

Adam, Heribert (ed.), *South Africa: Sociological Perspectives* (Oxford University Press, London, 1971).

Ashworth, Georgina (ed.), *World Minorities* (Minority Rights Group, Quartermaine House Limited, Sunbury, 1977).

Bagley, Christopher, *The Dutch Plural Society* (Oxford University Press, London, 1973).

Baker, Donald G. (ed.), *Politics of Race* (Saxon House, Farnborough, 1975).

Baxter, Paul, & Basil Sanson (eds.), *Race and Social Difference* (Penguin Books, Harmondsworth, 1972).

Benyon, John A. (ed.), *Constitutional Change in South Africa* (University of Natal Press, Pietermaritzburg, 1978).

Berger, Peter L., *Pyramids of Sacrifice: Political Ethics and Social Change* (Penguin Books, Harmondsworth, 1977).

Beshir, Omer Mohammed, *The Southern Sudan – From Conflict to Peace* (C. Hurst, London, 1975).

Blalock, Hubert M., *Toward a Theory of Minority-Group Relations* (John Wiley & Sons, New York, 1967).

Bluhm, William T., *Building an Austrian Nation: The Political Integration of a Western State* (Yale University Press, New Haven, 1973).

Botha, Roelf P., *South Africa: Plan for the Future – A Basis for Dialogue* (Perskor, Johannesburg, 1978).

Boulding, Kenneth E., *Stable Peace* (University of Texas Press, Austin, 1978).

Brady, Alexander, *Democracy in the Dominions* (third ed.) (University of Toronto Press, Toronto, 1958).

Brand, R.H., *The Union of South Africa* (Clarendon Press, Oxford, 1909).

Bryce, James, *Impressions of South Africa* (third ed.) (Macmillan, London, 1899).

Burns, R.M. (ed.), *One Country or Two?* (McGill–Queen's University Press, Montreal, 1971).

Campbell, Ernest Q. (ed.), *Racial Tensions and National Identity* (Vanderbilt University Press, Nashville, 1972).

Chaliand, G., *Revolution in the Third World* (Viking Press, New York, 1977).

Cillié, P.J., *Konstitutionele Verandering in Suid-Afrika (2)* (Instituut vir Suid-Afrikaanse Politiek, Potchefstroomse Universiteit vir C.H.O., Aktualiteitsreeks nr. 13, 1977).

Codding, G.A.Jun., *The Federal Government of Switzerland* (Houghton Mifflin, Boston, 1961).

Cohen, Abner (ed.), *Urban Ethnicity* (Tavistock, London, 1974).

Coser, Lewis, *The Functions of Social Conflict* (Routledge and Kegan Paul, London, 1956).
——, *Continuities in the Study of Social Conflict* (Free Press, New York, 1970).
Dahl, Robert A., *Polyarchy: Participation and Opposition* (Yale University Press, New Haven, 1971).
Dean, W.H.B., *The Riots and the Constitution in 1976* (Civil Rights League, Cape Town, 1976).
de Crespigny, A.R.C., & R.A. Schrire (eds.), *Government and Politics in South Africa* (Juta, Cape Town, 1978).
Dent, M.J., *Improving Nigeria's Draft Constitution* (Dark Horse Publications, Keele, 1977).
Department of Information, *Multi-National Development: The Reality* (Pretoria, 1974).
de St. Jorre, John, *A House Divided: South Africa's Uncertain Future* (Carnegie Endowment for International Peace, Washington, 1977).
de Smith, S.A., *The New Commonwealth and its Constitutions* (Stevens, London, 1964).
Despres, Leo A., *Cultural Pluralism and Nationalist Politics in British Guiana* (Rand McNally, Chicago, 1967).
Deutsch, Morton, *The Resolution of Conflict: Constructive and Destructive Processes* (Yale University Press, New Haven, 1973).
Dikshit, P.D., *The Political Geography of Federalism: An Inquiry into Origins and Stability* (Macmillan, London, 1976).
Dodd, Lawrence C., *Coalitions in Parliamentary Government* (Princeton University Press, Princeton, 1976).
Dreyer, June Teufel, *China's Forty Millions – Minority Nationalities and National Integration in the People's Republic of China* (Harvard University Press, Cambridge, 1976).
Dugard, C.J.R., *The Judicial Process, Positivism and Civil Liberty* (Witwatersrand University Press, Johannesburg, 1971).
du Toit, André, *Federalism and Political Change in South Africa* (University of Natal, 1974, Maurice Webb Memorial Lectures, Durban).
Earle, Valerie (ed.), *Federalism: Infinite Variety in Theory and Practice* (F.E. Peacock Publishers, Itasca, 1968).
Elazar, Daniel J. (ed.), *Federalism and Political Integration* (Turtledove Publishing, Ramat Gan, 1979).
Enloe, Cynthia H., *Ethnic Conflict and Political Development* (Little, Brown, Boston, 1973).
Finer, S.E. (ed.), *Adversary Politics and Electoral Reform* (Anthony Wigram, London, 1975).
Francis, E.K., *Interethnic Relations* (Elsevier, New York, 1976).
Franck, Thomas M. (ed.), *Why Federations Fail: An Inquiry into the Requisites for Successful Federalism* (New York University Press, New York, 1968).
Franklin, John Hope (ed.), *Color and Race* (Beacon Press, Boston, 1969).
Friedrich, Carl J., *Trends of Federalism in Theory and Practice* (Frederick A. Praeger, New York, 1968).
——, *Limited Government: A Comparison* (Prentice-Hall, Englewood Cliffs, 1974).
Gerhart, Gail M., *Black Power in South Africa: The Evolution of an Ideology* (University of California Press, Berkeley, 1978).

Glazer, Nathan, *Affirmative Discrimination: Ethnic Inequality and Public Policy* (Basic Books, New York, 1975).
Gordon, Milton M., *Assimilation in American Life* (Oxford University Press, New York, 1964).
Hanf, Theo, Gerda Vierdag & Heribert Weiland, *Süd-Afrika: Friedlicher Wandel?* (Kaiser Grünewald, Munich, 1978).
Harrison, J.F.C., The Early Victorians 1832–51 (Panther Books, St. Albans, 1973).
Heard, Kenneth A., *General Elections in South Africa 1943–1970* (Oxford University Press, London, 1974).
H.M.S.O., *British Guiana Conference, 1963* (Cmnd. 2203).
Hudson, Michael C., *The Precarious Republic: Political Modernization in Lebanon* (Random House, New York, 1968).
Hyam, Ronald, *Britain's Imperial Century 1815–1914: A Study of Empire and Expansion* (Batsford, London, 1976).
Jackson, Harold, *The Two Irelands – A Dual Study of Intergroup Tensions* (Minority Rights Group, London, 1971).
Johnson, R.W., *How Long Will South Africa Survive?* (Macmillan, Johannesburg, 1977).
Johnstone, Frederick A., *Class, Race and Gold – A Study of Class Relations and Racial Discrimination in South Africa* (Routledge & Kegan Paul, London, 1976).
Jordan, Winthrop D., *White over Black: American Attitudes Toward the Negro 1550–1812* (Penguin Books, Baltimore, 1969).
Kane-Berman, *Soweto: Black Revolt, White Reaction* (Ravan Press, 1978).
Kearney, Robert N., *Communalism and Language in the Politics of Ceylon* (Duke University Press, Durham, N.C., 1967).
——, *The Politics of Ceylon (Sri Lanka),* (Cornell University Press, Ithaca, 1973).
Kerr, Henry H., *Switzerland: Social Cleavages and Partisan Conflict* (Sage Publications, London, 1974).
Kuper, Leo, *Race, Class and Power* (Duckworth, London, 1974).
Kyriakides, Stanley, *Cyprus: Constitutionalism and Crisis Government* (University of Pennsylvania Press, Philadelphia, 1968).
Labour Party of South Africa, *Resolutions Adopted at a Meeting of the National Executive Committee Held at Stellenbosch on 10 September 1977* (mimeo).
Lakeman, Enid, *How Democracies Vote: A Study of Electoral Systems* (fourth edition) (Faber & Faber, London, 1974).
Laponce, J.A., *The Protection of Minorities* (University of California Press, Los Angeles, 1960).
Laurence, Patrick, *The Transkei: South Africa's Politics of Partition* (Ravan Press, Johannesburg, 1976).
Leggett, John C., *Class, Race and Labor – Working Class Consciousness in Detroit* (Oxford University Press, New York, 1968).
Lewis, Bernard, *Race and Color in Islam* (Harper & Row, New York, 1970).
Lewis, W. Arthur, *Politics in West Africa* (Allen & Unwin, London, 1965).
Lijphart, Arend, *The Politics of Accommodation: Pluralism and Democracy in the Netherlands* (University of California Press, Berkeley, 1968).
——, *Democracy in Plural Societies: A Comparative Exploration* (Yale University Press, New Haven, 1977).
Lively, Jack, *Democracy* (B.H. Blackwell, Oxford, 1975).
Macpherson, C.B., *The Life and Times of Liberal Democracy* (Oxford University Press, Oxford, 1977).

Marquard, Leo, *A Federation of Southern Africa* (Oxford University Press, London, 1971).

Mason, Philip, *Patterns of Dominance* (Oxford University Press, London, 1970).

Mackenzie, W.J.M., *Free Elections* (Allen & Unwin, London, 1958).

Macmillan, W.M., *Complex South Africa* (Faber & Faber, London, 1930).

McRae, Kenneth D., *Switzerland – Example of Cultural Coexistence* (Canadian Institute of International Affairs, Toronto, 1964).

McRae, Kenneth D. (ed.), *Consociational Democracy: Political Accommodation in Segmented Societies* (McClelland & Stewart, Toronto, 1974).

Mathews, A.S., *Freedom and State Security in the South African Plural Society* (S.A. Institute of Race Relations, Johannesburg, 1971).

Milnor, A.J., *Elections and Political Stability* (Little, Brown, Boston, 1969).

Neumann, Franz, *The Democratic and the Authoritarian State – Essays in Legal Theory* (Free Press, New York, 1964).

Noel, Donald L. (ed.), *The Origins of American Slavery and Racism* (Charles E. Merrill, Columbus, 1972).

Nordlinger, Eric A., *Conflict Regulation in Divided Societies* (Center for International Affairs, Harvard University, 1972).

Nwabueze, B.O., *Constitutionalism in the Emergent States* (C. Hurst, London, 1973).

Oberschall, Anthony, *Social Conflict and Social Movements* (Prentice-Hall, Englewood Cliffs, 1973).

Okun, Arthur M., *Equality and Efficiency: The Big Tradeoff* (Brookings Institution, Washington, D.C., 1975).

Oliver, John, *Ulster Today and Tomorrow* (PEP Broadsheet No. 574, London, 1978).

Palley, Claire, *Constitutional Law and Minorities* (Minority Rights Group, London, 1978).

Parkin, Frank, *Class Inequality and Political Order* (Paladin, London, 1972).

Parry, Geraint, *Political Elites* (Allen & Unwin, London, 1969).

Partridge, P.H., *Consent and Consensus* (Macmillan, London, 1971).

Pelzer, A.N. (ed.), *Verwoerd Speaks* (APB Publishers, Johannesburg, 1966).

Poliakov, Léon, *The Aryan Myth – A History of Racist and Nationalist Ideas in Europe* (Sussex University Press, London, 1974).

Powell, G. Bingham, Jun., *Social Fragmentation and Political Hostility – An Austrian Case Study* (Stanford University Press, Stanford, 1970).

Progressive Federal Party Parliamentary Secretariat, *Memorandum on the Constitutional Proposals* (1978, mimeo).

Rabushka, Alvin, & Kenneth A. Shepsle, *Politics in Plural Societies: A Theory of Democratic Instability* (Charles E. Merrill, Columbus, 1972).

Rae, Douglas W., & Michael Taylor, *The Analysis of Political Cleavages* (Yale University Press, New Haven, 1970).

Rae, Douglas W., *The Political Consequences of Electoral Laws* (Yale University Press, New Haven, 1971).

Ranney, Austin, *The Governing of Men* (third ed.) (Holt, Rinehart & Winston, New York, 1971).

Rapoport, Anatol, *Conflict in Man-Made Environment* (Penguin Books, Harmondsworth, 1974).

Report of the Committee on Alternative Constitutional Proposals (Coloured Persons Representative Council, Cape Town, 1979).

Report of the Spro-cas Education Commission, *Education Beyond Apartheid* (Johannesburg, 1971).

Report of the Spro-cas Political Commission, *South Africa's Political Alternatives* (Johannesburg, 1973).

Rex, John, *Race Relations in Sociological Theory* (Weidenfeld & Nicolson, London, 1970).

Rose, Richard, *Governing without Consensus: An Irish Perspective* (Faber & Faber, London, 1971).

——, *Northern Ireland: A Time of Choice* (Macmillan, London, 1976).

Rothchild, Donald, *Racial Bargaining in Independent Kenya – A Study of Minorities and Decolonization* (Oxford University Press, London, 1973).

Said, Abdul A., & Luis R. Simmons, (eds.), *Ethnicity in an International Context* (Transaction Books, New Brunswick, 1976).

Sawer, G.F., *Modern Federalism* (Watts, London, 1969).

Schermerhorn, R.A., *Comparative Ethnic Relations: A Framework for Theory and Research* (Random House, New York, 1970).

Schlemmer, Lawrence, *Black Attitudes: Reaction and Adaptation* (Centre for Applied Social Sciences, University of Natal, Durban, 1975).

Sherif, Muzafer, *Group Conflict and Co-operation* (Routledge & Kegan Paul, London, 1966).

Simons, H.J., and R.E. Simons, *Class and Colour in South Africa 1850–1950* (Penguin, Harmondsworth, 1969).

Smiley, Donald V., *The Canadian Political Nationality* (Methuen, Toronto, 1967).

Smith, Donald Eugene, *Religion and Political Development* (Little, Brown, Boston, 1970).

Smock, David R., & Audrey C. Smock, *The Politics of Pluralism – A Comparative Study of Lebanon and Ghana* (Elsevier, New York, 1975).

Steiner, Jürg, *Amicable Agreement Versus Majority Rule: Conflict Resolution in Switzerland* (University of North Carolina Press, Chapel Hill, 1974).

Stone, John (ed.), *Race, Ethnicity and Social Change* (Duxbury Press, Scituate, 1977).

Strong, C.F., *Modern Political Constitutions* (Sidgwick & Jackson, London, 1966).

Terreblanche, S., *Vernuwing en Herskikking – Op Pad na Nuwe Ekonomiese Instellings en Prioriteite in Suid Afrika* (Tafelberg, Cape Town, 1973).

Thomas, Wolfgang H., *Plural Democracy: Political Change and Strategies for Evolution in South Africa* (S.A. Institute of Race Relations, Johannesburg, 1977).

Thompson, Leonard, and Jeffrey Butler (eds.), *Change in Contemporary South Africa* (University of California Press, Los Angeles, 1975).

Thompson, L.M., *The Cape Coloured Franchise* (S.A. Institute of Race Relations, Johannesburg, 1949).

van den Berghe, Pierre L., *Race and Racism: A Comparative Perspective* (John Wiley, New York, 1967).

van Rooyen, Jan J., *Ons Politiek van Naby* (Tafelberg, Cape Town, 1971).

Verslag van die Kommissie van Ondersoek na Aangeleenthede Rakende die Kleurlingbevolkingsgroep (RP 38/1976, Government Printer, Pretoria).

Viljoen, Gerrit, *Ideaal en Werklikheid: Rekenskap deur 'n Afrikaner* (Tafelberg, Cape Town, 1978).

von Vorys, Karl, *Democracy without Consensus – Communalism and Political Stability in Malaysia* (Princeton University Press, Princeton, 1975).

Walshe, Peter, *The Rise of African Nationalism in South Africa: The African*

National Congress 1912–1952 (C. Hurst, London, 1970).
Walton, Edgar, *The Inner History of the National Convention of South Africa* (Maskew Miller, Cape Town, 1912).
Watts, Ronald L., *Administration in Federal Systems* (Hutchinson, London, 1970).
Wellman, David T., *Portraits of White Racism* (Cambridge University Press, Cambridge, 1977).
Welsh, David, *The Roots of Segregation: Native Policy in Colonial Natal, 1845–1910* (Oxford University Press, Cape Town, 1971).
Wheare, K.C., *Federal Government* (fourth edition) (Oxford University Press, London, 1963).
——, *Modern Constitutions* (Oxford University Press, London, 1951).
Williams, Robin M., Jun., *Mutual Accommodation: Ethnic Conflict and Cooperation* (University of Minnesota Press, Minneapolis, 1977).
Young, Crawford, *The Politics of Cultural Pluralism* (University of Wisconsin Press, Madison, 1976).

B. ESSAYS AND ARTICLES

Adam, Heribert, 'When the Chips are Down: Confrontation and Accommodation in South Africa', *Contemporary Crises* 1, 1977.
Arsel, Ilhan, 'Belgium', in Albert P. Blaustein & Gisbert H. Flanz (eds.), *Constitutions of the Countries of the World* (Oceana Publications, New York, 1973).
Barghoorn, Frederick C., 'Soviet Dissenters on Soviet Nationality Policy', in Wendell Bell & Walter E. Freeman (eds.), *Ethnicity and Nation-Building: Comparative, International and Historical Perspectives* (Sage Publications, Beverly Hills, 1974).
Barry, Brian, 'Review Article: Political Accommodation and Consociational Democracy', *British Journal of Political Science* 5, 1975.
Bastide, Roger, 'Color, Racism, and Christianity', in John Hope Franklin (ed.), *Color and Race* (Beacon Press, Boston, 1969).
Beinart, B., 'The South African Appeal Court and Judicial Review', *Modern Law Review* 21, 1958.
Bertsch, Gary K., 'Ethnicity and Politics in Socialist Yugoslavia', in *The Annals of the American Academy of Political and Social Science,* September 1977.
Blackwell, James E., 'The Power Basis of Ethnic Conflict in American Society', in Lewis A. Coser & Otto N. Larsen (eds.), *The Uses of Controversy in Sociology* (Free Press, New York, 1976).
Blenck, J., & K. von der Ropp, 'Republik Südafrika: Teilung oder Ausweg?', *Aussenpolitik* 3, 1976.
Blumer, Herbert, 'Race Prejudice as a Sense of Group Position', *Pacific Sociological Review* 1, 1958.
Briggs, Asa, 'The Language of "Class" in early Nineteenth Century England', in M.W. Flinn & T.C. Smout (eds.), *Essays in Social History* (Clarendon Press, Oxford, 1974).
Carnell, F.G., 'Political Implications of Federalism in New States', in U.K. Hicks et al, *Federalism and Economic Growth in Underdeveloped Countries* (Allen & Unwin, London, 1961).
Cohen, Percy, 'Race Relations as a Sociological Issue', in Gordon Bowker & John Carrier (eds.), *Race and Ethnic Relations: Sociological Readings* (Hutchinson

University Library, London, 1976).
Connor, Walker, 'Self-Determination: The New Phase', *World Politics* 20, 1967–8.
——, 'Nation-Building or Nation-Destroying?', *World Politics* 24, 1971–2.
——, 'The Politics of Ethnonationalism', *Journal of International Affairs* 27, 1973.
Daalder, Hans, 'On Building Consociational Nations: The Cases of the Netherlands and Switzerland', *International Social Science Journal* 23, 1971.
——, 'The Consociational Democracy Theme', *World Politics* 26, 1974.
Dahl, Robert A., 'Patterns of Opposition', in Robert A. Dahl (ed.), *Political Oppositions in Western Democracies* (Yale University Press, New Haven, 1966).
Davis, Rufus, 'The "Federal Principle" Reconsidered', in Aaron Wildavsky (ed.), *American Federalism in Perspective* (Little, Brown, Boston, 1967).
Dean, W.H.B., 'The Judiciary', in Anthony de Crespigny & Robert Schrire (eds.), *The Government and Politics of South Africa* (Juta, Cape Town, 1978).
Dekmejian, Richard Hrair, 'Consociational Democracy in Crisis: The Case of Lebanon', *Comparative Politics* 10, 1978.
Dugard, C.J.R., 'Legislative Preconditions for Peaceful Change', in S.A. Institute of Race Relations, *Papers given at the Forty-Eighth Annual Council Meeting*, Cape Town, 1978.
Eckstein, Harry, 'The Impact of Electoral Systems on Representative Government', in Harry Eckstein & David E. Apter (eds.), *Comparative Politics: A Reader* (Collier-Macmillan, London, 1963).
——, 'A Theory of Stable Democracy', in Harry Eckstein, *Division and Cohesion in Democracy: A Study of Norway* (Princeton University Press, Princeton, 1966).
Elazar, Daniel J., 'Federalism', in *International Encyclopedia of the Social Sciences*, vol. 5 (Crowell Collier and Macmillan, 1968).
Enloe, Cynthia H., 'Police and Military in the Resolution of Ethnic Conflict', *The Annals of the American Academy of Political and Social Science* 433, 1977.
Esman, Milton J., 'Malaysia: Communal Coexistence and Mutual Deterrence', in Ernest Q. Campbell (ed.), *Racial Tensions and National Identity* (Vanderbilt University Press, Nashville, 1972).
——, 'Communal Conflict in Southeast Asia', in Nathan Glazer & Daniel P. Moynihan (eds.), *Ethnicity: Theory and Experience* (Harvard University Press, Cambridge, 1975).
Ferguson, Clyde, & William R. Cotter, 'South Africa: What is to be done?', *Foreign Affairs* 56, 1978.
Gluckman, Max, 'The Bonds in the Colour Bar: South Africa', in Paul Baxter & Basil Sanson (eds.), *Race and Social Difference* (Penguin Books, Harmondsworth, 1972).
Gordon, Milton M., 'Toward a General Theory of Racial and Ethnic Group Relations', in Nathan Glazer & Daniel P. Moynihan (eds.), *Ethnicity: Theory and Experience* (Harvard University Press, Cambridge, 1975).
Heisler, Martin O., 'Managing Ethnic Conflict in Belgium', *The Annals of the American Academy of Political and Social Science* 477, 1977.
Hendrickson, Embert, 'New Directions for Republican Guyana', *World Today* 27, 1971.
Hewitt, Christopher, 'Majorities and Minorities: A Comparative Survey of Ethnic

Violence', *The Annals of the American Academy of Political and Social Science,* Sept. 1977.

Hodgkin, Thomas L., 'The Relevance of "Western" Ideas for the New African States', in J. Roland Pennock (ed.), *Self-Government in Modernizing Nations* (Prentice-Hall, Englewood Cliffs, 1964).

Horowitz, Donald L., 'Multiracial Politics in the New States: Toward a Theory of Conflict', in Robert C. Jackson & Michael B. Stein (eds.), *Issues in Comparative Politics* (St. Martin's Press, New York, 1971).

——, 'Three Dimensions of Ethnic Politics', *World Politics* 23, 1971.

Howell, John, 'Politics in the Southern Sudan', *African Affairs* 72, 1973.

Hutchinson, Bruce, 'Canada's Times of Troubles', *Foreign Affairs* 56, 1977.

Johnson, A.W., 'The Dynamics of Federalism in Canada', *Canadian Journal of Political Science* 1, 1968.

Kitromilides, Paschalis M., & Theodore A. Couloumbis, 'Ethnic Conflict in a Strategic Area: The Case of Cyprus', in Abdul A. Said & Luis R. Simmons (eds.), *Ethnicity in an International Context* (Transaction Books, New Brunswick, 1976).

Kuper, Leo, 'Political Change in White Settler Societies: The Possibility of Peaceful Democratization', in Leo Kuper & M.G. Smith (eds.), *Pluralism in Africa* (University of California Press, Berkeley, 1971).

Laponce, J.A., 'The Protection of Minorities by the Electoral System', *Western Political Quarterly* 10, 1957.

Latham-Koenig, Alfred, 'Shadow of Marxism over Mauritius', *Round Table* 266, 1977.

Leifer, Michael, 'Malaysia after Tun Razak', *Round Table* 276, 1976.

Lijphart, Arend, 'Cultural Diversity and Theories of Political Integration', *Canadian Journal of Political Science* IV, 1971.

——, 'Review Article: The Northern Ireland Problem: Cases, Theories and Solutions', *British Journal of Political Science* 5, 1976.

Livingston, William S., 'A Note on the Nature of Federalism', in Aaron Wildavsky (ed.), *American Federalism in Perspective* (Little, Brown, Boston, 1967).

——, 'Canada, Australia and the United States: Variations on a Theme', in Valerie Earle (ed.), *Federalism: Infinite Variety in Theory and Practice* (F.E. Peacock Publishers, Itasca, 1968).

Lorwin, Val R., 'Belgium: Religion, Class and Language in National Politics', in Robert A. Dahl (ed.), *Political Oppositions in Western Democracies* (Yale University Press, New Haven, 1966).

McKown, Roberta E., & Robert E. Kauffman, 'Party System as a Comparative Analytic Concept in African Politics', *Comparative Politics* 6, 1973.

Macridis, Roy C., 'Political Executive', *International Encyclopedia of the Social Sciences,* vol. 12 (Crowell Collier and Macmillan, New York, 1968).

Mahant, E.E., 'The Strange Fate of a Liberal Democracy', *Round Table* 265, 1977.

Mathews, A.S., 'Judicial Activism and Internal Security', in J. Midgley, J.H. Steyn & R. Graser (eds.), *Crime and Punishment in South Africa* (McGraw-Hill, Johannesburg, 1975).

Mayer, Kurt, 'Cultural Pluralism and Linguistic Equilibrium in Switzerland', in Pierre van den Berghe (ed.), *Intergroup Relations – Sociological Perspectives* (Basic Books, New York, 1972).

Mazrui, Ali A., 'Borrowed Theory and Original Practice in African Politics', in Herbert J. Spiro (ed.), *Patterns of African Development* (Prentice-Hall, Englewood Cliffs, 1967).

Melson, Robert, & Howard Wolpe, 'Modernization and the Politics of Communalism: A Theoretical Perspective', *American Political Science Review* LXIV, 1970.

Mendis, A.B., 'Sri Lanka', *World Survey* 89-90 (1976).

Milne, R.S., ' "The Pacific Way" – Consociational Politics in Fiji', *Pacific Affairs* 48, 1975.

Niblock, Timothy C., 'A New Political System in Sudan', *African Affairs* 73, 1974.

O'Brien, Conor Cruise, 'What rights should minorities have?', in Georgina Ashworth (ed.), *World Minorities* (Minority Rights Group, Quartermaine House Limited, Sunbury, 1977).

Olorunsola, Victor A., 'Nigeria', in Victor A. Olorunsola (ed.), *The Politics of Cultural Sub-Nationalism in Africa* (Doubleday, New York, 1967).

Patterson, Orlando, 'Context and Choice in Ethnic Allegiance: A Theoretical Framework and Caribbean Case Study', in Nathan Glazer & Daniel P. Moynihan (eds.), *Ethnicity: Theory and Experience* (Harvard University Press, Cambridge, 1975).

Petryszak, Nicholas, 'The Dynamics of Acquiescence in South Africa', *African Affairs* 75, 1976.

Pettigrew, Thomas F., 'Race Relations: Social–Psychological Aspects', *International Encyclopedia of the Social Sciences,* vol. 13.

'Questions and Replies on Constitutional Plan', *Pro-Nat,* Sept. 1977.

Rayside, David M., 'The Impact of the Linguistic Cleavage on the "Governing Parties" of Belgium and Canada', *Canadian Journal of Political Science* XI, 1978.

Rhoodie, Nic, 'Key Socio-Political Determinants of Intercommunal Power Deployment in a South African Plural Democracy', in S.A. Institute of Race Relations, *Papers Given at the Forty-Eighth Annual Council Meeting,* Cape Town, 1978.

Riker, William H., 'Review Article: Six Books in Search of a Subject or Does Federalism Exist and Does it Matter?', *Comparative Politics* 2, 1969–70.

Rimanque, K., 'Devolution in Cultural Affairs in Belgium', in Harry Calvert (ed.), *Devolution* (Professional Books, London, 1975).

Ronen, Dov, 'Alternative Patterns of Integration in African States', *Journal of Modern African Studies* 14, 1976.

Rose, Richard, & Derek Urwin, 'Social Cohesion, Political Parties and Strains in Regimes', in Mattei Dogon & Richard Rose (eds.), *European Politics: A Reader* (Macmillan, London, 1971).

Schlemmer, Lawrence, 'Theories of the Plural Society and Change in South Africa', *Social Dynamics* 3, 1977.

——, 'The Urgent Need for Fundamental Change in South Africa', in S.A. Institute of Race Relations, *Papers Given at the Forty-Seventh Annual Council Meeting,* Durban, 1977.

——, 'Conflict and Conflict Regulation in South Africa', in A.R.C. de Crespigny & R.A. Schrire (eds.), *Government and Politics in South Africa* (Juta, Cape Town, 1978).

——, 'White Voters and Change in South Africa', *Optima* 27, 1978.
Stavrou, Nikolaos A., 'Ethnicity in Yugoslavia: Roots and Impact', in Abdul A. Said & Luis R. Simmons (eds.), *Ethnicity in an International Context* (Transaction Books, New Brunswick, 1976).
Stein, Arthur A., 'Conflict and Cohesion – A Review of the Literature', *Journal of Conflict Resolution* XX, 1976.
Stein, Michael B., 'Federal Political Systems and Federal Societies', *World Politics* 20, 1967–8
Stoakes, Frank, 'The Civil War in Lebanon', *World Today* 32, 1976.
Taylor, Michael, & V.M. Herman, 'Party Systems and Government Stability', *American Political Science Review* LXV, 1971.
van Dyke, Vernon, 'The Individual, the State, and Ethnic Communities in Political Theory', *World Politics* 29, 1977.
Vosloo, W.B., & R.A. Schrire, 'Subordinate Political Institutions', in Anthony de Crespigny & Robert Schrire (eds.), *The Government and Politics of South Africa* (Juta, Cape Town, 1978).
Wagatsuma, Hiroshi, 'The Social Perception of Skin Color in Japan', in John Hope Franklin (ed.), *Color and Race* (Beacon Press, Boston, 1969).
Warburton, T. Rennie, 'Nationalism and Language in Switzerland and Canada', in Anthony D. Smith (ed.), *Nationalist Movements* (Macmillan, London, 1976).
Welsh, David, 'English-speaking Whites and the Racial Problem', in André de Villiers (ed.), *English-speaking South Africa Today* (Oxford University Press, Cape Town, 1976).
West, Katharine, 'Stratification and Ethnicity in "Plural" New States', *Race* XIII, 1972.

Index